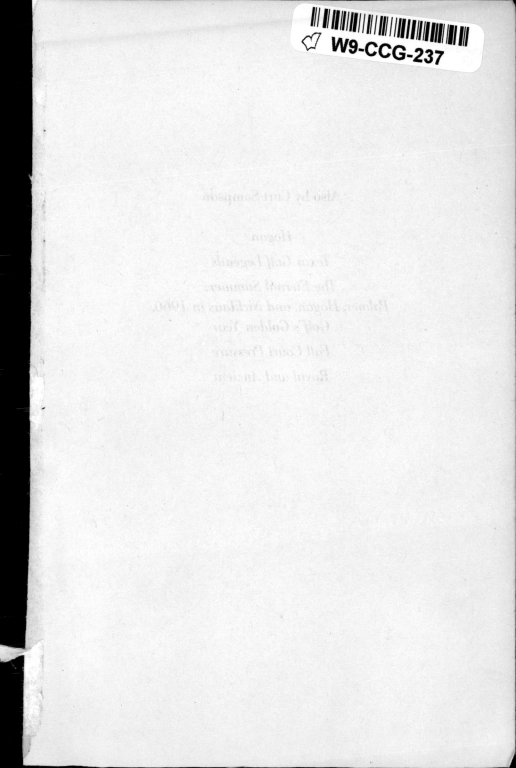

Also by Curt Sampson

Hogan

Texas Golf Legends

The Eternal Summer:
Palmer, Hogan, and Nicklaus in 1960,
Golf's Golden Year

Full Court Pressure

Royal and Ancient

THE
MASTERS

•

○

President Eisenhower poses with a few of his "Gang."

THE MASTERS

•

*Golf, Money, and Power
in Augusta, Georgia*

CURT SAMPSON

VILLARD
NEW YORK

Published in the United States by Villard Books, an imprint of
The Random House Publishing Group, a division of Random House, Inc.,
New York, and simultaneously in Canada by Random House of
Canada Limited, Toronto.

VILLARD BOOKS and colophon are registered trademarks
of Random House, Inc.

Originally published in hardcover and in slightly different form by
Villard Books, a division of Random House, Inc., in 1998.

Grateful acknowledgment is made to the following for
permission to reprint previously published material:

BANTAM DOUBLEDAY DELL PUBLISHING GROUP, INC.:
Excerpt from *The Story of the Augusta National Golf Club* by
Clifford Roberts. Reprinted by permission of Doubleday, a
division of Bantam Doubleday Dell Publishing Group, Inc.

LOS ANGELES TIMES SYNDICATE: "White as the Ku Klux Klan"
by Jim Murray. Copyright 1969 by Los Angeles
Times. Reprinted by permission.

Library of Congress Cataloging-in-Publication Data
Sampson, Curt.
The Masters: golf, money, and power in Augusta, Georgia /
by Curt Sampson.
p.   cm.
ISBN 978-0-375-75337-4
1. Masters Golf Tournament (Augusta, Ga.)—History.   2. Augusta
National Golf Club—History.   I. Title.
GV970.S25   1998
796.352'06'075864—dc21   97-49143

www.villard.com

Design by Robert Bull Design

Printed in the United States of America on acid-free paper

In memory of Dave Marr

"The reasonable man adapts himself to the world. The unreasonable one persists in trying to adapt the world to himself. Therefore all progress depends on the unreasonable man."
—*George Bernard Shaw*

"I forgot everything I remember."
—*Dan Williams, one of the builders of Augusta National Golf Club*

ACKNOWLEDGMENTS

The Club operates under established customs
(rather than rules) the spirit of which all
members are expected to observe. The
principal points are as follows . . .
2. The Club wants no publicity except with
respect to the Masters Tournament. Our
members wish to enjoy the seclusion of a private
club and prefer their visits at the Club not to be
publicized. . . . It is expected that [members]
shall actively discourage any form of publicity
pertaining to the Club, about which they
have advance knowledge, if it is unrelated
to the tournament—and especially if it
is to be commercial in form.
—*from the Annual Report to Members*

"**M**r. X, could you help me find out the year Jock Whitney
and Freeman Gosden joined?" Mr. X, like every Augusta
National member I've met, is a warm and gracious man,
quite the opposite of the club's cold, stuffy reputation.
"How's your golf game?" he replied.

A Masters employee sat with me at a table in the plaza near the main entrance while hundreds of people swirled around us. He swiveled his head left and right as we talked, and at one point he leaned so far forward that I thought he was going to take a bite of my sandwich.

The point of this preamble is that a lot of people who might have helped with this book didn't, and a lot of others who did didn't want to be identified.

A partial list of those I wish to thank must begin with Bill Earley, Danny and Jan Fitzgerald, Sid Matthew, John Strawn, Robert R. Sampson, and several indispensable Anonymouses, all of whom dropped what they were doing to come to my aid on numerous occasions. Thanks too, to:

Golfers: Al Besselink, Jack Burke, Jr., David Duval, Bruce Fleisher, Gilbert Freeman, Freddie Haas, Fred Hawkins, Bill Hyndman, Herman Keiser, Dave Marr, Byron Nelson, Jack Nicklaus, Arnold Palmer, Skee Riegel, Paul Runyan, Gene Sarazen, Charlie Sifford, Frank Stranahan, Art Wall, Tom Weiskopf, and Mickey Wright.

Writers: Jim Apfelbaum, Bill Babb, Ward Clayton, Jaime Diaz, Jim Dodson, Bill Fields, John Helyar, Mike Hiestand, Steve Oney, Mike Purkey, Rick Reilly, John Steinbreder, Mark Stewart, and Ron Whitten.

Historians: Robert Boyd, Reginald Butler, Edward Cashin, Burt Darden, Vicki Greene, Julie Ketterer, Lynn King, Jerry Matheis, Erick Montgomery, Patty Moran, John Naglich, Barbara K. Ordway, Caleb Roehrig, Mike and 'Lou Rucker, Bob Zimmerman, and from the Columbia University Oral History Research Office, Mary Marshall Clarke and Anne M. Gefell (for, among other things, allowing me to quote from Clifford Roberts interviews in the Eisenhower Administration Oral History).

Grass and tree experts: George Blakeslee, Ed Connors, Pete Cookingham, Lloyd McKenzie, Patrick M. O'Brien, Tom Schanher, Dr. Jim Watson, and Tim White.

France: Danielle DeLange, Andrée Fauchon, and Terry Stotts.

Architects: John La Foy and Desmond Muirhead.

TV: Frank Chirkinian, John Derr, Mitch Sado, Pat Summerall, and Ben Wright.

Medical: Dr. Allan Martin and Dr. Cheryl Sampson.

Fashion: Jan Strimple.

Finally, a special thank you to Glenn Greenspan of Augusta National; Doc Giffin; Scott Tolley of Golden Bear; Jim Donovan Literary; Peter Gethers and Amy Scheibe of Villard; and to Cheryl, Clay, and John.

CONTENTS

The 1934 Annual Invitation Tournament program.

INTRODUCTION

Charles de Clifford Roberts, Jr., sat in his apartment on Park Avenue and East Sixty-first, a seventy-four-year-old man with a polished scalp, blue eyes, and a whiskey-reddened nose. Never an imposing man physically—five-nine in his prime—Roberts had shrunk with age, surrendering about an inch. He drank a glass of burgundy in the late afternoon, and as he surveyed his domain, he moved his head in a birdlike way, trying to choose the right view through his trifocals.

His apartment building didn't impress much, either, just a fourteen-story brown brick rectangle with a plain-Jane façade. New York City had hundreds just like it. But 535 Park Avenue was a prestigious address, and expensive. Two uniformed doormen attended the entrance, and Central Park loomed just two blocks to the west. Roberts could go to his window, incline his head to the left, and if he wished to, see huge elms and oaks, prematurely crimson and orange in the cold fall of 1968.

Roberts sat alone. Once he'd been a social dynamo in his adopted hometown. His days between the wars and after World War II had been filled with business lunches and golf games at either of his two clubs, Blind Brook and Deepdale near New York City, or at Maidstone or National Golf Links, a hundred miles away on Long Island. At night, he played—expertly—in the Two-Cent Bridge Club. From time to time he took in a fight at Madison Square Garden.

Now, with so many of his cronies dead or retired to a warmer place, he didn't go out much.

He missed Bob Jones the most. Robert Tyre "Bobby" Jones, Jr., had been the second-brightest star in the glittering Golden Age of Sports—only Babe Ruth shone more brightly—and Clifford Roberts carried his spears. Other men's egos shrunk in the face of greatness, but Roberts's swelled. For years he counted on constant telephone and letter contact with Jones, his partner, his friend, his hero. Together they'd founded the Augusta National Golf Club and created the Masters. Later they'd gone into other business together. Now they rarely spoke. Disease had trapped Jones in his white-columned mansion on Tuxedo Road in Atlanta—a rare neurological disorder had made his spine as brittle and weak as an old stick, and it had curled his hands into unfeeling claws. Jones lived in a wheel-chair or in his bed. Someone had to light his cigarettes for him, and the only way he could sign his name was by grasping a tennis ball skewered with a pen. Roberts had recently told Jones that he no longer looked well enough to perform the traditional chat with the new Masters champion on TV after the tournament. This was true enough—Jones looked ghastly—but his feelings had been deeply hurt at having it pointed out. Jones excused himself from the tele-cast.

For almost forty years, Jones proposed and Roberts disposed, but time and decay had flipped their relationship upside down. Now Roberts was telling Jones what to do.

Together they had started the golf course in 1932, then the tournament in 1934, and had made both grow beyond anyone's ex-pectations, especially their own. Jones was president of the club, Roberts was chairman. Jones, cerebral, graceful, well educated, and above all enormously popular, provided the enterprise's guiding light. Roberts, whose formal education ended upon his graduation from a dinky high school in South Texas, was Jones's antipode; one Augusta National member referred to him as "our designated bas-tard." Yet everything this oddly complementary couple did together worked, including Joroberts, Inc., the company they formed to bot-tle Coca-Cola in South America. Pepsi couldn't keep up in Uruguay and Brazil, and the pesos and cruzeiros poured in. Thrilled to work with a man he idolized, Roberts gloried in their spectacularly successful early ventures, but even better ones beckoned.

In 1948, the year Jones was diagnosed with syringomyelia and began his long, slow decline, Roberts met General Dwight D. Eisenhower, who was to World War II what Jones had been to golf. One was born to command, the other to soldier, and they formed an immediate bond. Within months of their meeting, the general joined Augusta National, told Roberts to "call me Ike," and began to consider him one of his leading advisers and perhaps his closest friend. Within a few more months, Eisenhower received a staggering half-million-dollar advance for a book on the war in Europe; Roberts, the ultimate insider, helped arrange both the huge payment from Doubleday and the sales-boosting serialization of the book in the *New York Herald Tribune.* "He [Eisenhower] promptly handed the money over to me," Roberts later recalled proudly, "and asked me to put it in income securities for him." Roberts brokered stocks for Reynolds and Company, a New York investment banking firm (he owned one sixth of the company), and he was good at it; Eisenhower's portfolio quadrupled over the next fifteen years, with minimal risk. In one of his best gambits, Roberts got the general into Gulf Oil at sixty dollars in 1949. The stock raced up to ninety-five dollars a share within two years, then split two for one. Ike, along with several dozen other Augusta National members, also invested in Joroberts.

With Jones in decline, the pairing of Ike and Cliff solidified. Four years after they met, Roberts's wonderful new friend was elected president of the United States. Further glorious adventures unfolded: fund-raising, vacations, card games, conventions, campaigns, golf, and intimate counsel, all with or for the Most Powerful Man on Earth. Roberts hung a pair of pajamas and a toothbrush in the White House for eight years, and the staff at the presidential mansion came to refer to the Red Room as "Mr. Roberts's bedroom." Ike, in turn, visited Augusta so frequently that in 1953 Roberts arranged for the construction of a residence for his friend the president on the club grounds. The day after Ben Hogan won the Masters that April, Eisenhower flew in to Augusta and held his grandson David's hand as they watched a crew pour the foundation for his new house.

Because Eisenhower liked to fish, in the fall of 1949 Roberts built him a pond, not more than a skulled nine-iron from where the future First Hacker's house would stand. Store-bought bluegill and black bass soon swam in the shady little lagoon.

No subject was out of bounds between them. At least twice during the first presidential campaign, Roberts wrote to Eisenhower about religion. "[Several friends] urge me to advise you to join a church," Roberts wrote, although he believed Ike's "independence from formal affiliation with a particular denomination was an asset politically rather than a liability." Abraham Lincoln's parents were Baptists, Roberts informed Eisenhower, and Mary Todd Lincoln, his wife, had been Episcopalian, but Lincoln attended a Presbyterian church. Soon thereafter, Ike began gracing a pew. He never missed a Sunday at Reid Memorial Presbyterian over the scores of weekends he spent in Augusta.

Roberts, on the other hand, didn't attend. "Some think he was an atheist," recalls an Augustan who worked closely with the club chairman for many years. "At least, he never set foot in a church here."

"Dear Cliff," Eisenhower wrote in February 1951. "Anglo-Saxon men do not spend much time telling each other, face to face, anything of their mutual affection and regard," he began, then described at length his appreciation of his friend's thoughtfulness, devotion, and attention to the growth of the Eisenhower family fortune. The already profound friendship between Ike and Roberts grew even deeper during the presidential years.

When John F. Kennedy moved into the White House in 1961, Eisenhower departed for his farmhouse in Pennsylvania and for Palm Springs in the Southern California desert. From his most recent visit to Ike and Mamie, Roberts knew his dear friend had lost his vitality; by March 1969, in fact, Eisenhower would be dead. What with Vietnam, rioting students, and another Democrat, Lyndon Johnson, in the White House, the whole world was going to hell. Even the last Masters tournament had seemed a part of the larger chaos. There had been a rules dispute, and for twenty tortuous minutes after the conclusion of play, no one was sure who won.

Letitia Roberts provided no succor. Roberts and his second wife, the former Letitia Anderson Shearer, married since Christmas 1958, stood just three years away from a divorce court in Port-au-Prince. But the relationship ended long before 1964. Roberts knew one thing from his first divorce: a marriage isn't healthy one day and dead the next.

Roberts had also been denied the comfort that fatherhood and grandfatherhood might have provided. Or rather, he'd denied it to himself. Roberts didn't like children, and in fact believed that overpopulation would be the death of us all—believed it so profoundly that he left most of his fortune to Planned Parenthood. A man who'd sired five kids was once up for an invitation to join Augusta National. Everybody else at the club liked him, but Roberts looked over his dossier and vetoed the prospective member. "Anyone who is stupid enough to have five children isn't smart enough to belong to Augusta National," he said.

Roberts, golf's last autocrat, wielded power like the Old Testament God, with lots of rules—and no mercy.

Now, back in his New York apartment, Roberts waited for summer to end. The club didn't open until October, and Roberts wouldn't return to Augusta until then. The phone rang. John Mason, who ran the oral history department at Columbia University, would like to pay a visit. General Eisenhower's first postwar job had been as president of Columbia. As part of the Eisenhower Research Project, the amiable Mr. Mason explained, he would appreciate the opportunity to tape-record Mr. Roberts's memories of his time with Ike between 1948 and 1960. Mason seemed like a nice guy, and he was someone to talk to. Moreover, Roberts regarded himself as a historical figure, worthy of just this sort of recognition. So he agreed to the interview, but with one condition, which he announced on page one of the transcript: "I desire to place the following restriction on my memoir: that no use of any kind whatsoever is to be made [of it] until 20 years after my death."

The one interview Mason expected turned into fifteen, conducted over the next four years. The transcript of their talks fills 878 pages; if the interviewer hadn't run out of tape several times, it would have been more. By comparison, Clare Boothe Luce, Ike's ambassador to England, reminisced for 108 pages; Attorney General Herbert Brownell, Jr., 402; and Marion Bayard Folsom, Eisenhower's second secretary of Health, Education and Welfare, 163. Cliff Roberts, of course, had no official capacity at the Eisenhower White House. But the fact that he slept there overnight 120 times showed how close he was to the seat of power.

The obsessively organized Roberts brought notes to the tapings to refresh his memory. "Wasn't he a Republican?" Mason asked about some political figure. Roberts's reply required 1,200 words, four-plus double-spaced pages. Roberts spoke concisely, with no stumbles or repetitions—but with frequent pauses and *ah, ah*'s during which he searched for just the right word. He often interjected lawyerly turns of phrase: "I undertook to determine," for example, instead of "I tried to find out."

Professor Mason was struck by how lonely Roberts seemed and how anxious he was to talk—about almost anything.

The Eisenhower campaign needed money. "Well, I used to go over to Pete's office [Peter Jones, the preternaturally generous president of Cities Service, and a member at Augusta National] or he'd come over to my office and he'd give me $25,000 at a time in currency," Roberts recalled. "Pete and I were skirting around the fringes of the law [but] everybody violated those rules so regularly every year and nobody went to jail for violating them, so neither Pete nor I were worried too much."

Ike had woman trouble. Cliff met with the woman, Kay Summersby, who had written a book that hinted at a World War II romance with the general. "The Jewish writer that did the actual writing told a reasonably accurate story, as recited by Miss Summersby," Roberts said, "but there were a number of sentences in the book [*Eisenhower Was My Boss*, published in 1948] which, if lifted out of context and headlined separately, could be classified as double meanings, and the second meaning suggested a considerable degree of intimacy between the girl and Ike.

"I studied the woman rather closely during our two hour talk and came to the conclusion that she had never been General Ike's mistress. . . . I had sized him up as being one of those rather rare individuals like Bob Jones, for example, who was strictly a one-woman man. But I also felt that Summersby did not have sufficient physical appeal to tempt the average man, let alone a man such as General Ike."

Mason asked Roberts to comment on the 1957 civil rights disturbance in Little Rock, when, in perhaps the worst domestic crisis in his two terms, Ike sent federal troops to Arkansas to protect the black students who had enrolled at Little Rock's Central High. Roberts blamed the whole affair on the state's "worthless sort of a governor," Orval Faubus. "Southerners were very rational about most any other subject in the world, but when it came around to this thing, almost to a man they just said, 'Integration means one thing. It means mixed marriage.' . . . Those people were a lot more right about it than I thought they were at the time. . . . Where you had complete equality, since 1880 in Brazil, you go down there and look at the end result, I'll be damned if it's anything to look at being constructive.

"The mixed are the worst. But if [Brazilian businessmen] had their choice, they'd hire white people to work for them entirely, and secondly, their second choice would be 100 percent black people, and the third choice would be mixed, that they are the most worthless of all in every respect."

The Roberts tapes reveal a flawed and self-righteous man who harbored views on race that were and remain fairly common but are seldom so unashamedly revealed for the record. None of his views distinguished him from others of his class and age. His several compensating strengths also show through: loyalty, intelligence, a remarkable attention to detail, and brilliance at operating as a power behind the throne. In the behind-the-scenes string puller's traditional field, public relations, Roberts was somehow simultaneously a genius and an ignoramus.

The memoir disappoints in only two ways. Roberts didn't much discuss the Masters or Augusta National, where his peculiar talents helped create an institution golfers revere. And he didn't foreshadow his death.

Roberts killed himself five years after his final interview for the oral history. Researchers may open the five big, black binders expecting a confession, some preamble to Roberts's suicide note. But they won't find it.

* * * * * * * * * *

The golf tournament Roberts and Jones started is the only one that costs $20 to get in and $400 to get out. Some patrons are satisfied to leave with a few memories and a little green golf towel on a hook. But you always hear stories like this: A guy in the teeming retail complex by the main entrance finally reaches a cashier and presents three shirts. "How many of each of these are in stock?" he asks. The cashier taps computer keys. "At least fifty-four of this Slazenger," he says, "about forty of this Hickey Freeman, probably seventy of the green and white. Depends on how many are on the shelves." "I'll take all the mediums," the man says, "and I need hats and umbrellas, too." He pays his $10,000 tab in cash.

Just as the estimated per capita souvenir expenditure is skewed by corporate expense accounts, so too is the actual cost of a ticket. IBM ponied up $2,500 each for twenty gray-market badges in 1996, using them as the centerpiece for a week of entertainment for its top golf-nut clients. "I feel, as I'm sure you do, that sending your corporate clients to the 1997 Masters Golf Tournament would be a great way to reward them for their continuous business," reads the cover letter from a Colorado-based ticket broker. Page two has the prices: $150 for the Monday practice round, $200 for Tuesday,

$250 for Wednesday, and $2,900 for a badge for the four tournament rounds. But interest in the 1997 tournament overheated to boiling: season passes sold routinely for $8,000, and it was whispered that someone paid $12,000 for a clubhouse badge. In other words, the sixteen- to twenty-dollar-per-day face value of a ticket to the Masters is a laughable fiction—laughable, that is, if you've got a ticket.

"A thousand for your badge?" A stranger has fallen into step with you in the parking lot. He holds his hand over his mouth when he talks. As the spring twilight gathers, gentle as sleep, you notice the stranger at your side is dressed in a Full Augusta: green hat, shirt, jacket, and paper ticket, all rampant with the Masters logo, a chrome yellow outline of the continental United States with a flagstick poking out of the lower right corner, on a background of grass green. He wears green pants, the wrong shade, and carries a green, logoed lawn chair and a green, presumably logoed umbrella under his arm. The man is an army of dandelions on a field of clover, a getup that hints that he is picking up his own tab, that his Masters is more a religious experience than a mere tax write-off. The Thursday play is over; he wants to pay a grand for just three days inside the hallowed grounds. You hesitate. You've read the legalese: ANY-ONE ATTEMPTING TO RESELL THIS BADGE IS SUBJECT TO PROSECUTION UNDER APPLICABLE LAW. "Eleven hundred?" implores the stranger.

The next morning, the thoroughfare outside the main entrance to the Augusta National Golf Club buzzes with the ordered confusion of cars, cops, street vendors, and pedestrians. The ticketed enter the Masters Golf Tournament at Gate 3A through a break in the twelve-foot-high bamboo, pearlbush, and red-tipped photinia hedge. Blue-blooded Augustans, once-a-year customers of once-a-year scalpers, well-connected corporate types, the media, members, golf professionals (Class A PGA club pros get in free), and a sizeable cadre of repeat attenders come in off Washington Road with a self-congratulatory air. But anxiety paints the faces of the ticketless. They are refugees, and they can't cross the border because their papers are not in order. They lock their car doors with their left hands and immediately hold aloft the right, one or two or three fingers extended, hoping to find a surreptitious seller of the toughest ticket in sports.

How tough a ticket? Well, the Masters has been officially sold out since 1972, but demand exceeded supply as early as 1964 (Arnold Palmer shot 69 and 68 in the first two rounds that year, and thousands of his acolytes appeared for the final two rounds, many of whom were turned away). The waiting list grew so preposterously long by 1978 that it was simply abolished; Jesus will return before it is opened again. Scalpers in mirrored sunglasses and basketball shoes patrol the main parking lot and Washington Road, chanting their mantra, "Got an extra ticket? Got an extra ticket?" without moving their lips. To answer a plague of counterfeiting, the club recently began placing holograms on Masters ducats. Starting in 1997, the club conducted a lottery—*for the practice rounds.* And once two dozen CBS Television executives were caught wearing the Masters badges of two dozen dead men.

We love the Masters in part because it seems so pure. Sandwiches cost just a buck and a half, pairing sheets and parking are free, and the whole place is devoid of advertising. Then there is the course itself, golf's equivalent of baseball's Fenway Park. While British Open links look imposing and inscrutable, and you wonder if you could hit the typical U.S. Open fairway with your cautious cut five iron, Augusta National encourages uninhibited swings. With its elevated tees, no rough, and wide fairways, even the humblest among us feels he could be . . . Arnie. And not *just* Arnie, but *Arnie charging.* Such fantasy is wonderfully easy at Augusta.

Then there's the beauty.

As much theater as golf course, no athletic arena looks better on TV. Who can forget that shot of Jack Nicklaus with his blond hair and his green-and-white-patterned Hathaway shirt framed against the indigo blue of the pond in front of the sixteenth green in the final round of the 1975 tournament? In person, you appreciate that Augusta National was built on an ornamental-tree nursery and that it blooms like young love every April. Warm spring winds whisper through the pines, blazes of pink and white and scarlet on the background of flawless green make your heart ache, and what's that scent on the wind? Nandina? Tea olive?

Continuity counts for more than dogwood blossoms, however. Continuity is the reason for $8,000 badges and TV's willingness to pay the club $7 million per year to broadcast the tournament and Mizuno, Inc.'s payment of untold additional millions annually for the right to put the little yellow-and-green logo on golf equipment it sells in Japan. The other majors are erratic point-to-point races from Detroit to Seattle to Sandwich and seldom back again, but the Masters loops hypnotically back to East Georgia every spring. Not coincidentally, the tournament often ends on Christianity's celebration of rebirth and renewal, Easter Sunday.

"Isn't there a sameness to the Masters after all these years?" veteran golf writer Dick Taylor asked himself in a column in 1993, his thirty-first year of covering the tournament. "Never," Taylor wrote. "There is a 'high' experienced entering the gates each spring like no other in golf. It's anticipation of something great that is bound to happen."

Through decades of televised visits, we all know the course. We even know the commentator's patter: the tournament "won't really begin" until the back nine on Sunday, and we're certain that someone on the verge of winning will develop a disastrous case of threshold anxiety, while another competitor will discover untapped reserves of mental strength. The players we expect to play Augusta National well will be at the top. They will attempt shots that straddle the line between the heroic and the stupid, and sometimes they'll go over the line. The wrong man will win. Or the absolute right man.

During his annual pilgrimage, one gentleman from Arlington, Texas, saves his translucent green sandwich wrappers—chicken salad or pimiento cheese on white—always ritually purchased at the concession stand behind the sixteenth tee. In 1994, a club professional at his first Masters walked down the tenth fairway, recording the gorgeous scene with his camcorder. At the bottom of the steep hill the golf pro had to shut off the camera. He couldn't see; his eyes had filled with tears. On another sunny April morning, a sportswriter for *The Charlotte Observer* climbed the long rise between the press center and the first tee. At the top, he fell to his hands and knees, in the kiss-the-earth posture of Pope John Paul II. "Grass just doesn't grow like this!" Mike Purkey said to his companion. Purkey, now a senior editor at *Golf Magazine*, had been to several U.S. Opens and PGA Championships and to scores of PGA Tour events, but he'd never seen ground so smooth and tightly grassed or such a stunning, undulating immensity of emerald.

Purkey's employer fully understands Masters lust. So, like *Golf Digest* and every other golf rag, *Golf Magazine* publishes a Masters preview section in its April issue. The formula calls for an analysis of the favorites, a paean to the twelfth hole (or to the thirteenth, fifteenth, sixteenth, or eighteenth, or to the Par 3 course, or to the entire front nine), a recap of the previous year's tournament, and a profile of the defending champ. Perhaps a brief lesson in Augusta National syntax: members refer to the founding fathers as Bob Jones (never Bobby) and Mr. Roberts (rarely Cliff, never Cliffie). Their club is the National, which is sufficient to differentiate it from the (Augusta) Country Club, the course that borders the National to the south, behind the twelfth, thirteenth, and fifth greens. People who pay to watch the Masters are patrons, not customers. That stuff in the barrels is refuse, not trash, certainly not garbage. The semicircle of white, colonial-style buildings behind and to the left of the tenth tee are neither big houses nor small mansions; they are "cabins." One of the cabins has six bedrooms, another has eight bedrooms, eight baths, two saunas, and two living rooms.

Another staple of the Masters preview is a Masters trivia section, "Fifty Things You Didn't Know About the Masters":

What's the deal with those green jackets? Only members and Masters champions may wear them, and they are not to leave the Augusta National grounds—with the notable exception that new champions may keep their coats with them for the year of their reign, like Miss America's tiara. For a long time the jackets were made by the Brooks Uniform Company of New York City; they are now supplied by Hamilton Taylor, Inc., of Cincinnati. The fabric is 55 percent wool, 45 percent polyester; the coats are fully lined in rayon and silk, and the color of the green lining matches the outside. Single breast, single vent, three brass buttons on the front, two on each sleeve, and each button is embossed with the club logo. Augusta National ships the components of the coats to Hamilton Taylor for assembly, so no, you cannot get the same jacket for your club. But Hamilton Taylor will sell you a very similar après-golf garment for about $300 each. How about something in tan?

Who's finished second the most? Ben Hogan, Jack Nicklaus, and Tom Weiskopf, four times each.

What was the worst-ever eighteen-hole score in the Masters? Ninety-five, by George Kunkle, an amateur, in the fourth round in 1956, probably the windiest day in Masters history. He tripled the first hole and shot 49 on the front.

Has an amateur ever won? No. The best-ever finishes for an amateur were by Frank Stranahan, who tied for second in 1947; Ken Venturi, second in 1956; and Charlie Coe, joint second in 1961.

Didn't Roberts kick Stranahan out of the tournament the year after he took the silver medal and silver salver? Yes. Stranahan quarreled with a course worker, and Roberts settled their minor dispute in a very drastic, dramatic way. Stranahan and the other players could hardly believe it.

Did Roberts really require concession workers to cut holes in their pockets, to discourage them from walking with any of that sandwich money? Yes. *I'd like to join Augusta National, and I'd like to play next Saturday morning at ten. Who do I call?* You don't. To quote Roberts, "Every golfer in the country liked Bob Jones to an extent of almost considering themselves to be personal friends. . . . If such an admirer were turned down for membership in Bob's club, it was a tragedy, not just a disappointment. Accordingly, the club was obliged to adopt an 'invitation only' policy."

But Jones and Roberts died decades ago. Does the club still do everything their way? For the most part, yes.

Was there a parade during Masters Week in the old days? Yes; the players rode through downtown between floats and high school bands in white Oldsmobile convertibles.

And a beauty pageant? Yes; the Miss Golf Pageant featured competition in evening gown, talent, and swimsuit.

Is it true that the club sold building lots around the course and that houses were built? Strange but true, although only two houses were erected, by Mr. Jerome Franklin behind the first green and by Mr. Julian Roberts by the second tee. Roberts and Jones later decided the very idea was unseemly, and the two-story brick structures were eventually demolished.

The fifty factoids only lead to more questions, many of which transcend the Q-and-A format. As the only one of golf's four major championships to return to the same place year after year, there must have been considerable influence by the city on the tournament—and vice versa—over the years. How do Augustans feel about the National? Would Augusta be a dump without it, like Agra, India, would be without the Taj Mahal? Roberts referred to Augusta as "a little tank town," and you wonder if the locals can still feel that New York City haughtiness from behind the hedge.

And if you keep your ear to the Masters ground for even a little while you'll hear questions like these: Who owns the club? Who owns the tournament? If it's true that they don't give any money to charity, as all PGA Tour events do, then where does the money go? What's a pimiento? Are National members a secret society, like that Skull and Bones thing at Yale? Jimmy Demaret won the Masters three times, so why isn't he considered an Official Masters Hero? Why do the adoring essays in the most recent book on Bobby Jones compel you to look up the word *hagiography*? Was he really a saint? Didn't he ever have bad days or evil thoughts or nose hair? Was Roberts the careful, conniving SOB he seemed to be? Is it possible he actually relished the gradual decline in Jones's power, since it enhanced his own? Who or what shaped the shapers of the National and the Masters? Who was Bill Lane? Were Jones and Roberts racists? Does it matter?

As these questions imply, not everyone loves the tournament

and the club. "It's become the least of the four majors," says Johnny Miller, who never won there. "They're whores for one week, and then they say they're not whores for fifty-one weeks," says a former Masters champion. "What's really national about Augusta National beyond its elite reputation?" asks *Final Rounds* author James Dodson. "Their position as the shrine of golf in the U.S. is sad in a way. Only the chosen few are allowed to play the course. I wish every golfer who loves the game could play it, the same way anyone can play the Old Course." Novelist John Updike: "A Martian skimming overhead in his saucer would have to conclude that white Earthlings hit the ball, and black Earthlings fetch it, that white men swing the sticks and black men carry them," an observation that is somewhat dated, since the Augusta National caddie force is now integrated. Senior Tour pro Charlie Sifford disgustedly refers to the Augusta National establishment as "them motherfuckers." Concludes a member at the Country Club, "That's a strange atmosphere over there. Everyone's on pins and needles, afraid they'll do something wrong and not get their annual bill [in June]." The kiss of death at the National is what the mailman doesn't deliver.

Some of the caviling is warranted, some of it is not. While the Masters and the National have clung to a romanticized image of the Old South and one version of Old Golf, that could as easily indicate an admirable steadfastness as a dark conspiracy against change. And many critics have their own prejudices and agendas. Most of it comes down to the often hurtful and negative power of exclusion. Augusta National represents a birthday party everyone at school knows about and wants to attend. And the precious few who are invited are resented by the others. Dodson loves golf as it is played in Scotland, where the game was born and where it remains affordable and inclusive, quite the opposite of the National. Sifford, a black man, believes he was unfairly excluded from the tournament.

"Sure, Cliff Roberts and Hord Hardin were dictators," says Dan Jenkins, who has covered the tournament for either *Sports Illustrated, Golf Digest,* or the now-defunct *Fort Worth Press* since the early 1950s. "But I'd hate to see what the Masters would have been without them. And I'm not sure I want to see what happens when the new breed at Augusta starts putting committees in charge."

As for the hand-wringing columnists, they're forever wrapping everything in their standards of correctness, even antiques like the Masters. As British historian Denys Wistanley wrote in 1912, "Nothing is more unfair than to judge men of the past by the ideas of the present." But we do it all the time. For instance, in a 1993 column entitled "Politely White: Augusta Is Out of Touch," *Portland Oregonian* writer J. E. Vader decried the whiteness of the Masters' gallery and its players and the blackness of its concession workers and litter crews. Vader's tone puts you in mind of the scene in the movie *Casablanca*, when the bon vivant police captain played by Claude Rains is forced by the Nazis to close down Humphrey Bogart's bar.

> CAPTAIN LOUIS RENAULT: I am shocked, shocked! to find gambling is going on here.
>
> EMIL, THE CROUPIER: Your winnings, sir.
>
> CAPTAIN RENAULT: Thank you very much.

What? You mean racism lurks in the Georgia woods? Thank you very much for the very old news. The real surprise isn't that black serves white in some precincts of the Old South; it's that the two-hundred-year-old caste system is so durable.

But the Masters establishment doesn't want to hear any of it, the criticism or the caveats. The strangest part of the Jones-Roberts legacy is the pervasive worry about how the media depicts the club and the tournament. The teenager's self-consciousness in the nearly seventy-year-old institution seems startling and unwarranted. How many times must the queen be told she's the fairest in the land?

And like the queen in the fairy tale, Augusta National rules with fear. A cheerful publisher of cheerful golf books tells you he's got lots of great Masters stories—but he won't tell you any of them. "It's my ass," he says. "Besides, it's a private club, so they can do whatever they want. It's their tournament. All I know is it's the only tournament on TV I watch wall-to-wall, and it's gorgeous, and there are very few commercials. It's the start of the golf season."

"It's my ass" speaks to the widespread fear in the land of doing or saying anything that might provoke the Lords of the National and cause a press credential to be revoked, a source to dry up, an invitation to be withdrawn, or a membership to be revoked. "They can do whatever they want" is patently false. Example: after Augusta National member Hall Thompson spoke too frankly and too publicly about the absence of black members at his new golf course, Shoal Creek, the site of the 1990 PGA Championship, the PGA Tour issued an edict to all clubs: get a black or two paying dues or forget about hosting one of our tournaments. Augusta National fell in line. Its first black member, Ron Townsend, the president of the CBS TV affiliate in Washington, D.C., joined in 1991.

But of all the weapons-grade bullshit written and spoken about the Masters, "It's their tournament" is the biggest lie. Emotionally, the Masters belongs to the millions watching on TV and to the one hundred or so competitors and their caddies and their friends and families. Morally, a part of it belongs to the people of Augusta, who kept the event alive through the lean years before Arnie and TV. Legally, of course, the Masters is the property of Augusta National, Inc., which in 1996 paid Augusta-Richmond County property taxes of $207,425.96 based on its assessed value of $7,656,560. Still, you can imagine a lawsuit or two if the corporation ever decided "their tournament" had just become too damn much trouble and they weren't gonna have it anymore.

* * * * * * * * * * *

In Atlanta, the saying goes, the first thing they want to know is what you do for a living; in Macon, a new acquaintance asks what church you attend; in Savannah, they ask what you're drinking. But in Augusta, the first question is about your mother's maiden name. "Now *who* was you mama?"

This preoccupation with antecedents gives you the feeling that no one ever dies there. The culture looks backward for guidance. Confederate generals glare at you from parlor walls. The museums are excellent, and the historical society is active. Then there's that vibrant 365.64-acre monument to Bobby Jones on Washington Road. Clifford Roberts shot himself in the head by the pond he built for Ike, but he lives, too. So too do a surprising cast that make up the history of the place, men who shaped our view of an era and of the South.

Marginal figures like National members Jock Whitney and Freeman Gosden had a huge impact. When no one else would take a chance, Whitney spent three of his family's millions to finance what would become the most popular movie in history, a film of one of the most popular novels of all time, *Gone With the Wind*. Gosden and his partner, another white man named Charles Correll, developed and performed in a radio show called *Amos 'n' Andy*. No program was bigger; in the pre-TV thirties, the whole country stopped to listen to the two buffoonish "colored" voices, six times a week, for fifteen minutes, on NBC. Ty Cobb, the bigoted and violent baseball star, lived in Augusta, and frequently played the National. James Brown lives there still; the Godfather of Soul, of course, was never a member. Neither were Augusta natives Danny Glover, the actor, nor Butterfly McQueen, the actress. But they are part of the lore. So are Grantland Rice, O. B. Keeler, Henry Longhurst, Dan Jenkins, the presidents of Coca-Cola, Bethlehem Steel, General Motors, Singer Sewing Machines, and the United States; and Gene, Byron, Ben, Arnold, Jack, and Tiger; and Jack Whitaker, Frank Chirkinian, and Ben Wright; and caddies named Stovepipe, Dead Man, Marble Eye, and First Baseman. All of them still breathe Augusta air, or seem to.

William Faulkner, living two states to the left, explained the situation neatly. "The past isn't dead," he wrote. "It isn't even past."

THE
MASTERS

•

○

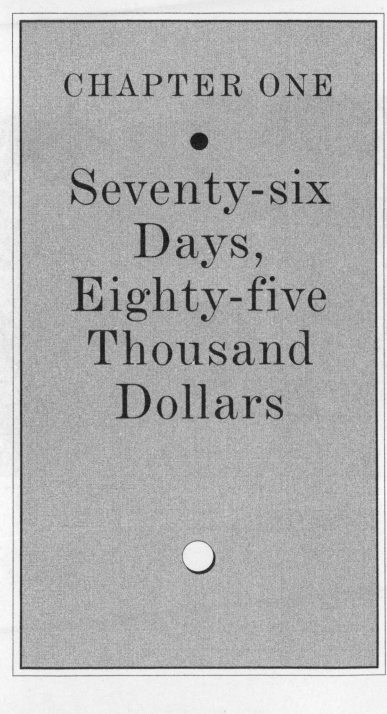

CHAPTER ONE

•

Seventy-six Days, Eighty-five Thousand Dollars

Promoters used bumper stickers in the thirties
and forties to try to raise attendance.

Cliff Roberts is our Bible.
—Augusta National chairman Jackson Stephens

Echoes and anticipation filled Penn Station. The intermittent slam of dropped suitcases mingled with the hail of shouted greetings, and the nasal loudspeaker drone of announced departures added counterpoint to the music of New York City's cavernous train terminal. But after the stock market crashed in October 1929, the railroad song was hushed. As the Great Depression deepened, people did less of anything that cost money, including travel.

Clifford Roberts stepped into this traveling buyer's market in January 1933. As he explained to the representatives of the revenue-hungry Southern Railroad System, he required comfortable conveyance for one hundred New Yorkers to and from Augusta, Georgia. At a discount. "Business was so bad," Roberts wrote in his history of the club, "that the railroad promised not only a special low rate, but all new Pullman equipment with two club cars for card players and two dining cars." Roberts accepted, and the big party for the grand opening of the Augusta National Golf Club began in a railroad station in New York City.

No event in the history of the club—not even the Masters—would be more important than this first gathering.

Eighty gentlemen had joined the new club by the eve of its formal opening; remarkably, about sixty of them lived in New York. The very idea seems bizarre in retrospect: a private enclave for rich Yankees in the heart of the South, just sixty-eight years after the

Civil War? But Augusta spread its arms in welcome for the National, largely because it was Bobby Jones's club. No Southern man had been so admired since Robert Edward Lee, the heroic but defeated Confederate general in the War of Northern Aggression. Another important factor in the civic embrace had to do with empty hotel rooms. Augusta was a resort town. But Northern tourists in recent years had begun to remain seated when their trains pulled into Union Station in Augusta; they'd discovered Florida. The Depression, of course, slowed commerce even further. Thus for one hundred dollars each, Cliff Roberts's New Yorkers—exactly one hundred of them—got three days' accommodation at the Bon Air Vanderbilt Hotel, local transportation in Augusta, and a round-trip ticket on the luxurious magic carpet of the rails, the Pullman.

Roberts took care of everything. He wrote and distributed an itinerary, organized a bridge tournament and made up the teams, made sure there was plenty of bootleg whiskey aboard (Prohibition's repeal was still a month away), and assigned bunks, giving the younger or more athletic travelers the uppers and the heavier or more mature gentlemen the lower beds. White-jacketed, black-skinned porters accompanied each Pullman sleeper. They made up the berths at nine or ten o'clock and helped those who needed a boost or a ladder up to the second story. The porters, living on tips, smiled a lot and called you "Mr. Smith" or "Mrs. Jones" and were customarily and carelessly called "George" in return—after George Pullman, the manufacturer of the Pullman car.

The three-foot-wide beds had curtains on one side, a window on the other, and a little hammock above, for holding wallets, jewelry, shaving gear, whatever. A sink and a toilet that flushed directly onto the tracks occupied a tiny room at the front of the car. No shower. Some found the clickety-clack sound track soothing at bedtime and nodded right off, but for most, the axiom "You can't sleep the first night on a train" held true. The trip from New York City to Augusta took eighteen hours.

Lawyers and investment bankers predominated among the southbound one hundred. Among them were Walton Marshall, the president of the Vanderbilt Hotel chain, who had arranged the sharply reduced room rate at the Bon Air Vanderbilt in Augusta; Walt played cards with Cliff in the Two-Cent Bridge Club. Marshall also knew Bobby Jones and his father, because both liked to stay at his hotels; he had, in fact, introduced Cliff and Bob. Another important passenger, dark-haired, handsome Melvin Traylor, the president of First National Bank of Chicago, had saved Roberts's financial bacon by warning him in 1929 of the impending crash on Wall Street. A former president of the United States Golf Association, Traylor had presented the 1928 U.S. Amateur trophy to Bobby Jones.

A third key figure on the train was Grantland Rice, America's most-read sportswriter. Tall, bald, and fifty-two, "Granny" Rice knew everyone, and everyone knew him. In those pre-TV days, the top writers of the perspiring arts enjoyed a considerable celebrity; Rice's name instead of the athlete's often made the headline, as in RICE PREDICTS TENNIS UPSET. He led a now-legendary story on a Notre Dame football game with "Outlined against a blue-gray October sky, the Four Horsemen of the Apocalypse rode again." He filled his column with similar classical allusions and with verse: "When the One Great Scorer / comes to mark against your name / he marks not that you won or lost / but how you played the game." Rice liked to tell stories, which made him a great guy to drink with: "Hey, Grant, what's Dempsey really like? . . . Have you talked to Babe Ruth lately? . . . What's the story on Tilden?" Roberts wisely made Rice his assistant in organizing the grand-opening party.

He did not fit the mold of most of the other capitalist Friends of Cliff who were founding members. Rice's connection was to the Jones family. Although they didn't play against each other, Rice had met Bobby's father, Big Bob (a.k.a. "the Colonel" or "Colonel Bob"), through college baseball. A good-field-no-hit shortstop, Rice majored in Greek and Latin at Vanderbilt in the Class of 1901. Big Bob, Class of 1897 at the University of Georgia, played outfield and first base. Rice did better in dead languages than Jones did in prelaw, but Big Bob was the superior athlete. Both were fraternity men and both, not coincidentally, enjoyed a cocktail. They would share quite a few over the years, cooling down after walking together in Bobby's gallery at scores of golf tournaments. Rice's pretty daughter Florence dated Bobby for a time, and they remained friends all their lives. Rice often featured young Bob in his nationally syndicated column, "The Sportlight." He'd been working in New York since 1911, for the *Evening Mail* and later for the *Herald*, but the big city never took the Tennessee out of his voice.

In his memoir, *The Tumult and the Shouting*, Rice recalled dozens of anecdotes involving Bobby and Colonel Bob, but neither Roberts nor Augusta National got a mention. The omission seems blatant for a founding member of the club, but is understandable in the context of the privacy and secrecy that enveloped the project from the start. It would have made a good story, but Rice was not inclined to write about a vital bit of deception on the club's first official day. Just a day after the party detrained in Augusta, Granny delivered a seemingly impromptu speech at the first meeting of the membership, an oration that decided the club's direction from that day forward.

The train arrived at Augusta's Union Station on Walker Street between Eighth and Ninth, a columned and ornamented edifice built at the turn of the century. White clouds billowed from under the steam engine's eight big wheels and a prolonged metal-on-metal shriek of brakes resounded in the domed station house. Porters slowly lowered step stools at each of the coaches, and the New Yorkers walked down them, claimed their bags, and tried to get their land legs back. Cars awaited outside in the square, as did, disappointingly, New York weather—a somber rain and temperatures barely in the forties. Some of the travel- and whiskey-weary checked in at the Bon Air and stayed there. Most, however, eager to meet Bobby Jones and see the new golf course, cabbed out to Augusta National.

Their route took them west, up the big hill on Walton Way, past stately houses flanked by big bare trees, still two months from blooming. A local might have informed them that this neighborhood was called Summerville. Wealthy Augustans built summer homes there to catch the cool breezes that were unavailable below in downtown and to escape the diseases that were assumed to float in the humid air by the Savannah River. The caravan turned right and downhill on Highland Avenue, onto Berckmans Road, dark with evergreens. Back up a hill, then right on Washington Road, Augusta National's northern boundary. Washington Road was a country address, bordered by big farmhouses with white picket fences, a dairy, thick stands of oak and pine, and a tree nursery. Cars coming from the west used to get stuck a mile down the road, where Interstate 20 now crosses Washington. Had to be hauled out by mule teams. Country. "You could kill all the rabbits you wanted here back then, with a rock and a stick," an old-timer says. Local historians can't remember if Washington's two lanes were paved in 1933 or not, but everyone recalls the huge flocks of birds flying in and around the trees by the road.

As the cars turned right into a break in a high border hedge and onto Augusta National's bare dirt driveway, a strange intoxication swept over the golfers. For the first few yards, little was visible in the passageway except the curled fingers of sixty eighty-year-old magnolias, and the world disappeared in the shelter and hush. The trees had not quite grown together overhead; a little rain and light penetrated the canopy, like a long, narrow hole in a roof. The rayon tires of the taxis turned a few more times and something at the end of the tunnel came into view, something white and solid. As the 275-yard driveway reached its end, the passengers beheld a symmetrical white mansion, a vision of antebellum glory.

The drama of the entrance suspended the New Yorkers' disbelief; it was 1857 again, and the welcoming arms of the plantation had made time and the Depression disappear. Within the graceful, concrete-walled manor house Master Bobby Jones awaited, and beyond Jones lay the virgin golf course, and the New Yorkers went out into the cold rain to have at it.

For warmth, "two of our local members provided some corn [whiskey] that had a little age," Roberts recalled. Kegs were placed beneath tents on the first and tenth tees. "However, some of those present had never drunk corn before, and did not know how strong it was until, let us say, it was too late."

That night after dinner at the Bon Air, club president Jones rose to his feet and tapped a glass. "But before he could proceed, Grantland Rice was on his feet demanding to be heard," according to Roberts.

> Grant explained that he had several times previously become a member of new clubs, all of which had gone broke. In looking back for a reason, he realized that all these promising new clubs . . . had made the mistake of holding a meeting, and he didn't want to see the Augusta National make this same mistake. Therefore, he proposed a resolution to the effect that Bob and Cliff be asked to run the club without the hindrance of meetings. Whereupon everyone stood and yelled "Aye," and Bob could do nothing but join in the laughter and capitulate. . . . The spirit of Grant Rice's resolution is still in effect.

The implication that Rice acted spontaneously and alone is credible only if you believe that the sportswriter and the Wall Street Machiavelli spent weeks together orchestrating the grand opening, then eighteen hours on a train with a bottle on the table between them, and failed to discuss either the best way and the best people to run Augusta National or their strategy to make the plan happen.

But did Roberts and Rice really keep Jones in the dark about their charade? Here, Roberts's account rings true. Bobby lived in Atlanta and wasn't on the train, for one thing. And Roberts's greatest skill and deepest instinct lay in divining ways to get important men what they wanted—usually more wealth, less trouble, and more privacy. Furthermore, those close to Jones had been "doing for Bobby" all his life. For example, Jones frequently did not appear for the press after his tournament rounds. In a unique arrangement, O. B. Keeler, a sportswriter for the *Atlanta Journal*, handled radio and the other writers for young Bob. Holding a towel around his waist, O.B. would recite some humorous or classical verse, charming the socks off the reporters in the locker room, then he'd tell them exactly what Bobby was thinking when he hit that niblick to the ninth. Jones, meanwhile, deflated as an old balloon from the stress of the day, would be elsewhere, sitting in twelve inches of bathwater and drinking three inches of corn.

Others competed for a chance to help him materially. The members of his club in Atlanta bought Jones a $50,000 house, which he declined when he determined that it jeopardized his amateur status. The president of Coca-Cola set him up in the bottling business at a time when filling Coke bottles amounted to printing money. Jack Warner pressed $120,000 into Jones's hand to get him to come to Hollywood to film a series of instructional movies. The wonder was that all the help did not spoil him. On the contrary, Bobby remained disarmingly humble.

Whether the result of a conspiracy or not, the Augusta National Golf Club decided on its first formal day of existence to be run by just two men. Jones, the spiritual leader not only of the club but of the game itself, gave Roberts his authority. He'd earned Jones's confidence; Cliff's ability to raise the money to buy the land ($70,000) and build the course (approximately $100,000) during the disastrous economy of the early 1930s impressed Jones enormously. They were quite a pair: the brusque Roberts symbolized the Yankee dollar and Northern, urban values while the modest golf champion embodied Southern gentility. Augusta National was a country of kings, with no confused or impoverished peasants accustomed to following someone else's rules, but the Jones-Roberts combination worked perfectly. The iron fist in a velvet glove has forever been the formula for successful dictators.

The velvet glove part was most important. Jones's courtesy was innate; politeness swims in a Southern boy's DNA.

Compared to the multiethnic, mercurial North, Southern attitudes and culture seemed better grounded and more substantial. Jones obeyed the South's informal code: a gentleman should be a crack shot, a good drinker, and courteous, especially with ladies. He should also cultivate his mind and should not appear too obviously concerned with matters of commerce.

Family matters had a more immediate impact on Bobby, of course, than his cultural inheritance. Two events in particular made him the man he became—the death of his infant older brother and the strange psychodrama involving four generations of Jones men.

* * * * * * * * * * *

Robert Tyre Jones, the grandfather, furrowed his brow and wore a high, stiff collar for his turn-of-the-century photograph. "R.T.," a thoroughly impressive man, mastered vertical business integration before the term was invented. He owned everything in Canton, Georgia, a little burg north of Atlanta: the biggest cotton acreage; the gin (which removed the seeds from the bolls); Jones Mercantile Company, where the cotton was woven into thread and dyed to make denim; and the bank, to loan the money to the growers and the mill. In 1925, R.T. grossed $1.5 million, a fabulous income worth about 100 million of today's inflated dollars. R.T. saw his success as virtue rewarded; he wrote extensively on business ethics and served as Sunday school superintendent at the Canton First Baptist Church for forty years. The church, in turn, named the R. T. Jones Bible Study Class in honor of the biggest man in the city. His life inspired a book entitled *A Man, a Mill, and a Town.* R.T. stood six feet five, and he must have looked like a giant to his oldest child, Robert.

Robert *Purmedus* Jones. "He didn't get his father's name, and he wanted it badly," says Jones biographer Sid Matthew. "As a result, he always struggled with his identity." Purmedus—the accent is on the second syllable—also did not inherit his father's stern look or outlook, and he led the faintly rebellious life of a preacher's son. He drank white lightning with his college and Canton friends, who took to calling him "Colonel," a nickname that stuck. The young Colonel's big hands and sturdy legs helped him rip into a baseball for the Mercer University Bears in Macon for three years, and for the Georgia Bulldogs in Athens for his senior season. But R.T. did not approve. Once someone told him of his son's great ability as a ball player. "You could not pay him a poorer compliment," he replied.

R.T.'s own father had been murdered. On December 1, 1888, when R.T. was thirty-nine, William Green Jones, sixty-six, a well-off farmer of about a thousand acres in Covington, Georgia, took a walk and never came back. He was alone on the road with $300 in his pocket, money intended for a further land purchase, when someone shot him in the back of the head and robbed him. The killer was never found. This tragedy could help account for R.T.'s stiff-backed morality and for his disdain of trifling activities involving sticks and balls.

R.T. never watched his son play a game. When a major professional team, the National League's Brooklyn Superbas (the successor of the Trolley Dodgers and the forerunner to the Brooklyn Dodgers), got his son's signature on a contract, the patriarch forbade him to fulfill it. You'll be a lawyer, not a playboy, R.T. said. Robert Purmedus obeyed his father.

"I can picture the Colonel saying to himself right then, 'I'll never be this way with *my* kid,'" says Matthew.

He wasn't. The Colonel moved to Atlanta, took a law degree at Emory and in 1900, at age twenty-one, a wife, Clara Merrick Thomas. Their first child, William, lived only three months. He couldn't keep food down, suggesting esophageal reflux—a sort of chronic vomiting—or pyloric stenosis, a narrowing of the end of the stomach. The Jones's second baby appeared to have the same digestive disorder. The Colonel gave the child the name he himself had wanted—Robert Tyre—and the attention and approval he'd craved. He carried his infant son around on a pillow and had no more children.

Despite his illness, life dealt Bobby Jones an unusually full deck. Handsome, articulate, and a genius with a golf club, Jones's accomplishments so impressed a New York publisher that he was invited to write his autobiography at age twenty-four. The resultant book was a rarity in two ways: it's readable and the athlete-author actually wrote it. Rice penned the foreword to *Down the Fairway* and Keeler served as coauthor, though he didn't do much; Jones wrote better than his writer friends.

His first memory, Jones wrote, was of "Camilla, our fat cook and nurse, and her fat brother, who was also blacker than Camilla, and her beau." The Colonel's successful law practice not only made the employ of servants possible, it enabled the family to rent summer homes by East Lake, a new country club that really was in the country, five miles out of Atlanta. In the summer of 1908, just a year after the six-year-old Bobby ate his first solid food, the Jones men took up golf. Within another five years, the doting Dad and his once-sickly son were traveling to tournaments together, tournaments young Bob soon began to win.

Their love was unmistakable. The Colonel—often in the company of, as Bobby put it, "a lively group from Atlanta"—rarely missed a chance to watch his son compete, and he agonized or exulted according to the results. They played together, too, most memorably in 1915, when thirteen-year-old Bobby beat his father in the finals of the club championship at East Lake. The Colonel idolized his son and was as much his friend as his father. Bobby repaid the tribute. Although he graduated from Technological High School; from the Georgia School of Technology (now known as Georgia Tech), in Mechanical Engineering at age twenty; and from Harvard with a degree in English literature a few years later, he shucked whatever career path those credentials might afford in favor of following his father into law. He needed just two years of law school, incidentally, to pass the Georgia bar. In another salute to his father, at about age eleven, Bobby began to refer to himself as Robert T. Jones, *Junior*—although, of course, he was not a junior. He did it to please his father. He obviously felt the Colonel's pain at the snubs and remoteness of R.T.

"Bob Jones was a quiet man," recalls Charley Yates, eighty-four, an Augusta National member since 1940. "But his father was the greatest extrovert God ever put on this earth. I was a locker room tenor, and he sang bass. 'O-o-o-ld Man River-r-r . . .' "

The foreword to Jones's last memoir, *Golf Is My Game*, reads "To my father, to whom I owe all this—and a lot more." The book was published in 1960. Robert Purmedus Jones had died four years earlier.

Bobby's personality presented a complex blend of the fun-loving Colonel and fun-shunning R.T. Like his father, he charmed everyone he met—"the kind of man," as British historian and Augusta National member Alistair Cook once said, "who sought out the stranger in the corner of the room and included him in the conversation." And just as his father had, Jones liked to drink. While serving as assistant manager for the Harvard golf team—his eligibility as a player had been used up at Georgia Tech—Bobby was once asked to take care of the whiskey supply for the post-match celebration. He took care of it, all right; he drank it himself. ("Jones was not an alcoholic," Matthew says, although "his tolerance declined later in life.") Despite such frolics, Bobby was, like his grandfather, perfectionistic and stern with himself and fiercely but politely competitive. And like the patriarchal R.T., he enjoyed the solitude and mental engagement of putting his thoughts into writing.

In 1918, R.T. shocked the family by coming down to Atlanta to watch his sixteen-year-old grandson play in a World War I Red Cross exhibition match. Was this a thaw? R.T. began to send his grandson messages from on high: "If you *must* play on Sunday, play well" and, on the eve of Bobby's first U.S. Open win in 1923, a telegram that read, "Keep the ball in the fairway, and make all the putts go down." Again, in 1926, at the first of his two New York City tickertape parades, R.T. was there. The show of support touched both Bobby and the Colonel, and the generational conflict gradually resolved.

Happy endings cropped up everywhere in the twenties. During the pleasantly crazy bridge between World War I and the Great Depression, Charles Lindbergh flew his single-engine plane from New York to Paris, alone, and was anointed a hero on two continents. And if sportsmen slipped into speakeasies for a cup or two of Prohibition brew, no one told. Sportswriters in the 1920s did not debunk, they glorified.

Harold Grange, for example, a very good college halfback, became mythic when a sportswriter rechristened him the Galloping

Ghost. A loutish young man named George H. Ruth drank and screwed and ate to mindboggling excess. But he pitched brilliantly and hit home runs at an astonishing rate, so everybody loved the Sultan of Swat. Heavyweight champion Jack Dempsey's nickname, the Manassa Mauler, hinted at his savagery, but the shorthand for tennis champion William Tatem Tilden II—"Big Bill"—gave no inkling of his private demon, homosexuality. "Emperor Jones" seemed appropriate for Bobby, who stood regally in the center of the stage in golf's sunlit theater.

But Jones protected a secret, too: the game had ceased to be all sunshine. The more he succeeded, in fact, the less he enjoyed the whole adventure. More friends bet increasing amounts on him to win and were decreasingly shy about telling him of their wagers. His galleries grew exponentially each year. "With his fans—and he played in championships when spectators could reach out and touch him—Jones' patience was monumental," wrote Charles Price in his 1986 book, *A Golf Story*. "He took them all in good-natured stride—favor-seekers, storytellers, party-crashers, name-droppers, social opportunists, self-promoters, kissin' cousins, drunks, and other assorted pests." Jones suffered stomach pains and occasionally burst into tears in private, but only his intimate friends—Keeler, Rice, and the Colonel—knew about it. While Bobby hid the effects of the mounting pressure and uninvited interaction, the Colonel grew so nervous that he often couldn't watch his son's tournaments and relied on word-of-mouth reports from the battlefield. Bobby could hardly have missed his father's agitation. Another clue that big-time golf was becoming a big-time drag for Jones was his atypical spat with another competitor, Chick Evans.

Their feud came to a head during the finals of the U.S. Amateur in August 1927. Jones versus Evans drew tremendous interest; if the planets aligned correctly, Chick might actually beat Bobby. The match took place at Minikahda Country Club in Minneapolis, where Evans had won the U.S. Open eleven summers before. A special train brought scores of Evans boosters up from his hometown, Chicago.

Sparks often fly in the hand-to-hand combat of match play, and any number of things might have set Evans off. Perhaps Chick resented Bob's breeding and relative wealth or his success. Maybe he disliked the precise part in Jones's hair. Evans sold milk, wholesale, to restaurants and institutions and had a salesman's grin and showmanship and memory of first names. Jones, on the other hand, maintained a polite reserve. After muttering privately about Bobby for years, Evans went public with his complaints in an Associated Press interview, which was published widely on his seventy-third birthday, July 18, 1963.

Jones clobbered Evans 8 and 7 in their big match. But "it wasn't the beating so much as the way it was done," Evans said. "On the first tee, Jones told me I had teed my ball in front of the markers. Later he called me for putting my finger into the grass.

"On what became the last hole of our match, I putted two inches from the hole. I thought he might concede the two-inch putt. . . . I looked at him and he just stood there, about a yard from me, and stared at me. I went up to my ball, and when I put my putter head down, it touched the ball.

"I looked up at Jones. 'The ball didn't move,' I said. 'It sure did,' Jones replied." Game, set, match Mr. Jones. Evans congratulated him sarcastically.

Jones, Evans said, used twenty-two clubs to his own seven (fourteen clubs were not the maximum allowable until 1938) and thus "developed his game with his clubs rather than his skull." The best part of Jones's game "was his ability to sink long putts. He had to, because from fifty yards out he was pitiful." Evans also hinted at flaws in Jones's character, from getting to be too big for his britches to dishonesty about his status as an amateur.

Jones responded gently. "Mildly amusing," he told the AP. "If he really meant to say these things, then I'm truly sorry he said them." His private reaction contained a lot more heat. Evans's accusations were "tripe," Jones wrote in a letter to United States Golf Association executive director Joseph Dey four days after the Evans interview was published. Jones played the first nine holes in thirty-one and began the second nine with two threes. This put him six up; Chick didn't have the wherewithal that day to make up such a huge deficit to the best player in the world.

Jones contradicted everything Evans said, especially his version of the contentious ending to their match. Already beaten, Jones told Dey, Chick "preferred being the apparent victim of a misfortune to playing the long twelfth hole up the hill away from the clubhouse.

"I do not recall that I have ever said anything about this thing before, and certainly do not intend at this moment, or ever, so far as I know, to make public any of these circumstances."

Whatever the particulars of the spat, Jones had an enemy, and he knew it. And though he obviously thrived in the formalized battle of a golf tournament—as he would prove for all time in 1930—conflict upset him terribly. Grantland Rice described him as having "the face of an angel and the temper of a timberwolf." Just before or soon after the Evans match, Jones decided to retire from tournament golf. He had tired of controlling the wolf.

Moreover, there was no money in amateur golf. While he was far from destitute, Jones was not wealthy, either. Bobby was twenty-eight, married, and a father of one child (a boy, Robert Tyre Jones III), yet he still lived in his parents' home.

On a sunny September afternoon in 1930, on the eleventh green at Merion Golf Club near Philadelphia, a man named Gene Homans missed an eighteen-foot putt and extended his hand to Jones. Jones shook the hand. "All at once I felt the wonderful feeling of release from tension and relaxation I had wanted so badly for so long a time," Jones wrote later. He had defeated Homans 8 and 7 to win the U.S. Amateur, thus sweeping all four of golf's then-major championships in one year. No one had done this before, or has since. Inspired by Jones's feat, people around the country picked up golf clubs in increasing numbers. "Augusta has gone golf crazy," the *Chronicle* reported a week after Jones's slam. Duffers were seen practicing on the Richmond Academy ball fields, on the lawn in front of the Arsenal, and "wherever there are no windows."

Two months later, Jones quit the game.

****

Dr. Alister Mackenzie, M.D., had the shanks.
In the finals of the Yorkshire Medical Cup in 1926, Dr. Mackenzie lay two on the eighth hole of the second round, and his ball was nearly on the green. But the golf architect—medical doctor lateraled his next three shots, circumnavigating when he only wished to land. He lost the hole and the match in a humiliating continuation of sockets, the absolute worst shot in golf. Afterward, as he recalled in his book *The Spirit of St. Andrews*, "a friend buttonholed me and said, 'Mackenzie, do you mind me giving you a bit of advice? You are just off to Australia to lay out golf courses. For God's sake don't let them see you play golf or you will never get another job.' "

Mackenzie doubtless told this story many times and would have punctuated each telling with his booming, operatic laugh. He loved golf, but couldn't play it worth a flip until the last few years of his life. Like most hackers—but unlike most golf architects—he abhorred long grass, narrow fairways, small greens, and water hazards. "I am by nature a revolutionary," Mackenzie said.

He was also a bit of a rogue. "Being a Scotsman, I am naturally opposed to water in its undiluted state," he wrote. His rich Scottish burr hinted at haggis and single malt, but Mackenzie grew up in Leeds, in Yorkshire, England, and while his father was a physician from the Scottish Highlands, his mother was English. Still, Mackenzie always represented himself as being Scottish, for the same reason chefs so often hail from France and watchmakers are Swiss, or say they are. Alister Mackenzie, born *Alexander* Mackenzie, made a gift to each of the courses he designed of a photograph of himself in a kilt, looking pleased.

It was rumored that he ate roast beef for lunch every day and washed it down with a tumbler of scotch. His ruddy face and beefy body—and his death of an apparent heart attack at age sixty-three—hinted at high living. His golf courses were equally exuberant, but unlike the man who made them, they do not die. Some of the roller coaster greens he designed were dizzying even to look at and might be fun to ski; although most of his greens were quite reasonable, Mac often designed a surface that could require a five-yard putt to travel twenty yards to reach its target. The typical Mackenzie bunkers looked like reproducing amoebae or a wallpaper pattern popular in girls' bedrooms in 1970.

How and why did Jones hire a doctor who'd given up medicine to play in the dirt? Why not Alfred Tillinghast or George Thomas? Most of all, why not Donald Ross, the most popular and prolific golf course architect of the day, a former golf pro who really was from Scotland? Jones could have had his pick.

In the standard telling of the tale, Jones first got to know Dr. Mackenzie in 1929, in California. Bobby had just lost in a stunning upset in the first round of the U.S. Amateur at Pebble Beach, and with time on his hands and his lodging reserved for the week, he played a round at a new course down the street from Pebble on the headlands above the Pacific, Cypress Point. Mackenzie had designed it, and Jones loved it. Mac, age fifty-nine, was then employed at laying out another course on the Monterey Peninsula and at romancing a local widow, Mrs. Edgar Haddock. Mackenzie interrupted these duties to spend the next several days with Jones, discussing what should go into a great golf course and what should be left out. Jones would have been pleased to be reminded that Mackenzie, the consulting architect at the Old Course at St. Andrews, considered the Old to be a sacred place, subtle, complex, and by far the best golf course on earth. In this, Jones agreed wholeheartedly.

While Bobby may have mentally chosen Mackenzie in 1929 as the architect of Augusta National, he had become susceptible to the man two years earlier. Mackenzie had written a book published in 1920 entitled *Golf Architecture*. On the half-title page of the copy Mac sent to Atlanta he wrote:

> *TO/ Robert T. Jones (Jun)*
> *The World's finest*
> *sportsman and greatest*
> *golfer—*

With the author's
compliments. A.D. 1927

Here Jones, already thinking about the golf course he would build some day, could read what amounted to the résumé of a brilliant prospective designer of his course, combined with the man's thoughts on construction, deception, Bolshevism, bunkers, and the fine art of manuring (don't put it in too deep, Mackenzie advised). In *Golf Architecture*, he also mused on a profound and difficult subject:

> Beauty means a great deal on a golf course; for even the man
> who emphatically states he does not care a hang for beauty is
> subconsciously influenced by his surroundings. . . .
> All the famous holes and greens are fascinating to the golfer
> by reason of their shape, their situation, and the character of their
> modelling. When these elements obey the fundamental laws of
> balance, of harmony, and fine proportion they give rise to what
> we call beauty [which is] more felt than fully realized . . . and in
> course of time [the player] grows to admire such a course as all
> works of beauty are eventually felt and admired.

In this, Mackenzie spoke directly to Bobby Jones's heart. Jones considered himself an artist and golf an art rivaling the aesthetic appeal of ballet. While Sam Snead and other American pros looked around St. Andrews and saw random hills in need of mowing or excavation, Jones saw an intriguing series of solvable puzzles. The Old Course looked and felt as much like public sculpture as public golf course to him, and in its undulations and bumps he felt the breath and character of the men who'd built it over many centuries.

Part of his art appreciation had to do with myth, and with myth's first cousin, illusion. Not the myth of "Old Tom used to hit it up there" or "Vardon made a two here once" but the emotional force of imagination set free. For example, the ideal landing area for the drive (or the second shot) on the fourteenth at the Old is known

as the Elysian Fields, which in Greek mythology was a paradise assigned to virtuous people after their deaths. But to reach this
heaven, one must clear a yawning sand bunker called Hell. The idea
of the heroic but optional carry to paradise enthralled both Jones
and Mackenzie. As Mac put it, "What pleasurable excitement there
would be in seeing one's second shot sailing over Hell!"

Jones hired Mackenzie to design his course because Mac was
Bobby's educational and intellectual equal, as Donald Ross was not,
and because they agreed on a hundred little things and on one big
thing: the spirit of St. Andrews.

The subtitle to Mackenzie's *Golf Architecture* hinted at another factor in his favor: *Economy in Course Construction and
Green-Keeping.* The Depression was raging by the time Bobby was
ready to build his golf course, and he needed to have it done on the
cheap.

****

To get his own financial house in order, Jones signed a contract
on November 13, 1930, with Warner Brothers to star in a series
of ten instructional movies, costarring a score or more of movie actors playing themselves as fair-to-poor golfers. Since taking money
to teach golf on celluloid might technically make him a professional, Jones simultaneously renounced his amateur status and retired from competitive golf four days after accepting Jack Warner's
check for $120,000. He and O. B. Keeler took the train to Holly-
wood in February 1931, and Keeler, apparently concerned about
the booze situation in Southern California, brought along eleven
typewriter boxes filled with bottles of Georgia corn whiskey.

"In the foist place . . . this little shot . . . oughta be played . . .
like a long putt. Stand up . . . fairly erect . . . comfortableh . . . then
knock it up . . . close to the hole." For clarity, Jones often spoke in
short phrases in the films, in his North-Georgia-meets-Harvard accent. "Swing nice and easileh," he said, showing a rare understanding of adverbs. "My aim isn't to make a few average golfers out of
their class but to make the average of the whole somewhat bettuh."

But what Jones said and how he said it was less remarkable than his grace and command in front of the camera. Movie stars such as W. C. Fields, Joe E. Brown, Harold Lloyd, Walter Huston, and Guy Kibbee hung on every word. He looked faintly silly in makeup and lipstick, but the stars—America's royalty—worked for free and treated him with obvious deference.

Jones apparently did not take advantage of his intimate contact with movie people, one of the few classes of American Depression society with any money, by asking W. C. Fields or the others to help underwrite the construction of his new golf club. Fund-raising was Cliff's bailiwick, anyway, and he seemed to have it in hand. But the new golf course had to be on his mind; when Jones returned to Hollywood later in 1931 to make a second set of instructionals (for another $120,000) after the success of the first, Mackenzie came down from his home on the Monterey Peninsula for a visit. Perhaps he showed Jones some holes he'd sketched or a routing plan. For by this time, a site for Bobby's dream course had been selected: a former indigo plantation and defunct ornamental-plant nursery in Augusta.

Augusta was Cliff's idea. Just after Jones won the Slam in 1930, "I suggested to Bob that Augusta was the logical place," Roberts reported in his club history. It was warmer than Atlanta, Cliff pointed out (it is, by a few degrees), which was important because the club they contemplated would be open only in the winter. The members simply didn't need a summer place; they already had their Winged Foots or Shinnecock Hills, their primary clubs back up North. Augusta also had rail lines, plenty of hotel rooms, and other healthy golf courses, which Jones had played and liked. So, according to Roberts, he called slick-haired Thomas Barrett, Jr., the future mayor of Augusta, to ask if he knew of a likely site. And Barrett immediately recommended the old Berckmans place, Fruitlands. Cliff looked at it, then called Bob. Jones confirmed this chain of events, but some dispute it.

"Baloney," a long-time Masters employee and Augusta resident says today. "They searched everywhere in Cobb County [Jones lived in Atlanta, which is in Cobb]. The club is only here because this was the best acreage they could find. They didn't care about Augusta then, and they don't care now."

Whether Jones and his scouts ignored his own backyard or looked only to Augusta remains in doubt. What is known, however, is that Jones met Roberts in Augusta soon after his return from Hollywood in the spring of 1931. "This is the place," Brigham Young said when he came over the Wasatch Mountains and saw the Great Salt Lake; Jones drank in the very different beauty of vernal East Georgia and expressed the same sentiment. "Perfect! And to think this ground has been lying here all these years waiting for someone to come along and lay a golf course upon it."

The Berckmans nursery did already resemble a golf course, an astonishingly beautiful one. But it wasn't just the vista of rounded hills and oaks and pines and blooms that floated Jones's boat. This place was *private*. Jones felt the same seductive sense of enclosure the New Yorkers would feel at the grand opening a year and a half later. None of the adoring, annoying crowds he'd been drawing even for casual rounds could easily breach these green walls. Jones could laugh and swear and drink and helicopter his mashie on this side of the pearlbush and photinia, and who would know except the other guys in his foursome and their caddies? "I don't throw clubs any more, in public, though once in a while I let one fly, in a friendly round with Dad and Chick Ridley and Tess Bradshaw," Jones admitted in *Down the Fairway*. "And [I] get a great deal of relief from it, too, if you want the truth." But for several years, almost all of Jones's golf had devolved into exhibition matches, and he was sick of it.

Privacy in golf was a distinctly American idea. Lord knows Bobby needed it, and the executives who joined him in investing in Augusta National thought they did. "Our aim," Jones wrote, "was to develop a golf course and a retreat of such stature, and of such excellence, that men of some means and devoted to the game of golf might find the club worthwhile as an extra luxury where they might visit and play with kindred spirits from other parts of the nation."

Exclusion contradicted the St. Andrews model, of course.

Golf is a melting pot in Scotland—except at the country's two private clubs, both owned by Americans. Anyone with the necessary pounds and pence could play the Old Course, and still can (although you'd better have a starting time nowadays). Townspeople pause and watch the play or walk their dogs across the nearly treeless links to the sea, and hotel guests hang their heads out of their windows and comment on the golfers and their shots. *Come play*, says St. Andrews. *Stay away*, says Augusta National. *Unless you know a member.*

Two days after Bob and Cliff announced their intent to build Bobby's dream course, Roberts wrote a letter to Olmsted Brothers, a golf course construction company. He already had some letterhead, which showed the Augusta National headquarters address as Suite 201, The Vanderbilt Hotel, New York City. Roberts wrote that he and his partners planned to immediately construct a golf course on a portion of their 364 acres in Augusta. The rest of the ground would be used for a second course (never built) and for building lots for Northern members.

The construction of the course was a financial high-wire act, a dangerous race to get the thing built and producing income before the underwriters' money ran out. Construction started late in November 1931 and was completed 124 days later, on May 27, 1932. Subtract Sundays, when no one worked, and thirty days when rain prevented progress. Incredibly, Augusta National was built in seventy-six frenzied working days.

After Mackenzie and Jones settled on the routing, a contract for clearing and grubbing the land was given to a local firm, and the first part of the race began. Prosper Berckmans and his crew sprinted in front of the men with axes and mattocks, and transplanted over 4,000 small trees and shrubs from fairways into roughs and around certain greens. Berckmans had been born on the property and would remain as the club's first manager; his grandfather had started the nursery seventy-three years before.

One hundred thousand dollars had been budgeted and borrowed to build the course, but a variety of factors enabled the project to come in at least $15,000 below that. (The "extra" money was

spent on facilities not in the original estimate.) Not including the
land or any buildings, Augusta National was built for $85,000. "One
thing in our favor was the opportunity to make each dollar do double duty as the result of so many business people wanting to be identified with 'Bobby's course,'" Roberts wrote. About all some
suppliers got out of the association was a muted trumpet blast: an ad
(a *free* ad, by rights) in the first Masters program, in March 1934.

> *We point with pride to the remarkable results obtained at*
> *the Augusta National Course from the use of more than*
> *600 tons of FLORIDA PEAT HUMUS in their soils for greens*
> *and fairways. Humus is the very foundation of*
> *soil fertility and plant life. . . .*
> *Florida Humus Company, Zellwood Fl.*

The owner of Florida Humus was the president of the New York
Stock Exchange and, inevitably, a friend of Cliff's. He donated eight
freight cars full of decayed organic matter; the National paid only
the shipping cost.

> *Southern States Phosphate and Fertilizer Company,*
> *Augusta and Savannah*
> *Our Berckmans' Golf Special is used exclusively for*
> *fairways and greens by the Augusta National Golf Club*

> *Scotts Seed was selected for the Augusta National and has*
> *been sowed on one-fourth of all other American courses*
> *O. M. Scott & Sons Company, Marysville, Ohio*

Scotts supplied the National with 8,000 pounds of heat-loving common Bermuda, *Cynodon dactylon,* about the only grass anyone used
for a golf course or a lawn in the South in 1932. Bermuda turns tan
in the late fall, so for winter color the club planted domestic rye—
a winter grass—directly over the dormant Bermuda on its greens
and tees.

AUGUSTA NATIONAL GOLF CLUB'S GREENS AND FAIRWAYS
Always in Perfect Condition! 32,000 feet of McWane cast iron
pipe in sizes 8, 6, 4, 3, 2, 1¹/₄ inch installed to
provide a constant water supply
McWane Cast Iron Pipe Company, Birmingham, Alabama

Only a few golf courses in the world had underground sprinkler systems, which eliminated the need to pull hoses long distances and made very thorough watering possible. The McWane pipe, "purchased at a price that was below manufactured cost," according to Roberts, was not replaced with modern plastic until the winter of 1970–71.

A City of Augusta raw water line running from the Savannah River to the Augusta Reservoir cut across the property's southeast corner, near the fifth hole. This undrinkable water irrigated the golf course.

You are invited to inspect BUCKNER HOSELESS FAIRWAY
WATERING *on fairways of* AUGUSTA NATIONAL GOLF CLUB
Buckner Mfg Co. New York, N.Y.

Buckner plugged its sprinkler heads into quick-disconnect valves in the underground pipe. Little underground heads popped up under pressure to sprinkle greens and tees. Big heads squirted water in 200-foot diameter circles, plenty to cover the 170-foot-wide fairways.

****

Other things besides discounted raw materials helped keep construction costs down, and first among these was the Depression. Between the irrigation system and a spider web of drainage pipe submerged beneath almost every fairway, Augusta National required a mind-boggling amount of ditch digging. But plenty of out-of-work human mules were available to labor for, as Dan Williams recalls, "ten cent a hour, ten hours a day. Six days a week. And a lot of men standin' right there, waitin' for you to fall out, so they can take your job."

A dime an hour was actually pretty good for such work in Augusta in 1932. "The farms was payin' sixty cent a day, for hoein' or pickin' cotton, and that was all day," the old man says. "Forty cent for women."

Williams, eighty-seven and as comfortable-looking as an old upholstered chair, sits by the window in his nephew's auto glass shop on Washington Road and thinks about the good and the bad of building a golf course. His was the out-of-the-loop point of view from the bottom rung; for example, he and the other black laborers thought Cliff Roberts was the pro at the club. "We didn't know then he owned half of Wall Street." And he believed then and believes now that the Depression was caused by "five big men on Wall Street who froze up all the money.

"Me and Joe King ran a shovel pan. Two mules in the front— I drove the mules—and Joe in the back holding on to the two handles of the pan. We cut that bank out of number thirteen and spread the dirt out on the fairway."

The old swamp at the bottom of the property—what would become the twelfth green—was the main trouble spot. At one point eight mules and two tractors were stuck in the mire there.

Dan Williams and the others transplanted about 4,450 small trees and shrubs and fifty large magnolias and hollies from fairways to rough, according to *Contractors and Engineers Monthly* of October 1932. Other trees they just cut down. "Sometimes we dug up stumps. Some were so big it might take you two days to do one. It was so hot you could feel the water squishin' in your shoes. And with that foreman standin' over you, it was like slavery again."

A bunch of the workers would chip in to buy a half gallon of moonshine on Saturday after work; usually it cost a dollar, sometimes as little as seventy-five cents. "You shake it up and if it don't bead [form bubbles], you don't buy it," Williams explains. "That bead better stay there, too." Predictably, a lot of mule drivers and ditch diggers started back to work on Monday dead broke and with monstrous hangovers.

Mackenzie's design saved money, too, perhaps as much as the cheap labor. Sand bunkers cost a lot to build and maintain, and Mac was not disposed from a strategic or artistic standpoint to litter the landscape with too many of them; he sketched in only twenty-nine, about a third fewer than average. Mac, a frugal sort of Scotsman, coached the construction engineer, Wendell Miller, in his myriad other shortcuts in carting, drainage, seeding, sanding, labor, and manure. But probably the greatest savers of time and money in the construction of Augusta National were machines. A small fleet of Caterpillar track-driven tractors pushed over trees, graded fairways, and pushed up or hollowed out the heavy clay soil for greens, tees, valleys, and mounds. Georgalina Tractor Company supplied three Cat Sixties (sixty horsepower), three Thirties, a Twenty, and two Fifteens. The big one, the Sixty, looked substantially like a modern earthmover, except that its engine was slung forward, like the hood on a Buick. The unmuffled motor was also loud as hell and was exhausted through a pipe next to the operator's seat. Comfort aside, subtly sculpting earth with heavy metal is akin to doing needlepoint while wearing boxing gloves, but something or someone inspired the heavy equipment shapers of the National.

Roberts visited the construction site just once, on a hot, cloudless day in the spring of 1932. Diesel exhaust scented the air as Cliff and Augusta mayor-to-be Thomas Barrett, Jr., toured the grassless golf course. Picks, shovels, mules, and Cats attacked the earth, kicking up dust. Roberts and Barrett kept their coats on. They reached number nine, and something in the hole's design made Roberts uneasy. He paced 220 yards or so from the tee, the length he expected from his typical drive, and found the ground there to be unpleasantly sloped. Cliff hated the idea of a downhill, sidehill lie on a hole where bets are often doubled. In a vintage example of throwing his weight around, Roberts requested that a level area be graded into the fairway to coincide with his tee shot. "The engineer was not at all enthusiastic about accommodating me, but finally agreed to bring back the tractor and do the job," he wrote. "I have many times had occasion to congratulate myself on winning this particular argument."

Jones and Mackenzie stood sweating nearby, collaborating. As in the famous photograph of them on the eighth tee, Bobby socked out a few drives on various holes, trying to show Mackenzie the outer limits of a heroic carry. The architect might then adjust the location of the tee, bunkers, or mounds. Sean Connery definitely plays Mac in the movie: "C'mon, now, laddie, let's r-r-really give this one a r-r-ride."

Who was in charge? Mostly Mac. "Mackenzie and I managed to work as a completely sympathetic team," Jones wrote in *Golf Is My Game*. "Of course, there was never any question that he was the architect and I his advisor and consultant. No man learns to design a golf course simply by playing golf, no matter how well." On the other hand, Jones was a big hitter, and he played a high hook. So the preponderance of dogleg left holes on Augusta National and the tremendous advantages it offered the long driver, particularly on the par fives, could not have been a coincidence.

The digging done, the laborers planted the Scott's Bermuda seed, turned on the Buckner Hoseless watering system, and drenched ninety acres of bare fairway with unfiltered Savannah River water. The grass grew gratifyingly quickly and luxuriantly. Seeded on May 27, mowed on June 10. Dan Williams and others from the construction crew were rehired to push reel mowers, their pay increased to fifteen cents an hour. Jones and a few intimates played the course for the first time on August 26, 1932. Bobby shot 72, even par. Augusta National—the name was Bobby's idea—opened informally in December and formally a month later, when Roberts and the New York One Hundred came down on the train.

But Mackenzie never saw Augusta National wreathed in green. On January 7, 1934, at about the time Grantland Rice was proposing that Bob and Cliff run the club as they saw fit, Mackenzie died at his home in California.

* * * * * * * * * * *

Within months of its opening, Augusta National's members started talking about hosting the U.S. Open. Roberts wrote to

Rice on March 30, 1933, confirming that this was not possible; the Open had always been held in June or July, and Augusta National was to be closed every summer. Two weeks later, in a letter to founding member Alfred S. Bourne, Roberts announced his and Bob's determination for the National to start its own tournament.

The tournament was Cliff's idea. He even came up with a name for it: the Masters. But Jones thought the name immodest, and he would not go along.

CHAPTER TWO

•

The Squat
Italian
Shot-maker

Courtesy of Neil Ghingold

Beau Jack, the world lightweight champion, got his start
in the Augusta National Battle Royals.

Horton Smith, 1934 . . . Gene Sarazen, 1935 . . .
Horton Smith, 1936 . . . Byron Nelson, 1937 . . .
Henry Picard, 1938 . . . Ralph Guldahl, 1939

Gene Sarazen sits like a sun-tanned Buddha on an upholstered chair. Horizontal stripes of soft light penetrate the venetian blinds in his fourth-floor Florida beachfront condo, revealing his amazingly unlined face, crisp new clothing—white, hard-collared golf shirt over navy plus twos—and his air of gentle amusement. Sarazen, ninety-four, has been telling for the ten thousandth time how he holed out a full four-wood shot on the fifteenth hole of the final round of the second Masters ever played, a shot that allowed him to tie Craig Wood, forcing a play-off he would easily win.

The *second* Masters. With the retirement of Bobby Jones, Sarazen—né Saraceni—became the best player in the world. He won eight tournaments in 1930, Jones's retirement year, and by the end of the summer of 1933, he'd won the U.S. Open twice, the PGA three times, and the British Open. So why didn't he play in the first Masters in 1934?

"I remember the return address on the invitation had Cliff Roberts's name on the envelope. 'Aw, the hell with this,' I said. I thought it was some kind of promotion, to sell stocks or real estate." Sarazen didn't even consider changing his scheduled exhibition tour with trick-shot artist Joe Kirkwood for some first-year tournament in East Georgia. "But the invitation the next year said Bobby Jones on it. Now *that* was something."

The *Chronicle* noted his arrival: "Swarthy, sawed-off Gene Sarazen, the squat Italian shot-maker, and Robert Tyre Jones, Jr., golfdom's greatest hero, arrived here yesterday morning . . . getting in some intense practice in the second renewal of the classic Masters Invitational Tournament." The squat Italian shot-maker shot seven-under-par 65 of his first tour of Augusta National, prompting this headline: STOCKY ITALIAN EQUALS RECORD MADE BY JONES.

In three subsequent practice rounds, Sarazen scored 72, 67, and 67, which leads you to conclude he loved the course. "No, I wasn't impressed. I didn't care for it. It was not a good course when Jones and Mackenzie finished it—a very poor design. Hell, number eleven was a *drive and a pitch.* They used to drive the seventh hole. Sixteen was a terrible hole, one hundred yards over a ditch. And the first hole should have been like St. Andrews' [wide-open] first, but it wasn't anything like it."

But Sarazen did not complain at the time; in fact, he complained out loud about those who did. The new guys on the pro tour, he told a writer, "play a lot of pansy golf. They get on the greens and they say, 'It's a little slow, Paul. It's a little fast, Charles.' "

Bettors, noting Sarazen's low practice scores and pugnacious attitude, made him second favorite, at seven to one, during the tournament's Calcutta betting party in the ballroom of the Bon Air Vanderbilt Hotel. (Calcuttas—the equivalent of win-place-show parimutuel wagering on racehorses—were a more or less official part of the Masters scene until 1948, when the USGA formally disapproved of them.) Jones went off as the favorite, at six to one, but this was money bet with the heart, not the head. The hands of golfdom's greatest hero shook as if palsied when he putted under tournament pressure now. Jones appreciated the irony: he couldn't win his own tournament on his own course. He'd lost his edge, forever, in the three-and-a-half years between the Slam and the first Masters. He and Mackenzie had made the greens too fast and too steep for a once-a-year competitor.

Play in the 1935 Masters began Thursday, in twosomes, which Sarazen liked, because two get around faster than three or four, and Gene always played as if he had a train to catch. In an exceptionally odd-looking pairing of golfer and caddie, a lanky, fune-really dressed man named Stovepipe carried Sarazen's bag and tried to keep up. The top of the caddie's Abe Lincoln hat towered over his employer by at least two feet. "Stovepipe used to minister in the colored church in town," says Sarazen. "We talked a lot. 'How are things at church?' I'd ask him. 'Oh, they're not putting anything in the pot [collection plate], Mr. Gene,' he'd say."

Sarazen's form held in the first round, as he shot 68, tied for the lead with Ray Mangrum. But that night he woke with a start. Someone had entered his room at the Bon Air and stood staring at him from the foot of his bed.

"Who are you? What do you want?"

Silence.

Finally, a woman's voice: "I beg your pardon. I must be in the wrong room." Armed with a Wilson driver, young Gene hustled the mystery woman from his boudoir.

He recovered from that unsettling experience—and from the unseasonably raw, wintry weather—to shoot 71 and 73 in the next two rounds, just three behind the leader, Craig Wood. With nine holes to play, he'd closed to within one. But Wood, the pro at Winged Foot in New York, finished with a rush. His birdies on fourteen, fifteen, and eighteen took him to six-under, three better than Sarazen, and good enough, apparently, to win.

Sarazen drove into the right-center of the fifteenth fairway, a par five with a tiny pond in front of the green.

"Hagen says to me, 'Come on, Gene, hit it, will ya? I've got a date,'" Sarazen says, mimicking his playing partner's high tenor. Sarazen fiddled for a minute, uncharacteristically indecisive, and considered his situation. His Wilson K-28 lay about 230 yards from the hole; Wood had been snug and dry in the clubhouse for an hour, with a score three shots lower than Sarazen's own current standing; he and the twenty-five or so people watching—Sarazen's estimate—were beginning to freeze; and the most ardent ladies' man on the tour was standing nearby with his arms crossed, antsy to finish a lousy 79 and get out of his wet clothes and into a dry martini. And was that Bobby Jones watching up there by the green? It was. A three wood would never hold the green, and a four wood didn't seem like enough club. Sarazen took the four wood—a Wilson Turfrider—closed the club's face to decrease its loft, looked at the target once, waggled once, and crushed it.

"His spoon [three-wood] shot from 220 yards electrified a gallery of 2,000," the *Chronicle* reported. Double eagle! He walked to the green in a daze. "Not until I pulled the ball out of the cup did I realize what I'd done," he says.

Sarazen had tied Wood with one wonderful wood, but he still had three holes to go.

"No one ever asks about the last three," he says.

"The short hole was a cinch—you often got a two there. Just a wedge pitch. I parred. Seventeen wasn't bad, either, because the trees were much smaller then." He parred seventeen, too.

"But eighteen played against the north wind. I played the tee shot way left." And way short. Mackenzie's narrow eighteenth green resembled three stair steps surrounded front and sides by sand-filled bomb craters, an intimidating target under pressure, even with the seven-iron shot it was designed for. Again, Sarazen took the four wood from Stovepipe. And given the stress of the moment, he hit a shot almost as brilliant as the one on fifteen.

"I made the green, but I was up and the pin was down. That green was like glass—they didn't pour water on them like they do now. I just touched it and walked along while the ball rolled. It reminded me of curling." The K-28 stopped its languid turning three feet past the cup. Sarazen holed it: "The hardest three-footer I ever made."

The newspapers went crazy over the double eagle, of course; THE SHOT HEARD ROUND THE WORLD was an obvious and popular headline the next day. Sarazen won the thirty-six-hole play-off on Monday, 144 to 149. He accepted a fifty-dollar bonus from Roberts for his exhausting 108-hole victory and accepted the applause from the four hundred or so spectators who'd watched the play-off. Among them was Jones. There could be no doubt as to who he pulled for: Sarazen.

Gene's win in Bobby's tournament added links to a preexisting chain. "Jones and I were born two weeks apart, and we married two Marys, and in the same year," he says. The two best players of their era exchanged conversational letters in later years and had at least one reunion in Georgia every spring. "I'd go down to his cottage after my [Masters] round. 'I can always tell when you've played well,' he says to me. How? 'You come down here for a drink.'

"Once he said to me, 'You know, we didn't do so bad.' And he's this way." Sarazen hunches his back and curls his hands into trembling claws.

Years went by and Jones and other friends died, and some of the pleasure of the old man's annual return to Augusta disappeared. Retired as a competitor since 1973, the Squire's presence now is strictly ceremonial and nostalgic. Since 1987, in golf's equivalent to throwing out the first pitch on Opening Day, Sarazen, Byron Nelson, and Sam Snead each hit drives from the first tee in the eight o'clock chill on Thursday morning. The night before, Gene, Byron, Sam, and all the other past champions dine together in the clubhouse. In a tradition started by Ben Hogan in 1952, the defending champ selects the menu and picks up the tab.

"The dinner used to be fun," Sarazen says. "But now the room's too small. There's too many of them [other former winners] and they all want hats and everything else signed, so they can take them back to their clubs and sell 'em. [Henry] Picard and [Herman] Keiser and I get there a half an hour early and sit down at the table." The autographing takes place in the Champions Locker Room, where the past Masters have a drink before dinner; but it's understood that no one may sign or ask for signatures in the dining room.

"I'm not sure what I like best about the Masters, or least," Sarazen says. "At ninety-four, you're not sure of anything. The reason I go is Mr. Spanos takes me there on his airplane."

****

If only Sarazen's friend Mr. Spanos could fly his corporate jet back to the Masters in the 1930s. When it was just a game. When Sam

Snead had hair. When a ticket cost two dollars a day or five-fifty for the week and could be bought at any of the leading drugstores or cigar counters in Augusta or at hotels in Aiken, Millen, and Waynesboro. Most years before World War II they couldn't give them away—the Depression, no interstate highway system, and chronically rotten weather during Masters week—but Augustans bought badges anyway, more than they needed, as a civic duty. Augusta National papered the house, and the mayor and Cliff Roberts exaggerated the attendance shamelessly, which the *Chronicle* printed straight-faced.

The ensemble cast of golf's most colorful era gathered. They played cards. They drank. None of them knew his cholesterol count. Most were ex-caddies on holiday from their real jobs, giving lessons and selling Dots and K-28s at some country club up North. Only Walter Hagen had sufficient magnetism and *cojones* to survive as a full-time touring pro, giving exhibitions around the globe. He oiled his hair, never wore a hat, drank champagne, dressed like a prince, rented limousines, made and lost fortunes, and rarely played a practice round.

Hagen displayed another of his trademarks—fashionable lateness—in the 1936 Masters. He'd drawn Japanese golfers Chick Chin and Torchy Toda as playing mates for the second round, and Ambassador Hiroshi Saito came down from Washington to watch. Chick, Torchy, and Hiroshi-san arrived at the first tee fifteen minutes early for the twelve-thirty starting time, but no Hagen. Finally, two long minutes late, the crowd parted and Sir Walter made his entrance, smiling like he'd just been named king.

Tommy Armour, another larger-than-life type, let it be known that he'd strangled a German soldier during the Great War with his huge, bare hands. He'd had quite a war: as a machine gunner in a Scottish regiment of the United Kingdom's tank corps, he'd been wounded in battle, losing the sight in one eye, and was promoted to Major Armour by the Armistice. "I never won a big tournament," he said, holding court in the locker room before the 1937 Masters. "The other guys lost." The Silver Scot ran a hand through his magnificent mane of gray hair and applied himself to his usual trio of drinks, consumed in order, for health reasons: a shot of whiskey, a gin buck, and a Bromo.

"So who's gonna win this year, Tommy?" someone asked. "Who do you like?"

"Ky Laffoon," Armour said.

Laffoon, a florid man from Zinc, Arkansas, was known to the other pros as Chief, for his real or perceived Native American blood, but he was not known as a guy who might win a major tournament. Ky had the worst temper on the tour, except for Lefty Stackhouse, a self-flagellant who never got a Masters invitation. Sarazen the contrarian wore long pants when the other guys were sporting plus fours and switched to knickers when his fellow professionals went to pants. Horton Smith showed up before any of the other contestants at the first tournament and won, and won again in the third Masters, and wooed and won the daughter of Augusta National founding member Alfred Severin Bourne in between. Paul Runyan was a magician with a fairway wood. He had to be; his maximum drive flew only 210 yards. Jittery Leo Diegel sometimes jumped up and down after hitting a shot, like a kid on a pogo stick, the better to see where his ball stopped. Hagen recognized the perfect foil in poor Leo and psyched him out unmercifully.

The rough edges on certain of the professionals were smoothed by the genteel would-you-care-for-another-bourbon-sir? environment and by the presence of lots of amateur contestants, men who belonged to clubs as opposed to those who worked at them. Foremost among these, of course, was Jones. In his speech at the dinner he hosted for the amateur contestants every year, Jones reiterated his fondest wish, that one of them would win.

"I was nineteen when I was personally invited by Bobby Jones to play in the Masters," recalls Freddie Haas. "He had heard that I had won the Southern Amateur, which was his favorite tournament. So when he came down to Metairie [Louisiana] Country Club for an exhibition, he asked me to play with him. He told me about the tournament he was putting on, and asked if I'd like to come, and I said, 'Boy, would I.' "

Jones might have seen himself in Haas, a Southern boy and a

student at LSU, articulate, courteous, and winning college and amateur tournaments left and right. He'd make a perfect champion. Unfortunately, Haas shot 87-74-WD in his first Masters in 1936, and didn't do particularly well in subsequent appearances as an amateur. (He turned pro at age twenty-nine, after the war.)

"Well, there was some awful rain in the early years," Haas says. "And not to detract from the thing, but we were all critical of the course. Augusta National was designed with Jones in mind. He played a high hook, which was a tremendous advantage, particularly on the par fives. Those of us who played the ball left-to-right couldn't reach any of the par five greens in two. . . . Perhaps we were really criticizing our own inability to hook the ball."

No amateur would come close to winning the Masters until 1947. But the mere presence of a dozen or so men who played the game for fun and not for money helped give the Masters the light, nonmercenary feeling Jones wanted. So did the two-ball foursomes match on Wednesday, the approach-and-putt contest on Thursday morning, the iron competition on Friday morning, and the driving contest on Saturday morning.

So did the drinking contest all week. "Drinks were on the house for everyone at the first tournament, including the gallery," recalls Paul Runyan, who competed in the first thirteen Masters. "I remember this vividly, that they had one hundred and fifty gallons of white lightning in the clubhouse, and by the morning of the third day, they ran out. Yes, they got some more."

Wednesday was Calcutta night. No one evinced the slightest embarrassment at the organized public gambling. In 1936, for example, Tommy Armour and Horton Smith were the auctioneers and were assisted by another pro, Wee Bobby Cruickshank. The *Chronicle* quoted odds and betting amounts on the front page. "At the very first Calcutta, I had eight of my members from Metropolis Country Club there," Runyan recalls. "I made them stop when the bidding for me reached $1,800. But I finished third in the tournament, so they got back $2,200. Jones sold for $13,800, three times more than anyone else."

Thursday night of Masters week, the club hosted a chicken dinner, with biscuits, sweet potatoes, and collard greens on the side. "Wonderful," Runyan says. Local members fed the golfers one or two other nights, with country ham or barbecue as the feature. "Mighty good," remembers Byron Nelson. In short, Jones made sure none of his guests thought this was just another Akron Open. "They only had $5,000 of prize money," says Runyan; twice that was available at many tournaments in the mid-1930s and early 1940s. "But the course was almost as beautiful then as it is now. And they treated you so well, and Bobby Jones was playing in it. That gave it more appeal than almost anything else."

O. B. Keeler turned on the gas and caught some of the grand member–guest atmosphere:

> A simply terrific warming up of the more or less golfing
> socialites in advance of the tournament . . . the mere dropping
> of Paul Patterson [the owner of the *Baltimore Sun*], Grantland
> Rice, George Morse, Leonard Shearer, and Big Bob Jones, to go
> no further and fare no worse into the seething maelstrom, is quite
> sufficient to upset a considerable portion of maelstrom.

Roberts entered the maelstrom nineteen days before the first round of the first Masters. While Cliff took care of a thousand administrative details—such as trying to find $1,000 of Augusta money to pay NBC Radio to broadcast the event and building the broadcaster a little tower by the eighteenth green when he did—Jones struggled with the conflicting roles of host and competitor. He relished the reunion with old friends he hadn't seen since his retirement four years before, but he didn't want to play. Roberts convinced him the Masters would fail without him, that it was virtually his duty to participate. Jones relented; "I doubt that anyone else could have talked him into it," Cliff said. Bob found the pressure-free practice rounds "provided the most enjoyable golf I had ever had," and he played like the Bobby of old during warm-ups, shooting a course record 65 in 1934 and breaking it with a 64 in 1936. But he performed like an old Bobby in the tournament proper, with the quiver in his long, ornate putting stroke leading to lots of 74s and 78s. In eleven tournaments between 1934 and 1948, he never broke par for eighteen holes.

Jones reversed the nines soon after Mackenzie died; some have speculated that he did not want to risk a confrontation with Mac on the issue. The first Masters was played back nine first; after that, the original Mackenzie order was returned. Jones insisted that the event not be called the Masters but was ignored by Roberts and by the newspapers, even the *Chronicle*. Annual Invitation Tournament, the generic name Jones preferred, was printed on the cover of the first two tournament programs and in the invitations until 1939. And nowhere else. As late as 1963, Jones referred to the tournament in a letter as "the so-called Masters."

The picture of a nonconfrontational, somewhat irresolute man emerges. But a more profound issue involved who would belong to Augusta National. The original understanding between Cliff and Bobby had Roberts recruiting men he knew in New York and men from financial circles—most of his friends belonged to both groups. Jones's members were to come from his natural constituencies, the world of golf and his hometown. It didn't work out that way, however. Founding members from New York outnumbered Atlantans by about sixty to one—or sixty to three, if you include Jones and his father, the Colonel. The only founding member from Atlanta not named Jones was gray-haired Harry M. Atkinson, the CEO of the Georgia Power Company.

One hundred thousand adoring Atlantans had lined the city's streets when Bobby came marching home from the Grand Slam. But he perceived that his homeboys were miffed with him for building his dream course in faraway Augusta. So Jones, no salesman, simply decided not to ask anyone from Atlanta to join. "I know Bob was keenly disappointed that only one of his Atlanta friends became an underwriter," Roberts said, which was undoubtedly true. But the passive-aggression of not asking, then being disappointed, revealed a flaw in the great man's personality. By default, it made Augusta National more Cliff's club than Bobby's.

Clearly, Jones had other interests: he wrote for a magazine

Rice had started called *The American Golfer*; he did a half-hour weekly radio golf show with Keeler; he practiced law; he designed golf clubs for Spalding Brothers; and he helped, a little, with the up- bringing of three small children, Clara, Robert Tyre III, and Mary. The Masters and the National were peripheral.

But Augusta quickly became the center and the focus of Clif- ford Roberts's life.

****

A string of naked lightbulbs bathes a boxing ring in harsh light, its canvas floor stained with sweat and blood, its three cotton ropes sagging. The boxing platform sits incongruously in the center of the elegant ballroom of the Bon Air Vanderbilt Hotel. Several dozen white gentlemen sit at white-clothed tables, drinking, smok- ing after-dinner cigars, watching the primitives in the ring hit each other, and shouting the way men do at fights. "I'll take the short guy for twenty. Come on, throw the left!" Waiters circulate silently. Glasses clink, men yell, and the combatants pant and grunt. Landed punches cause pearls of sweat to jump off the fighters' heads, the droplets catching the light in the smoky air for an instant. George Bellows—*Stag at Sharkey's, Dempsey and Firpo*—could have painted the scene.

The spectators are members of the new Augusta National Golf Club. In that more formal era, the men wear coats and ties to dinner and keep them on for the boxing match, as they would for any after-dinner entertainment in Augusta: bridge or poker games, musical groups, gospel singers, dancers, minstrel shows. Back home in New York, a typical boxing card began with middleweights and ended with heavies, but Augusta National fight nights conclude with a demeaning spectacle called a battle royal.

The battle begins. Six blindfolded black boys who have been recruited from "the Terry"—Augusta's Negro territory—are shoved into the ring, their hands encased in boxing gloves. Sometimes one hand is tied behind each warrior's back, to prevent any defensive jabbing. Someone hits a brass bell with a ball peen hammer and the combatants start throwing haymakers. They hit air, ring ropes, ring posts, and each other. Last one standing wins.

Augusta's most famous citizen, soul shouter James Brown, recalled what it was like to fight in a battle royal: "I'd be out there stumbling around, swinging wild, and hearing people *laughing*. I didn't know I was being exploited; all I knew I was getting paid a dollar and having fun."

Ralph Ellison evoked much more sinister images of the battle royal in his book *Invisible Man*: "Blindfolded, I could no longer control my motions. I had no dignity. I stumbled about like a baby or a drunken man. The smoke had become thicker and with each new blow it seemed to sear and further restrict my lungs. My saliva became like hot bitter glue. A glove connected with my head, filling my mouth with warm blood . . ."

The white men laugh and gamble and watch the black boys blindly beat the shit out of each other.

By no means did the National keep this quaint barbarism alive by itself. For example, the city-owned Bell Auditorium in downtown Augusta staged free-for-alls on Saturday nights from time to time. But the private exhibitions indicated the taste some of the early members had for raising hell at night after a day of golf. Most of them were far from home, unencumbered by spouses, in an unfamiliar, almost exotic locale. Picture college boys on spring break, but with more worldly tastes and a lot more money. You hear of the parties they had, and of the whores, and in the context of the vaguely sinful excitement of the battles royal, the stories have some credence.

Chairman Roberts chose the entertainment at Augusta National. Where and how he developed his taste for golf, bridge, and the fights is the story of his life.

Charles de Clifford Roberts, Jr., first drew breath on his grandfather's farm in Morning Sun, Iowa, on March 6, 1894. Morning Sun is in the southeastern part of the state. To get there from Iowa City, go south about thirty miles on 218, then east on 78 past Olds, Swedesburg, and Winfield. Speed limit's forty-five through town. You can't miss the Morning Sun Methodist Church (established 1871): white siding, stained glass windows with flat bottoms and curved tops, and a big fir tree by the front door. The tank on top of the erector-set water tower looks like the head of the tin woodsman in *The Wizard of Oz*. The Iowa countryside is pleasant, mostly flat, and uninspiring. The town existed primarily because two railroads ran through it, the Iowa-Central and the Chicago-Rock Island-Pacific. Nine hundred and forty-eight people resided in Morning Sun in 1900, when little Cliff was six.

His father, a native of West Virginia, described his occupation as "self-employed real estate agent" for the census taker in 1910. Mrs. Roberts, the former Rebecca Scott Key, was a cousin of Francis Scott Key, the composer of "The Star-Spangled Banner"; her side of the family had a little money. Charles de Clifford had an older brother named John Dorias and younger sibs named Dorothy, Robert, and Alpheus. Dorothy and Robert Roberts were twins. In about 1910 or 1911, the family left Iowa for Kansas, then moved again. They got on a southbound train and didn't get off until four days and 1,300 miles had passed. Their new home would be in Palacios (almost rhymes with molasses), Texas, on the Gulf Coast, north and east of Corpus Christi.

In his Eisenhower oral history interviews, Roberts was vague and evasive about his early life, which is understandable in view of the premature and violent deaths of his parents.

WHERE DID YOU ORIGINATE, SIR?
I'm a Middlewesterner. Having spent a considerable amount of time in the South, I have acquired possibly a Southern accent as well as a Western drawl.
WHEN AND WHERE WERE YOU BORN, SIR?
I was born on my grandfather's farm in Iowa. My folks had a number of homes. My father always was interested in seeing what was on the other side of the next hill. . . . The only part of my life that is most easily told is that I've been in the same business, at the same location, since the end of the First World War.

The Roberts family did not migrate alone. Railroad companies and people with Texas land for sale had joined forces to entice thousands of people from the upper Midwest to come south. The big draws for the Iowa, Nebraska, and Illinois farmers were the chance to raise a crop during the winter—perhaps something tropical, like figs or oranges—and, as one ad claimed, "the purest drinking water. No mosquitoes. Cool Gulf Breeze." Full disclosure would have included humidity. Mud. Hurricanes.

Nonetheless, the real estate–railroad joint venture quite obviously worked. You can see it in the lap siding, gable windows, and the needlessly steep, snow- and ice-shedding roofs on the houses the newcomers built, an architecture that came down on the train from Swedesburg. One "immigration company" claimed to have brought 40,000 people to South Texas between 1900 and 1915, eighty of whom bought property. The railroads discounted tickets and got a pleasing volume of passengers, and the Texans got real estate buyers—and real estate agents, like Cliff's father, Charles Roberts.

The founders of Blessing, a little town twelve miles north of Palacios, had wanted to call their town Thank God, such was their joy at the arrival of the railroad.

The Roberts clan settled into a house in Palacios with ten acres and an orchard, but they weren't there long. One Sunday, as the family left the house to attend services at the Christian Church, Cliff realized he had forgotten his gloves. He went back into the house and hurriedly grabbed the gloves off a table, accidentally knocking a kerosene lamp into the curtains behind it. Charles managed to push the piano out the front door, but not much else was saved.

The family moved to a modest frame house on East Bay Street in Palacios. East Bay traced the letter C and ran alongside the Gulf. The frame house was rented and cramped. But as difficult a time as this obviously was for the Roberts family, things were about to get incalculably worse.

Cliff went to Palacios High School and tried to absorb the newness of the place. Iowa had not been particularly liberal, but Baptist- and Methodist-dominated Texas seemed robustly right wing. Politics and morality intersected in the debate over strong drink: "Mrs. Nannie Webb Curtis, the great Prohibition advocate," the weekly *Palacios Beacon* reported, "put herself on record as being squarely against Coca-Cola and other dope drinks." (Coke then marketed itself as a "temperance drink," an alternative to liquor.) The teenaged Cliff Roberts possessed no antecedents for the weather, the ocean, the heat, the hurricanes, or the people. Especially the people. Southeast Iowa had had few, if any, blacks, but a third of Matagorda County's 15,000 residents were Negro and many more came from Mexico. The people with darker skin shucked the oysters, picked the rice and cotton, and lived poor. Seemingly the only group with a lower status were the CUSSED REAL ESTATE MEN, as the newspaper noted in a front-page editorial. Not that we condemn them all, the paper said evenhandedly: "a negro commits a fiendish act and public opinion has sometimes hanged the wrong nigger."

But Palacios and Blessing had a newly rich upper class, too, the likes of which young Cliff also had never seen. Shortly after the Spindletop gusher in 1901, oil was discovered in Matagorda County. Derricks sprang up everywhere. Operating companies like Pay Streak Oil and Swastika Oil punched holes in the ground, and drillers and land men got rich. Cliff graduated from Palacios High and worked for a time with his older brother in a dry goods store in Palacios. Later he opened up his own place, a men's clothing store, up in Blessing. The oil men, he'd noticed, liked to dress up.

Young Cliff was an important enough personage to rate this mention in the *Palacios Beacon* on February 21, 1913: "C. D. Roberts, Jr., of Blessing was in the city on Sunday with his family."

Rebecca Roberts celebrated her forty-fourth birthday on July 31, 1913. Eight days later, she turned a shotgun around and killed herself. "The deceased had been a constant sufferer from ill health for more than a year," the *Beacon* reported. "The death might have been an accident, but it is supposed to have been suicide for relief from continued suffering." Cliff's father found the body by the garage at five A.M. that Friday morning; the gunshot had not awakened any of the sleeping children. Rebecca left notes to each of the five kids, each, according to the paper, "an expression of affectionate farewell."

The whole thing happened so fast: Reverend J. H. Bristor, pastor at the Christian Church, held a short funeral service at the family home on Saturday. On Sunday, just two days after the tragedy, the bereaved husband gave notice to the landlord and loaded clothes, kids, and his wife's body on the train back to Iowa. Cliff stayed behind. The family broke up.

Some have speculated that his mother's suicide thrust the mantle of parenthood on Cliff, but that didn't happen, at least not in an overt way. First of all, his father remarried. Besides, it was geographically impossible. Cliff's younger sister and brothers lived in Kansas, and he rarely saw them over the ensuing decades. In fact, the five children wouldn't stand in the same room together for thirty-seven years, until Alpheus's twenty-fifth wedding anniversary. Others believe his mother's death turned Cliff into an overachiever. Perhaps it taught him that self-murder is the ultimate act of revenge—against life, God, illness, those left behind, whatever. Probably it caused a steep decline in his capacity for sympathy or empathy: how could he feel for anyone else, when he himself had been through so much? And what of his vindictiveness and his tendency to intimidate, qualities he passed on to the Masters and Augusta National? Couldn't those qualities be traced to the manner of his mother's leaving?

One lesson of his mother's death was very simple. Suicide was not unthinkable. It worked. The survivors' confrontation with these simple, horrible truths is one reason why suicide often runs in families; so too do potentially fatal mood disorders.

Cliff closed his haberdashery, bought a Model T, and hit the road as a suit salesman. He sold so many suits that the manufacturer couldn't keep up. Take a break, his employer urged. So Cliff spent his twentieth and twenty-first summers with his mother's parents, the Dorias Keys, at their 1,300-acre vineyard in Encinitas, California. He sat in the cool of his grandfather's library and read his collection of biographies and autobiographies of great men.

Soon after the United States declared war on the Central Powers in April 1916, joining the Allies in the Great War in Europe, Cliff enlisted in New York City and trained for the Army Medical

Corps at Fort Hancock in Augusta, Georgia. Like authors Ernest Hemingway and John Dos Passos, who later made it seem like a romantic activity, Private Roberts drove an ambulance in the war. When not ferrying wounded men away from the trenches during his ten months at the French front, Cliff busied himself with soldierly pursuits: a Parisian girl named Suzanne Verdet, and wine.

He returned to Texas after the war, ready now to make his fortune. Selling clothes had provided a good income, but Cliff Roberts had bigger things in mind. Remembering the industry that had provided Matagorda County with its wealthiest residents, he marched into the oil field. The *potential* oil field, that is; Cliff became a land man. It's a simple part of the business, really: a land man approaches a farmer or rancher and offers to lease the stuff below his 5,000 acres for, say, two dollars per acre. He then sells the lease to a big company for four dollars. One can picture Cliff, an impressively serious young man in a suit, obsessively clearing his throat, speaking flat, Yankee accents with a slow Southern cadence. His target is a man wearing bib overalls and a sunburn. "Ahem. This could be of great benefit, uh, uh, to you, sir, and to your family. You will retain a one-eighth interest in the mineral rights. Which is, ahem, twelve point five percent. Which, ahem, which will enrich you still further if oil is found. And, ah, the disturbance to your cotton crop will be minimal." Cliff worked the flatland around Goose Lake and Humble, near Houston. He'd deliver his pitch, produce various forms and contracts from his briefcase, and demonstrate an impressive familiarity with the legalese. Not every farmer signed, but a lot did. Cliff advanced to oil- and gas-lease trader, in which he probably had land men working for him. The stakes and the risks for a land man were high, but a good run could make you rich overnight.

Charles de Clifford Roberts, Sr., came south in 1921, probably at his son's invitation. Kenneth Roberts believes his grandfather was attempting to duplicate Cliff's success as a land man. But the experiment ended tragically. "I never told anyone this," Cliff told his nephew Kenneth fifty years after the fact, "but when your grandfather came down after the war, I supported him." In October

1921, Charles moved to a little town near Brownsville, Texas, at the southern tip of the state. And there he died. An accident, or another suicide?

SAN BENITO MAN IS RUN OVER, KILLED BY RAILROAD TRAIN

C.T. [sic] Roberts, 50 [sic] years old, was run over and killed by a Brownsville-bound Gulf Coast Lines passenger train Tuesday night at San Benito. The accident occurred about 9:00 P.M. [on November 1]. The train had been gone about twenty minutes when the mangled body was discovered, near the passenger station. Wheels had passed over the body just below the chest, practically cutting him in two. Physicians said instant death was caused.

Mr. Roberts, a victim of locomtorataxia [sic], came to San Benito from Kansas City some weeks ago for the benefit of his health. He had shown some improvement, but recently suffered a relapse.

The body is being held pending instructions from the family.

Locomotor ataxia is a chronic disease of the nervous system, often caused by syphilis, stroke, or alcohol abuse. It's intensely painful at first, then slowly debilitating. Its sufferers lose their reflexes and coordination. But ataxia does not compel its sufferers to walk in front of trains.

****

Cliff made his big score in 1923, when he packaged a number of desirable mineral leases and profited an astounding $50,000 on their sale. "I think he realized that deal was a fluke, that he'd never get that much at one time again," says Kenneth Roberts, who, like his uncle, became a successful land man. Cliff scooped up his winnings and took them to the biggest poker game in the world, the business big time: New York City. He bought into a stock brokerage business; his $50,000 ante gave him a 16 percent share of the Reynolds Company. When the city held confetti-filled parades for returning heroes, Cliff could have opened his office window at 120

Broadway and flung a handful of ticker tape onto the heads of Charles Lindbergh or Bobby Jones.

He developed a taste for suitable pastimes. Man's man stuff: baseball, boxing, something to take a client to. A fever for contract bridge swept the country in the twenties; Cliff caught it and played it for two cents a point. Jones's exploits caused a similar spurt in golf's popularity. Cliff joined the very posh Deepdale Golf Club on Long Island and whittled his handicap to eight in 1928. He also paid dues at Blind Brook Country Club in Purchase, north of the city, in Westchester County. He and the boys took golf vacations, too, occasionally to Augusta, Georgia. They stayed at a bridge buddy's place, the Bon Air Vanderbilt, and played Forest Hills and Augusta Country Club. Roberts's future came together when the hotelier, Walt Marshall, introduced him to Jones in New York, probably in 1925.

Cliff cultivated Bobby as if he wanted to sell him a suit or stock or buy his mineral rights. He became his confidant. "I was one of the few who knew of Bob's idea about [building] a new type of golf course," Roberts wrote. What he didn't write, but many believe to be true, was that Bob's golf club was really born on a friend's yacht. Cliff and the gang occasionally cruised to their golf engagements on Long Island. And in the golden glow of a sunset and a glass of scotch, Cliff proposed that they help Bobby Jones get a golf club together.

Walt Marshall was on the boat; he put up $25,000. Alfred Severin Bourne, who lived in Augusta and whose family owned Singer Sewing Machine, Inc., pledged another $25,000 for the new golf course. In time a score more Friends of Cliff came up with $5,000 each of cash or credit.

As Cliff sunk his teeth and increasing chunks of time into Augusta National, sportswriters and authors speculated on the perceived financial cost of his devotion. He could have been back in the financial district, as Charles Price wrote, "putting together what inarguably would have been an estate much larger than it actually was." Roberts allowed the perception to live, and even encouraged it. "I have no regret for lost business opportunities," he wrote in his grand and wordy style in his club history. "My life has been so enriched by the working association and joyous companionship of Bob Jones and Ike Eisenhower, and many other Augusta National members, that I consider myself to be far richer today than could have been possible by any other measure of success." But if Cliff suffered, he didn't suffer much. In addition to his apartment on Park Avenue in New York, according to his nephew Kenneth Roberts, Uncle Cliff also owned a penthouse on the beach in the Bahamas, an apartment on old-money Grandfather Mountain in western North Carolina, and an apartment in Beverly Hills. When he died, his stocks were worth about $76 million, and his share of the Reynolds Company— by then Dean Witter Reynolds—was valued at around $25 million.

Profit was not his motivation for getting close to Jones, however; by Cliff's standards, Bob was a pauper. What drew Cliff to Bob was the same impulse that would draw him to Ike twenty years later: the power and ego boost that accrues from an affiliation with a great man. And within the delicious feeling of authority lived a kind of altruism. Roberts had given up on religion, but he made his own. He would wield his power like a righteous sword—for the Good of Bob, or for the Good of the Masters, or of Ike, or of the National, or of the Game.

CHAPTER THREE

•

Tank Town

The first five Masters champions: (*left to right*) Gene Sarazen,
Horton Smith, Ralph Guldahl, Byron Nelson, and Jimmy Demaret.

Georgia governor Eugene Talmadge once showed up for work at the capitol building wearing his socks over his shoes. "Just a good old country style during snow and sleet storms," he explained on that frigid February day in 1936. "You can't slip and fall with socks outside your shoes." His Honor wore his country-boy banner proudly. When rising pig prices threatened the traditional Southern New Year's Day meal of hog jowl and black-eyed peas, Talmadge announced his intention to eat pig chin despite its increase to nineteen cents a pound. "I sort of like potato puddin' with it, too," he said. On occasion he visited his constituents in his state-provided limousine, and farmers would stick their heads in the back window and whistle softly at the luxury of the thing. "Shee-it," the governor would say, and squirt a stream of tobacco juice on the vehicle's carpeted floor.

As its elected leader demonstrated, culture often ran second to agriculture in Georgia. But the perception of the state as a mere breeding ground for peaches and peanuts changed drastically and permanently as the Depression thirties slipped into the war-torn forties. Three things—a book, a drink, and a game—forced everyone to rethink Georgia. Augusta's involvement in the state's emerging identity was intimate and complicated.

The book, of course, was *Gone With the Wind*. The epic story of the fall of the Old South enjoyed unprecedented success all over the world, selling 1.5 million copies the first year. It was translated into eighteen languages, including German. Half a million Germans bought it, among them Adolf Hitler. Der Führer read it and loved it, then banned it from occupied Europe; he did not want his conquered countries thinking secession and civil war. *Gone With the Wind's* love-during-wartime theme proved to be universally attractive, but the most important reason for the book's astonishing popularity was nostalgia. That it was nostalgia for a time that never existed didn't lessen its power. Slavery was brutal, not, as Margaret Mitchell depicted it, benign and paternalistic; agricultural life in the South was exhausting, not gracious; and plantation butterflies like Scarlett O'Hara, with her "magnolia-white skin" on "breasts well-matured for her sixteen years" lived almost exclusively in fiction and in fantasy. The movie was filmed at Busch Gardens and studio backlots in Southern California—not in Georgia—and the massive oak in front of Tara, the O'Hara plantation, was made of concrete.

Despite the popularity of the book, no one wanted to make the movie, because Civil War films were then considered to be box office poison. But John Hay "Jock" Whitney, chairman of the board of Selznick International Pictures, saw the synopsis and wanted to take it on. Author Mitchell accepted Selznick's offer of $50,000 for the film rights.

A starlet-dating millionaire playboy, Jock Whitney stood with one foot in Hollywood and the other in Old New York. As a member of Augusta National, he also had a toe in Georgia. "Nice fella, not much of a golfer," recalls Charley Yates, the club's oldest member. Whitney's father had died while playing tennis in 1927, leaving him the largest gross fortune ever appraised in the United States up to then. As the film's predicted costs soared up to $4 million, Whitney money continually pulled the project out of the fire. Jock sold his interest in *Gone With the Wind* to MGM for $1.5 million before it was released; surely not the smartest move he ever made, because interest in the film grew even faster than the cost to make it.

Butterfly McQueen provided another Augusta connection to the movie when she landed a minor role as Scarlett's maid Prissy, a squeaky-voiced, infuriatingly ineffectual slave. Ms. McQueen moved from Tampa to Augusta in the sixth grade, in 1926, as one of her classmates recalls. "But she moved to New York after high school, and I didn't see her for a while," Dr. Ike Washington says. The first time Dr. Ike saw the movie, at the Imperial Theatre on Broad Street, he blurted out, "I know that girl!"

Butterfly cut short her acting career by refusing to continually portray maids who sounded like they'd been inhaling helium, and she lived in Augusta from her middle years until her death in a fire at her home in 1996. She was no lightweight. In one of *Gone With the Wind*'s climactic scenes, Prissy says, "I don't know nothin' 'bout birthin' no babies!" and is then slapped across the face by an angry Scarlett (played by Vivien Leigh). But Ms. Leigh proved incapable of pulling her punches in rehearsals, and Ms. McQueen stormed off the set. "She's hurting me, she's hurting me!" she said. "I'm no stunt man, I'm an actress!" After Leigh apologized, Butterfly returned.

Georgia governor E. D. Edwards felt the frenzy in the land about *Gone With the Wind* and declared a state holiday for the premiere of the movie just before Christmas 1939. Atlanta mayor William B. Hartsfield scheduled three days of events; thousands of Atlantans milled around in Civil War period costumes, hoping for a glimpse of a movie star. The governors of Tennessee, Alabama, Florida, and South Carolina donned evening dress and attended the premiere. So too did Bob and Mrs. Jones, Margaret and Mr. Mitchell, and Clark Gable, Leslie Howard, Olivia De Havilland, Leigh, Whitney, and all their Hollywood retinue. The premiere was not just a regional event, it was the most celebrated, anticipated party in memory.

But Butterfly McQueen and the other black costars did not attend. They couldn't. They were not invited. The insult stung a second time when Hattie McDaniel won a Best Supporting Actress Oscar for her portrayal of Mammie, becoming the first black woman to win an Oscar.

Gone With the Wind was to become the most watched, most profitable movie in history. Almost 200 million people in the United States have gone into a theater to see it (obviously, many saw it more than once). If a fourth that many people watch a film today, it's considered a blockbuster. If you adjust ticket revenues for inflation, the film has taken in about $859 million; the second-place movie, *Star Wars*, is way behind, with about $630 million.

The ubiquity of *Gone With the Wind* caused a rebirth of Confederate pride and a surge of Yankee guilt at destroying the lovely, imaginary antebellum world. But in one small corner of the South, the gracious life seemed to live on. "The dark cedars on either side of the graveled drive met in an arch overhead, turning the long avenue into a dark tunnel," Mitchell wrote. "And the beautiful white-columned house crowned the hill like a Greek Temple." The author was referring to Ashley Wilkes's plantation, Twelve Oaks, but to anyone who'd been there, it sure sounded like Augusta National Golf Club.

TV came to Augusta in 1956, and it played the *Gone With the Wind* card more strongly each year. In its fifteen-second February and March promos in the 1990s, CBS shows the clubhouse and a dogwood in bloom, while we hear a few mellow chords from an acoustic guitar. "A Tradition Unlike Any Other—The Masters," the voice-over coos, but you might wonder which tradition is being referred to.

* * * * * * * * * * *

Someone from out of town could have noticed Robert Winship Woodruff's absence from the movie premiere and found it odd. Woodruff, after all, had supplanted his friend Bob Jones as the first citizen of Atlanta and, thus, the first man of the New South. But savvy locals knew that the man who ran Coca-Cola paid a public relations man to keep his name *out* of the news; he reportedly told the publisher of the *Atlanta Constitution* he didn't expect to see his name in the paper unless he was convicted of rape. His nickname was Mr. Anonymous, both for his staggering philanthropy and for his strict avoidance of the limelight. He was also known as the Boss.

Bob Woodruff had known the Jones family for years. In the early 1920s, when he ran a Cleveland-based truck cab manufacturer called White Motor, he'd retained Colonel Bob to do some legal work. And back when Bobby had been thrilling Atlantans by winning all those golf tournaments, Woodruff often watched the play and celebrated with father and son afterward. When Jones holed the final putt of his 1930 Grand Slam, he handed his golf ball to Woodruff. Once he'd called Bobby's hotel room after a big win and invited him to his own room for drinks. "Well, no, Bob, I've got some friends here with me now," Bobby had replied. "Why don't you come join us?" Turn down the great Robert Woodruff? The friends, Charley Yates and Eugene Byrd, still tell the story, both of them proud of Bobby's loyalty and lack of pretense.

Woodruff was no stuffed shirt himself. "Flattery is like chewing tobacco," he said. "It tastes sweet, is very satisfying, and does no harm. Unless you swallow it." He smoked a cigar, wore a fedora, and *always* picked up the check. Byrd, one of Bobby's law partners, remembers his amazement the day he had lunch in Woodruff's office, and the Boss ate only a plate of collard greens and black-eyed peas, the most modest food imaginable.

One of his biographers wrote that Woodruff never read, looked at art, or listened to music. But friends contradict that image of a dressed-up good ol' boy. The Boss gave original and very costly bird drawings as Christmas cards, and a rumor persists that he gave millions upon millions to the United Negro College Fund, on the condition that his donation remain a secret. Using Coca-Cola profits to teach black kids might not play in the South.

He probably would have been a founding member of Augusta National, if only Bobby had asked. As it turned out, Woodruff joined just a little later. Not that he really desired a club membership; he rarely took time away from work for golf or male bonding. But Cliff Roberts, Bobby, and another National member, Dwight Eisenhower (who joined in October 1948), took their places in Woodruff's very small inner circle. Roberts became a minor financial adviser, Jones took his place as a de facto Coca-Cola employee, and Ike, well . . . During a rare interview conducted in 1950, a reporter asked Woodruff about the picture of Eisenhower on his wall. "Some of us want to see him made president," the Boss said. "We sent him overseas [to Paris, as the chief military officer of postwar Allied Forces] to give him an international flair, then we made him president of Columbia so the eggheads would like him." No, he said, they hadn't decided yet if Ike should run as a Republican or a Democrat.

Woodruff owned five houses, his favorite being Ichauway, a 30,000-acre plantation–hunting preserve near Newton, in Southeast Georgia. Ichauway resembled a theme-park Tara or Twelve Oaks even more than Augusta National did. "The place and its people are of another time," wrote John Huey in *The Wall Street Journal*. "Matched pairs of mules hitched in brass studded harness haul dog wagons with leather benches to the hunt. Black servants in crisp white smocks serve lunches of dove pie with nutmeg, corn pancakes sopped in sorghum syrup, and cold home-churned buttermilk in figurined ceramic mugs. Afterwards, they stoop to offer moist Havana cigars from fine-grained humidors." Cliff, Bob, and Ike joined Woodruff there a couple of times a year to shoot at birds. Ike so loved the spirituals the Ichauway field hands sang that he'd call from the White House to hear them.

The threads connecting Coca-Cola and Augusta National couldn't be missed. Neither adhered to the Madison Avenue adage that there's no such thing as bad publicity. Both were based on secrecy. Both grew to become mighty institutions that symbolized vigorous, prosperous Georgia. And both sold themselves as products pure and undefiled, throwbacks to a more innocent age. You could interchange their slogans: "Coca-Cola–A Tradition Unlike Any Other." "Enjoy the Masters–It's the Real Thing." There is even a hint of Coca-Cola's Spencerian script in the cursive writing of the Masters logo.

And while neither needed the other to succeed, a Coke–Augusta National symbiosis developed. Club membership gave Woodruff an occasional break from his workaholism, access to and influence over the president of the United States, and eventually, a significant customer (just try ordering a Pepsi at the Masters). Woodruff owed Ike. As the Supreme Allied Commander in Europe during World War II, Eisenhower, apparently with no ulterior motive, gave Coca-Cola a tremendous boost. Like Generals George Patton and Omar Bradley, Ike loved the stuff. He also believed the men would fight for Coke, a wholesome symbol of the American Way. "On early convoy request three million bottled Coca-Cola," he cabled from North Africa, in June 1943, a year before D-Day. He also asked for "complete equipment for bottling, capping, washing same quantity twice monthly." Ike gave Marshal Zhukov of Russia a case of Coke at the Potsdam conference at the conclusion of the war in Europe. Sixty-four Coca-Cola bottling plants were built around the world during the war, fifty-nine of them at U.S. government expense. The company retained them all.

In partial payment for Ike's important role in promoting his product, Woodruff climbed out on a political limb. He began wearing I Like Ike neckties; by supporting Eisenhower's Republican candidacy in 1952, the Boss broke with decades of Georgia Democratic tradition. Ike didn't win Cobb County or Atlanta in 1952, but he came closer than any Republican had in twenty years.

Roberts also benefitted from the association with Woodruff. The Boss knew how to handle power, and Cliff Roberts was an observant man. Don't be too accessible, he learned. Don't explain. Sue the hell out of anyone who infringes on your trademark. (Georgia was a good state to sue in if you treasured privacy, since plaintiffs are not required to reveal their assets to claim damages.) Above all, as Woodruff demonstrated, powerful men control perceptions. That meant controlling the newspapers. A case in point occurred on November 8, 1957—"Black Friday" to company oldsters—when Coca-Cola dismissed about a quarter of its headquarter's employees. Yet nothing about the mass firings appeared in the Atlanta papers, not even after several laid-off Coke workers killed themselves. For his part, Roberts controlled the information flow by declaring himself the sole spokesman for Augusta National and the Masters—and by offering a membership to William Morris Senior, the owner of the local newspaper.

"I knew of course that we could not entirely escape the millionaire club label with which we had already been tagged," Roberts recalled in the oral history, speaking of his information control during the eight years one of his members was the president of the

United States. "But I was determined for Ike's protection not to feed the socialistically-minded press boys any ammunition that it might be possible to prevent them from receiving." Such as what Eisenhower shot, who he played with, and who Augusta National's members were.

"To further improve relations with the press, I authorized Jim Haggerty, the president's press secretary, to invite all of them to a dinner given by the club at which time I made a brief talk outlining the club's policies."

Cliff's draw-in-the-enemy strategy succeeded brilliantly. The biggest names in politics, sports, and business came to town to play Augusta National, and the nation's press rarely commented. Inevitably, the kid gloves treatment spilled over onto the Masters. Not since Pravda covered the Kremlin did a golf club or a tournament enjoy such a sweetheart press—not just in Augusta, but around the country.

Coca-Cola–Augusta National mutualism reached a crescendo after the war with the formation of the Joroberts Corporation. World War II—and the years preceding it—had been a bonanza for Coke, when its vital interests and those of the United States had become intertwined. The government's theory was that Woodruff's slightly addictive mix of kola nuts and sugar water and his measles rash of Coke signs helped make the world safe from Nazism and communism. Joroberts was formed to continue Coca-Colonialization by owning and operating bottling plants in Scotland, England, South Africa, and in the world's last big untapped cola markets, Central and South America. With Jones as Joroberts president and secretary and Roberts the vice president and treasurer, the company looked like Augusta National all over again. And, in fact, it was. Almost all the thirty stockholders belonged to the club. Among them were Eisenhower and his son John; Woodruff and his nephew Morton Hodgson; Albert Bradley, chairman of the board of General Motors; and Ben Farris, the president of United States Steel. This club within the club cost $7,000 to join.

Joroberts profit margins were quite thin in the early years, due mostly to South American poverty and government price controls. But Roberts took care of business in person and things improved; net income for 1950, for example, was $127,157.81. Sales through Embotelladora Andina in Chile were particularly strong throughout the 1940s, but the performance of São Paulo Refrescos in Brazil was disappointing. Profits improved, however, after Cliff met with Brazilian dictator Getulio Vargas. His Excellency amended the law to allow the use of phosphoric acids in soft drinks (which were part of the Coca-Cola recipe), and he reduced the tax on soft drinks in six-and-a-half-ounce bottles by 44 percent.

No one but Coke used six-and-a-half-ounce bottles.

* * * * * * * * * * *

Until Ike became president in 1952, the Masters played Prissy to Coca-Cola's Scarlett. Although newsreel and newspaper summaries gave Bobby's tournament a toehold in the national consciousness, few actual spectators showed up, and gate receipts fell miles short of covering costs. Roberts blamed the Masters' money problems on Augusta's remote location, on bad luck with the weather, and on the indifference of Jones's golf game.

Crowds had been pretty good for Bobby's comeback in the first tournament, but revenues declined as Jones's scores rose in each of the next five Masters. Prize money had to be raised by passing the hat among the members. Rotund Bart Arkell, owner of a meat-packing business, donated the $1,500 first-place prize, and Jay Monroe, another founding member, gave the $800 check for second.

"They counted every penny," recalls William Hyndman III, a ten-time Masters contestant, now in his eighties. "If you asked for some extra crackers with your soup, you'd find an extra two cents on your bill."

When Roberts wrote in his club history "that the [early] financial results were a bit disastrous," he understated the problem. The course had cost more than expected to finish, maintain, and operate, and the Annual Invitation Tournament had provided very little, if any, financial help.

Augusta National couldn't pay its bills.

On March 20, 1933, Cliff wrote:

TO THE CREDITORS: AUGUSTA NATIONAL GOLF CLUB

A small group of sportsmen advanced to the club one hundred and twenty thousand ($120,000) dollars, and this need not be repaid for a period of years. The Augusta National is embarrassed, however, by current debts amounting to approximately thirty-one thousand ($31,000) dollars.

Although our President, Mr. Robert T. Jones, Jr., was not expected to do more than contribute his efforts and influence, he has voluntarily made available to this project the sum of ten thousand ($10,000) dollars. We can ask him to do no more. It is likewise impossible to secure, at this time, further assistance from the small group that advanced one hundred and twenty thousand ($120,000) dollars for construction. For this reason, we are forced to say to you that the club can not now pay the sum that is due to you.

If trouble is made by any owner of current obligations, [the] mortgage will be foreclosed, the enterprise wrecked, and the sponsorship of Mr. Jones will be lost.

In other words . . . don't embarrass us. If you do, we'll take our ball and go home. Roberts's petulant and bullying tone seemed to lay the club's money problems at the doors of those who were owed money instead of those who owed it. By this time, Cliff and the others may have realized they'd blundered royally by failing to incorporate from the start. Under the loose partnership used to found and build the club, Roberts, Jones, and the rest could each have been sued for debts or for hospital bills and lost income from a mule kick or a shovel accident. The beauty of a corporation, of course, is that none of its owners bears any personal liability.

A year later, the club's bills still unpaid, Roberts put on a happy face and wrote another letter to the club's creditors. This letter (February 6, 1934) offered ad space in the first Annual Invitation Tournament program. But not for free: "It will be agreeable with us for you to mention in your advertisement the fact that you supplied

materials to this Club, and we shall be willing to have you use the
credit balance standing in your favor on our books, as a means of
making payment for the advertising space." Cliff had some gall.

A number of suppliers took advantage of the offer. Why not?
They must have wondered if they were ever going to get paid anyway. Members filled up the empty spaces in the program. Coca-Cola
bought a full-page ad for $200; Jay Monroe paid $500 for the back
cover. "The Monroe Adding-Calculator is a handy little machine
that sits upon the desk . . ."

After the second Masters, the original members took a hard
look at the red numbers on the balance sheet. Should we have an
assessment and pay off these debts? they asked themselves. Hell, no!
the loudest voices answered. We've put enough money into this
thing, and have you noticed there's a Depression going on? Well,
someone said, there's another way we can get out of this.

In June 1935 the club pulled its big switcheroo, simultaneously shafting its debtors and insulating itself from lawsuits. Beneath a tangle of *witnesseth*'s and *whereas*'s the deed transfer
reveals what happened:

> Whereas the Fruitlands Manor Corporation failed to pay the
> interest which became due on January 1, 1934, and quarterly
> thereafter, and such default continued for more than thirty
> days; and Georgia Railroad Bank and Trust . . . declared the
> entire outstanding indebtedness . . . to be due and payable;
> Whereas Georgia Railroad Bank and Trust . . . advertised the
> property . . . for sale at public outcry to the highest bidder for cash
> at the door of the County Courthouse on the first Tuesday in June
> 1935 . . .
> When said property was then and there cried off and sold to
> Jerome A. Franklin, Alfred S. Bourne, Jay R. Monroe, William
> H. Wallace and Henry B. Garrett . . . for the sum of $30,000,
> that being the highest and best bid submitted . . .

Step one in the legal swindle was allowing the bank to fore-
close on Bobby Jones's dream course (that the bank had remained

unpaid for a year and a half may be a clue that the Nationals controlled the timing).

Step two was buying the "old club" back under a new name, one with "Inc." on the end. This canceled the debt and cut off the debtors' right to sue.

Step three was to tell those people to stop sending any more bills stamped "past due":

TO THE UNDERWRITERS AND CREDITORS OF THE AUGUSTA NATIONAL GOLF CLUB (DECEMBER 2, 1935)

In 1931, the Fruitland Manor Corporation acquired a tract of land situated near the City of Augusta, comprising approximately 364 acres.

The Augusta National Golf Club was organized at about the same time. . . . The necessary land for the golf course, club house, garden and grounds, comprising 207.77 acres, were leased from the Fruitland Manor Corporation . . . Construction costs of approximately $25,000 could not be met, and the creditors holding these claims still remain unpaid.

The Fruitland Manor Corporation was uanble to meet the interest payments on its first mortgage bonds, and last summer, interest coupons for a period of approximately two years were in arrears . . . The holders of the bonds [the bank] exercised their right of foreclosure. . . . A Protective Committee for the Bondholders purchased the property. . . . The Committee made settlements with local women who held eleven of the outstanding bonds and who were unwilling to assent to a plan for the future operation of the property, but these women gave up and cancelled all of their claims for the unpaid interest.

The bondholders who participated in the plan and acquired the Fruitland Manor property at foreclosure sale have formed a new corporation known as THE AUGUSTA NATIONAL, INCORPORATED, and have taken Class A non par preferred stock in exchange for their former holdings.

While there is no legal or moral obligation to make any provision for the underwriters and other creditors of the old Club, the former bondholders, through their Committee, have unanimously

determined to offer the Class B stock of the new corporation to the
unpaid creditors and underwriters of the old Club . . .

The offer here communicated will remain open only until Saturday, December 28, at Twelve o'clock, noon . . .

Lawyer Lansing B. Lee, of Lee, Congdon and Fulcher, an Augusta law firm, wrote the letter (Lee belonged to the National). He offered the creditors and bond-holders a simple choice: a piece of The Augusta National, Inc.—or nothing. In simple terms, the club settled its unpaid bills by trading stock for the money it owed. One share of Class B stock per $100 of debt. Ownership of Class B stock in the company definitely did not include membership in the club, of course, or voting rights, and could not be passed down to an heir on the holder's death. At the top of the Augusta National, Incorporated, stock certificate was a lovely scene of lady golfers, an image that may or may not have been significant. Was a share of this stock as worthless as it seemed? Did it ever pay a dividend?

And who were the "local women" who at first declined to go along with the plan? One doyenne of Augusta golf history indignantly refuses to believe either that the National ever effectively fell into bankruptcy or that women held any of the paper. "I've never heard of any of that! I knew Bobby Jones and he was a gentleman from the top of his head to the tips of his toes! You'd better check your facts. Someone is pulling the wool over your eyes." But the middle piece of the puzzle, the deed transfer, is hidden in plain view in a file cabinet at the Richmond County Courthouse.

Although Congress had passed "blue sky" laws in 1933 to protect unsophisticated investors, Augusta National Incorporated's stock-for-debt swap was neither illegal nor particularly unusual.

But its knee-jerk secrecy makes its deification of the founding members seem a little spurious. It also makes one wonder what else it's been hiding.

* * * * * * * * * * *

Of the club's and the Masters' later glory, Roberts said, "I never thought it would be possible in a little tank town such as

Augusta." "Tank town" is a disparaging phrase not used much these days, derived from the water tanks in a thousand no-account settlements huddled by the railroad tracks, identical and anonymous, existing only to dispense water for the train's engines or for its sanitation. Down-and-out boxers fought in tank towns, low minor league baseballers played in tank towns. Urban, cosmopolitan gentlemen like Roberts distrusted such smallness. Cliff had been to Paris and lived in New York. Was that why a policy evolved that no more than 10 percent of club members could be from Augusta? For a short time, local members were required to house their out-of-town golf guests in one of the club's cabins, not in their own homes. Out-of-town members generate more revenue for the club, of course—they eat more meals, entertain more guests, and rent more of the club's ninety-four rooms. But are they smarter, better leaders, too? Chairmen of the club have come from, in order, New York City, Houston, St. Louis, and Little Rock; the heir apparent is also from Arkansas. No Augustans.

Roberts was dismissive of the city but got love in return. Even after a number of local people received stock of dubious value instead of money for the labor, materials, or cash they'd given the club, Augusta nurtured the National like a little child. When it had little of its own money to spare, the city donated $7,500 to each of the first three Masters. Augustans bought extra tickets that they quite literally couldn't give away.

BUSINESSMAN STRESSES VALUE OF GOLF EVENT headlined the *Chronicle* in 1939. The Masters, the man said:

> gives advertising the value of which is inestimable. It brings
> visitors here that would probably never see the city . . . at a time
> when the city is really at its best—all the flowers are in bloom and
> the weather is just right. Among the visitors are executives of the
> largest corporations in the country. The business firms of Augusta
> realize the value of this tournament and are taking a real interest
> in promoting it.

Obviously, Augusta was not too proud to make a buck. Yet if the National boarded up its clubhouse and indigo bushes and rabbits again ruled its fairways, the city would find another hook on which to hang its hat. It always had.

****

"'Slow-talkin', slow thinkin', backward, barefoot, racist.' That's what Northerners think and write about the South." The gray-haired lady from Augusta is leaning forward in her chair, her eyes bright behind her glasses. Her guest had expected a soft-spoken lady of the Old South; their meeting had been delayed because she'd been suffering from "the vapors." "You know those bumper stickers that say 'FORGET, HELL!'? Well, we really feel that way. Would you like some more Diet Coke?"

Like many Augustans and virtually all the members and staff at the National, the woman ("Don't use my name!") assumes a writer's evil intent. "There's entirely too much tearing down," she says. "Why shouldn't people who like to write or paint or play golf get together, free from gawkers, and enjoy each other's company? The Assembly [a members-only Augusta society that holds debutante balls for its daughters] is *not* elitist. It's birds of a feather.

"You could write all kinds of lies and they'd be believed thirty years from now, just because they're in a book."

And thirty years from now the fascination of readers and writers with the Gothic South will still be deep and wide—and still unwelcome. "We are aware that visiting reporters will want to tour the entire freak show of Southern stereotypes—snake handlers, Klansmen, and *Deliverance*-style pinheads," wrote Tom Chaffin, a journalist and historian at Emory University in Atlanta, on the eve of the 1996 Atlanta Olympics. "Race, of course, is the underlying focus of such preoccupations by the media, and the South clearly bears a burden for its historical racism. But by 1996, it should be clear that neither the South nor the United States holds a lock on racism."

No one could question the existence of racial injustice in the northern United States. But actual buying-and-selling-human-beings slavery both fascinates and appalls us, like Lenin's desiccated body under glass in Red Square. An unusually high percentage of Augustans owned slaves 150 years ago, which did not lead to a ghetto riot in May 1970 and did not cause Augusta's currently paralyzed, five black–five white city council that disagrees along racial lines about almost everything. But slavery led to war, and war led to the continuing, amazingly vigorous cultural battle—FORGET, HELL!—between the Visigoths from the cold, crude North and the cavaliers of the civilized South.

Augusta became Augusta because of some rocks in the Savannah River. Deer, buffalo, ground sloths, and woolly mammoths walked back and forth on the below-water sand bridge the rocks made, Indians followed, and a westward trail as well worn and obvious as Interstate 20 resulted. So many tribes pitched their tents in the area that when an ancient burial ground was discovered underneath the twelfth green at Augusta National during its construction, no one could say for sure whose bones and artifacts had been found. Creek? Cherokee? Iroquois? Catawba? Chickasaw? Those tribes and others lived by the trail at different times.

The English under General James Oglethorpe arrived in Savannah in 1733. Oglethorpe made nice with the natives, who might help keep the Spanish and the French from getting their hands on Carolina. An upright man, Oglethorpe took issue with the popular business and social lubricant, rum, and opposed slavery. He brought English-style order to what looked to him like wilderness, ordering surveyor Noble Jones to go up the river in 1736 to lay out a town and a fort. But not everything went the way the general pictured it. Rum and slavery proved too popular to legislate away, and the Indians gradually moved out as whites moved in. Creeks and Cherokees "owned" a lot of the area around the Augusta sand bar, not that they knew from fences or survey marks; they ceded two million acres to the Royal Colony of Georgia in 1773 to retire debts already owed to traders.

The upriver town Oglethorpe ordered got its name from a homely German royal who had recently married Frederick of England and who later gave birth to King George—yes, *that* King

George—the Third, the one who later lost the Revolutionary War. The woman was the princess of Saxe-Gotha.

White and black émigrés from Virginia and North Carolina made Augusta boom. "Slaves were so numerous that free white laborers complained that they could not find work," wrote Edward J. Cash in *The Story of Augusta*. According to the first census, in 1790, about 20,000 of the Augusta area's 80,000 residents were slaves. While the Virginians brought culture, devotion to honor, and religiosity to their new home, "slavery and social snobbery were the darker sides of [their] influence." Honor and snobbery ran amok in the early 1800s when white, male Augustans settled even innocuous disputes through dueling.

While handguns-at-thirty-paces seems charmingly Old World and Old South, in reality Augusta was to *Gone With the Wind* what London was to *Mary Poppins*. For example, not all the local slave owners were white. The Richmond County Register of 1818 recorded twenty-five black Augustans who owned slaves. Caesar Kenedy owned eight, as did Judy Kelly. About half the free black slave owners on the list were women. And unlike the lords of Tara or Twelve Oaks, Augusta plantation owners tended to live in town, not on their acreage. The typical Richmond County farmer owned five or fewer slaves and worked with them in the fields, raising corn, sweet potatoes, turnips, hogs, and cotton. And a little hell. Poor whites and slaves drank and gambled together in Augusta and, on rare occasions, married each other. Some slaves hired themselves out to the highest bidder, keeping some of the proceeds for them selves and giving some to their owners. Black and white mixed far less on the big plantations across the river in aristocratic South Carolina or in nearby Georgia counties such as Hancock, sixty miles to the west.

Short-staple cotton united the country on both sides of the Savannah, and Augusta, in the middle, grew as a port and merchant city. So much cotton was stacked on the side streets by the river-front, a horse and buggy could hardly pass. Cotton was speculated on in the factoring houses on Reynolds Street, and it was ginned, graded, weighed, baled, burlapped, warehoused, carted, and floated down the muddy river to Savannah, where it was shipped to New York or to Liverpool, England. The city and private investors built a canal in 1840—"a very Yankee thing to do," says Professor Cashin—to provide the thread mills with the water they needed to turn their turbines. The mills wove cotton into thread and thread into denim cloth and dyed it blue, with indigo. America needed blue jeans. If the mills bought locally, they might have used the indigo grown on one particular plantation on Washington Road. Pretty place; looked almost like a golf course.

Augusta was of at least two minds about slavery as the Civil War inched near. "No pure Republic can exist without the slavery of an inferior race as the basis of society," editorialized the *Chronicle*. But the paper seemed to be speaking to the big planters on the outskirts of its circulation area. Augusta was both more ambivalent and less emotional about the issue than other areas. Some wanted an abrupt end to slavery, some a gradual phasing out, and others of both races didn't particularly mind the status quo. No slave uprisings occurred in Augusta, although insurrections took place nearby, including a particularly violent one in Hancock County. The city fathers increased the tax on owners who hired out their slaves from ten dollars to one hundred dollars, and slapped a twenty-dollar tax on free blacks. One slave owner, James Henry Hammond, made a point of keeping his slaves away from Augusta, because there were "more abolitionists there than took Harper's Ferry."

South Carolina seceded quickly in 1860, but Georgia left the Union only after a bitter, public debate. The North is "rotten and corrupt, and based on *wrong*," huffed the *Chronicle* during the secession campaign. "Its downfall will be speedy, and its destruction complete."

Augusta armed the South, and its shoe and clothing factories clothed and shod it. The Arsenal, built in Summerville (against the neighbors' wishes) in 1829, manufactured fuses, percussion caps, and grenades. The Confederate Powder Works, a big brick edifice down by the canal, produced 2.75 million tons of gunpowder during the war. A part of it still stands in front of one of the denim mills. The only surviving structure built by the Confederate States of America is a tall, obelisk-shaped chimney with a Sputniklike lightning arrestor on the top, bearing inscriptions sad and proud. "Conserved in honor of a fallen nation, and inscribed to the memory of those who died in the Southern Armies during the War Between the States." "GEORGE WASHINGTON RAINS Brigadier General Ordinance, C.S.A. Brevet Major U.S.A. Captain, 4th Artillery, who under almost insuperable difficulties erected, and successfully operated these powder-works, a bulwark of the beleaguered Confederacy."

Refugees and wounded soldiers doubled Augusta's population in 1864, a considerable number of them arriving from the west in the fall, fleeing the Union's fiercest general, William Tecumseh Sherman. Sherman torched Atlanta in November and massed his troops. Where next? Scouts warned of an eastward advance along the railroad. Four of the Confederacy's top generals—Braxton Bragg, P.G.T. Beauregard, Wade Hampton, and James Chesnut—joined about 10,000 soldiers reinforcing Augusta. Streets were closed. The Powder Works was fortified. Soldiers built breastworks; part of the city's earthen defensive perimeter can still be detected near where the railroad station used to be.

But Sherman did not attack. Instead he and his 60,000 troops marched quickly in a wide path southeast—raping and pillaging along the way in Confederate accounts, merely feeding themselves according to Union versions. They took undefended Milledgeville, the state capital, and moved east to Sandersville the next day. Sherman then ordered part of his force under General Kilpatrick to engage the rebels in Waynesboro, "thus keeping up the delusion that the main army was moving toward Augusta," as Sherman recalled in his *Memoirs*. But the Union army marched to Savannah instead.

Why Sherman skipped past Augusta has been debated ever since. Most historians concluded he needed a seaport for resupply or that he really was happy to avoid a fight on his way to the coast, to conserve his resources for more important battles ahead. But why bypass the arsenal of the Confederacy, the biggest prize in Georgia? Perhaps the fact that Sherman had been assigned to the garrison at Augusta Arsenal exactly twenty years earlier had something to do with it. Then-lieutenant Sherman was twenty-four and single, and Ellen Ewing, his girl back in Lancaster, Ohio, had been lukewarm toward his proposal of marriage. According to legend, "Cump" Sherman had had an Augusta girlfriend, perhaps even a child. He spared the town to spare them. Or so many Augustans believed, and believe still.

Sherman explained his apparent mercy variously over the years. An important factor in his strategy, he said once, was that his men were on fire to have at the South Carolinians, the dirty bastards who had started the war in the first place.

* * * * * * * * * * *

Augusta prospered for several decades after the Civil War, then slumped. Yankee capitalists bought so many of its businesses that the Southeast became almost a colony of the Northeast. Natural disasters—floods, fires, an earthquake, and several outbreaks of typhoid fever—took a more dramatic toll on the city. An untended tailor's iron ignited the big fire of 1916, burning thousands of bales of highly flammable cotton and scores of the big homes near the cotton district. Downtown was devastated, and the Augusta cotton industry never fully recovered. A new electric trolley car line enabled Augustans to live out, uphill, away from the disease-ridden, unreliable Savannah. Gradually, the city turned its back on the river.

But it never turned its back on its past. A ghostly, white marble monument on Greene Street unveiled in 1875 became the focal point for war and remembrance. Carvings of four generals—Lee, Jackson, Cobb, and William Henry Talbot Walker of Augusta—surround the lower level of the cenotaph; an Augusta enlisted man, Berry Benson, posed for the figure at the top. "No Nation Rose So White and Fair None Fell So Pure of Crime," reads the oft-quoted inscription on one side. "Our Confederate Dead," a sadder, simpler phrase, is chiseled into the other. Benson took part in all the Memorial Day and Confederate Memorial Day parades until his death in 1923, but he never looked at the statue while marching past.

Some Southern cities wallowed in the Lost Cause and their lousy economies, but Augusta revealed a hustle and boosterism that only Atlanta was thought to possess. City fathers petitioned Uncle Sam for military bases and got them; Fort Hancock, Daniel Field, Fort Gordon, Bush Field. A brewery for Belle of Georgia beer was opened at Thirteenth Street and Walton Way, by the canal, an appropriate business for an army town.

Dr. William Tutt was an Augustan familiar with making something out of nothing. He manufactured and sold Tutt's Liver Pills, Tutt's Improved Hair Dye, Queen's Delight (for feminine complaints), and Tutt's Syrup of Sarsaparilla. His next big idea was to lure moneyed Yankees into town by giving them a place to sleep. He asked around; yes, there would be objection to a tourist hotel on the Hill. So he proceeded, discreetly, to buy the perfectly placed four-acre estate of Mrs. Anna McKinne Winter for $12,500. In 1889 he built a big brown hotel on the Hill in 1889 and called it the Bon Air. He added an eighteen-hole sand-green golf course in 1901 and a tennis court, a swimming pool, and riding paths. Suddenly, thanks in part to Dr. Tutt, Augusta was a tourist destination and a breathless advertiser of itself. "The future playground of the country. . . . Just 24 hours from New York City and the East. Just 24 hours from Chicago and the West. . . . France with her chateau district has nothing to offer like Augusta."

Other entrepreneurs followed Tutt into this new kind of snake oil. Morris Partridge opened the Partridge Inn across the street from the Bon Air; with no room for a golf course, it featured an indoor putting course instead. The Bon Air burned down in 1921, and was rebuilt and reopened three years later. White stucco and marble this time, a seven-story ocean liner beached on a hill, but fireproof. "The Bon Air has three hundred guest rooms," its brochure bragged, "and over a hundred baths." The Richmond Hotel opened on Broad Street, handy to the railroad station. West of downtown on Wrightsboro Road, the eight-story Forrest-Ricker Hotel opened, with a Donald Ross–designed golf course named

Forrest Hills, which you can still play today (though it is now called Forest Hills). Another architectural disappointment, the Forrest-Ricker resembled exactly what it would later become: a hospital.

The big hotels shut down for the summer back in those pre–air conditioning days, as did Augusta National.

"Hogan, Nelson, Mangrum, and Snead stayed with us sometimes, for two or three weeks at a time," recalls Carlton "Beanie" Morris, who was a bellboy at the Forrest-Ricker before the war. "No, they weren't good tippers. This was before they got money. . . . I remember I carried their bags two at a time from the back door of the hotel down to the first tee. Big leather bags, with their shoes and practice balls inside. Heavy as lead. Like to kill me." Beanie–short for Beanpole–weighed barely 115 pounds in his heavy uniform, grayish blue with a dark blue stripe down the side.

Augusta's hotel and real estate market bombed spectacularly in 1926, and the future site of the Augusta National Golf Club was ground zero. When a Florida financier and hotelier named J. Perry Stoltz announced his intention to build a hotel and golf course on the defunct Berckmans nursery on Washington Road, speculators from Ohio and Canada bid the surrounding real estate to absurd heights. "Commodore" Stoltz came to town, enrolled his son in Richmond Academy, and finalized plans for the project. He decided to build the hotel behind the manor house, use the old building as an office during construction, then tear it down when the new Fleetwood Hotel was complete. Workers dug the foundation in or near ground that would later become Augusta National's ninth and eighteenth greens, first and tenth tees, and putting green. But before the concrete trucks arrived, a hurricane blew away Stoltz's hotel in Florida, and all his money, and all his plans.

****

Other winds blew many of Augusta's blacks out of town, mostly to New York and Philadelphia. Boll weevils, lynchings, segregation, and the black-hearted night riders–the Ku Klux Klan–provided the push. Money delivered the pull. "Henry Ford started paying five dollars a day, when these people were making five dollars a *week*," says Dr. Ike Washington, Ph.D. Ed. "The agrarian South became like France before the French Revolution. White people owned everything, not because they bought it, but because they inherited it." The exodus of the descendants of former slaves to the industrial North between 1910 and 1930 was big enough to have a name: the Great Migration.

But what could you say about the people who stayed behind, and their children? Were they less ambitious or less talented than those who went north and sent money back home? Or more committed to friends, family, and community? The lives of three successful black men from Augusta do not provide a simple answer. Their names were Bowman Milligan, Sidney Walker, and James Joe Brown, Jr.

Cliff Roberts hired Milligan just minutes after meeting him, making the "large, strong and fine-looking black man" the club's steward and the first clubhouse employee. Milligan never missed a day of work for the next forty years, and Roberts invested him with increasing responsibility and authority. Cliff undoubtedly came to love Bowman, in a master-to-servant way. He gave his steward four paragraphs and two pictures in the club history and left him $5,000 in his will. Five thousand was tip money to Roberts, but the gesture spoke of the genuine bond between them.

"Sure I knew Bowman! Powerful man. Powerful as Joe Louis. Powerful enough to slap a white woman, if Mr. Roberts told him to. And back then, we didn't even *look* at a white woman." Dan Williams, who helped build and then maintain Augusta National so long ago, guffaws along with everyone else in his nephew's auto glass shop. Slap a white woman!

"Back in the early days, any black man could just walk right into the Masters tournament," says Dr. Ike Washington. "Everybody assumed you were a caddie. And you'd go right to the back door of the kitchen, and Bowman would give you somethin' to eat.

"I remember going north with Bowman once, right after the war [Augusta National closes from May to October; Milligan had a summer job at Longmeadow Country Club in Springfield,

Massachusetts]. We stopped at the Monmouth race track in New Jersey, and Bowman gets on the phone. 'Hello, Mr. Fruehauf? Bowman Milligan. What should I do?' [Harvey C. Fruehauf, the country's biggest manufacturer of truck trailers, was a member at the National.] Mr. Fruehauf had a horse running that day. But he says, 'Don't bet.'

"Bowman made some more calls. And he picks three winners in a row, one of them at fourteen to one. I bet two dollars, but he bet two hundred at a time. And he's got so much money it didn't even look like money."

One of Bowman's myriad duties at Augusta was procuring the entertainment suggested by his boss. On fight nights, Bowman made sure to visit the shoeshine boy who worked the corner of Ninth and Broad. The kid's name was Sidney Walker, a bouncy, heavily muscled 140-pound teenager, and a regular in the National's private battle royals. He never lost.

"The reason I started fighting, I went home and told my grandmother that a boy had taken my shoeshine polish and my money, and I was crying," Walker recalled. Grandma spanked little Sidney for not fighting back. A week later, the same boy returned to extort more polish, but this time Sidney fought and "kind of knocked him out a little bit." In his grandmother's joyous eyes, the child had been reborn. "My grandmother gave me the name Beau Jack."

"The boy was a waif," Roberts wrote, who "could not read or write, and was in doubt about the identity of his parents." Bowman hired him to black boots at the club because the members liked him from the battle royals so much, but Walker believed his future lay in the real thing, in prizefighting. "I asked Milligan would he take me north with him," recalled Walker; big-time boxing resided in the Northeast, particularly in New York. "I wanted to be a fighter. I think I asked him about five years and he never gave me a chance to go.

"So I asked Mr. Bobby Jones and he said, 'Well, I'll speak to some of the members when they come in off the golf course tonight at dinner and we'll see what we can do for you.' He called me downstairs and said, 'I finally spoke to the members and fifty of them will give you fifty dollars apiece to start your boxing life.' "

Boxing writer Peter Heller elicited those memories from Jack at his shoeshine stand at the Fontainebleau Hotel in Miami Beach in 1971. In 1997, Jones's role had expanded in Beau's memory: "They put up $50 apiece. . . . Everybody but Bobby Jones, and he put up $500." Jones has no role in Roberts's version, however; Cliff portrayed himself as the hat passer "not because any of us at the club thought he was a qualified fighter, but rather because Bowman had faith in him." He also credited Bowman with inventing Sidney Walker's famous *nom de ring*.

Fans loved Beau's windmilling battle-royal style and his power; he was a lightweight with a heavyweight's punch. "He was especially popular with his backers," Roberts wrote, "the majority of whom made a practice of having dinner together, going in a body to see Beau Jack fight, and then celebrating together in a private room at the Park Lane Hotel. On several occasions Bowman was asked to bring the Beau and join us."

Once, after Beau 'n' Bowman had hit the big time, they took a check for $45,000 to Roberts's office in New York. Would he please invest their fortune for them? Cliff looked at both sides of the check. "Boys," he said after a long pause, "I don't have the time for amounts like this. But since I know you, I'll see what I can do." Roberts set up trust funds for both. Without them, he said, Bowman would have gambled it all away at the $50 window, and Beau would have squandered his winnings on young women.

Beau Jack earned a fight for the vacant lightweight title against Tippy Larkin on December 18, 1942. Cliff and most of the other New York–Augusta National investors attended, their hearts beating hard in the supercharged atmosphere of a title fight, made still more electric because of their personal and financial interest. In the third round, Beau Jack interrupted the rhythm of his attack with a bolo punch, a showboating overhand right thrown from the floor and aimed at Larkin's noggin. "I let it went and that was it," Beau recalled. Tippy remained seated and senseless for the count of ten. The Georgia Shoeshine Boy was the new champion, and a hero to the nine-year-old who'd inherited his corner at Ninth and Broad in Augusta.

"What I really wanted to do was box," recalls James Brown, the Godfather of Soul. "My idol was Beau Jack, the lightweight champion of the world."

Brown had reasons to dream. He lived in a whorehouse run by his aunt, Handsome "Honey" Washington. He'd stand in the road out in front of the house at 944 Twiggs Street when Camp Gordon–bound soldiers walked by. He'd sing and dance to get their attention—and the change they threw—presaging one of his nicknames, the Hardest Working Man in Show Business. "I wouldn't let 'em say no," Brown recalled. " 'Come on,' I'd say, 'there's some real pretty [girls] in that house yonder.' I'd hook my arm in theirs and start tugging, pulling them toward the house. When they'd finally say yes I'd lead 'em right inside." Those not interested in fornication could buy half-pints of moonshine corn liquor for twenty-five cents; like a lot of the South, Georgia stayed dry for years after the repeal of Prohibition.

From his point of view on Twiggs Street, "Augusta G-A was sin city: plenty of gambling, illegal liquor, and a lot of houses like the one I grew up in," wrote Brown in his autobiography. "The local government then was corrupt, the police could be bribed, and the law was whatever they said it was.

"Sometimes the Ku Klux Klan held parades right through the Terry [local shorthand for the 130-square-block Negro territory]. The funny thing was all the black folks turned out to watch. I never paid much attention."

Augmented by James's regular raids on a food wholesaler's garbage bin and by the steady stream of cash customers, life at 944 Twiggs improved slightly during the war years. An uncle provided James his first store-bought underwear, replacing the stitched-together flour sacks he'd worn up to then. But a spiritual poverty remained. He saw his father, Joe, only occasionally, and his mother had left her husband and son years before.

So it was no surprise that like hundreds of other kids in the Terry, James became a hustler and a minor thief. At age fifteen, he was caught stealing clothes from cars parked on Broad Street—four cars, the police said. He turned sixteen, after two months in jail, and was then tried as an adult. Judge Grover C. Anderson gave James Joe Brown, Jr., no less than two and no more than four years at hard labor for each offense, the sentences to run consecutively. Eight to sixteen years, total.

* * * * * * * * * * * *

World War II romance had a far more civilized air just two miles from where James Brown shilled for his Aunt Handsome.

The girls wore their hair high on top, tight at the sides, and down to the shoulders. They frowned into mirrors before going out, applying makeup and bobbing their hair so that the ends flipped under. Pads filled the shoulders of their gossamer-weight challis dresses, which buttoned in front and ended in the shortest skirts in twenty years. Entire calves were visible. Showing some leg during wartime was considered almost a patriotic duty, "something for the boys," the girls said.

The young men who held the young ladies wore tan ties tucked into tan shirts tucked into tan pants, highly polished brown shoes, and had military haircuts. The tall windows in the Bon Air ballroom were thrown open on warm evenings, but couples watching the dance from the narrow window seats blocked most of the breeze. When the band finished "Moonlight Serenade," the clarinet and trumpet players found handkerchiefs to wipe the sweat from their faces. The dancers pushed gently apart and applauded. Some held hands and walked up a couple of steps to the double doors and down a dim, echoing corridor to the lobby, past potted plants and wicker furniture, then out the front door. Across the driveway and into the dark the couples strolled, and the blossoms on the huge magnolias perfumed the air and glowed like pale moonlight.

Some nights during the war years the gentlemen from the Augusta National Golf Club engaged the ballroom for boxing matches or other entertainment. But their Masters tournament and all the attendant excitement were on hiatus for, in the suddenly common phrase, "the duration." A shame, because after nine years the golf and the golfers had really taken their place on the Augusta social calendar. The Masters had become a novel published in serial form, with an exciting new chapter revealed each April, starring an increasingly familiar cast. "Everybody talked about Jimmy Demaret and his clothes," recalls a woman who was a girl at the dance. "Byron Nelson was so nice. Ben Hogan was Mr. Cool. And we all thought Sam Snead was really cute. . . . I had a friend who went out with Sam Snead." Many of the golfers stayed at the Bon Air and ate and drank and danced there. The big white hotel hosted the Calcutta party on Wednesday and the after-tournament soiree on Sunday.

But the dancing stopped in 1942—except for men in uniform. Soon after Nelson beat Hogan in a play-off in the tournament in 1942, the Masters was suspended and Augusta National was closed. Two hundred head of Hereford cattle grazed the course, and the superintendent, with no grass to cut, spent his time raising turkeys. Cliff had some of the gobblers smoked and shipped to the members and sold the rest. At a loss.

Jones applied for duty in the Army, though he was three times exempt: by age (forty), dependents (Mary and the three kids), and medically (two varicose vein surgeries on his legs). "War appeal[ed] to his competitive instincts, far more than the probable prospects of being an entertainer giving golfing exhibitions to sell war bonds, as Bob Hope and Bing Crosby did," wrote Dick Miller in his biography of Jones, *Triumphant Journey*. With a choice between being on display and being in harm's way, Jones took the hard way out.

He was commissioned a captain in the Army Air Corps in June 1942 and reported to Mitchell Field in New York, then studied aerial photographic interpretation for ten weeks at an intelligence school in Harrisburg, Pennsylvania. And, since he was a lawyer and had read Goethe in the original German while at Harvard, Captain Jones learned prisoner interrogation. But the Army frustrated him by assigning him to the aircraft warning service, a bunch of civilian sky-watchers. He took some courses in identifying airplanes and helped train hundreds of volunteers. He referred to this time disparagingly as "fighting the Battle of the Atlantic Seaboard." Jones had been in the Army reserve since 1931; he wasn't a rookie. "When I entered the Army it was in the hope of seeing really active duty," he told a reporter from the *Atlanta Journal*. He hectored several superiors until they sent him overseas.

* * * * * * * * * * *

In 1943, now-Major Jones shipped out to England, to look at photographs of the damage done by B-25s and B-26s on their bombing raids on the Germans in France. Usually a fighter pilot escorting the medium-range bombers took some snaps, and Jones would look at the photos, debrief the photographer or someone else who'd been on the mission, and fill out a form. Flak over the target heavy, medium, or light? Enemy aircraft? How many? What type? Did you see where they took off from? He may have helped analyze the "after" photos as well, a process known as BDA (bomb damage assessment). "The truth is," says an Air Corps combat veteran, "those guys didn't have that much to do."

But things changed for Jones and his unit. According to Sid Matthew (*The Greatest of Them All*) and other biographers, Bobby's unit found themselves dug into foxholes on the beach at Normandy just one day after D-Day in June 1944. Although it's difficult to ken why the Army would put middle-aged intelligence officers in the line of fire, apparently Major Jones spent two months at or near the front. He saw destruction and death and experienced the strange insult of being shot at.

But Jones would carry at least one pleasant memory of his time with the Ninth Air Corps. On March 17, 1944, his forty-second birthday, Roberts somehow got a fifth of twenty-five-year-old bourbon delivered to him, an amazing feat during wartime. Jones wrote to Cliff to thank him for the bottle, which he said "proved to be a very good companion indeed."

You picture Jones in olive drab, a glass in his hand, lulled into contemplation of his future.

CHAPTER FOUR

•

Jimmy, Frankie, and Herm

Miss Augusta floats down Broad Street in the Masters Week Parade.

Herman Keiser, 1946 ... Jimmy Demaret, 1947 ...
Claude Harmon, 1948 ... Sam Snead, 1949 ...
Jimmy Demaret, 1950

Certain guys they liked, certain guys they didn't. Gene, Byron, and Ben they liked, and their glory and grace sweetened the tournament's ritual. Back-nine bridges were named in their honor: the Hogan spans Rae's Creek on the twelfth; Nelson's Bridge is on thirteen; and the Sarazen runs alongside the water hazard on the fifteenth. Hogan started the Tuesday night Champions Dinner in 1952, and it has been a permanent part of the Masters landscape ever since. Byron long held the honor of partnering the tournament leader during the final round, "and brought home seven winners," he says proudly. The nonagenarian Sarazen strikes the first tee shot and makes the first comment about how far these kids today hit the ball. A country boy amateur named Billy Joe Patton finished a close third in 1954, and in subsequent years showed himself to be humble, funny, well met, and well-off. Later Billy Joe received the club's ultimate accolade: an invitation to join.

"I've been going there since I was twenty-three," Nelson says. "Every year except when Louise was paralyzed [Byron's first wife died in 1985]. And I still get that feeling, that nostalgia. It's kind of like old home week.

"Every Wednesday, Peggy and I amble down to Amen Corner, just to look at those holes. The course is closed for the par-three tournament, but there are always a hundred people in the stands behind the twelfth tee. And they applaud me."

Byron is eighty-five now and jowly, and he needs a cane to ease the pain of walking with hips made of titanium and polyethylene. But sixty-something years ago, as a skinny, apple-cheeked young man of twenty-five, he won the Masters. "In 1938, the year after I won, I asked Cliff if he'd suggest some stocks I might buy. 'Well, what have you got now?' [He imitates Roberts by slowing and lowering his voice to a growl.] So I told him—I had a few thousand dollars in some penny stocks. He says, 'Where'd you get those dogs?'" Roberts informed Nelson that he didn't normally handle accounts under one million dollars, but for him, he'd make an exception.

"As you know, Cliff's company, the Reynolds Company, later became Dean Witter Reynolds. No, I never sold those stocks. They're what I live on now."

Ben Hogan ascended to Augusta National sainthood on a different arc. Byron enjoyed almost immediate success in the Masters, winning the tournament before Ben had even been invited to it. But Hogan failed, practiced, failed again, practiced some more. He improved enough to tie Byron in 1942, but lost in a play-off. Again he finished an excruciating second in the first postwar Masters, to the former storekeeper on the light cruiser USS *Cincinnati*, Herman Keiser. He eventually won, of course, in 1951 and in 1953, the latter a performance so brilliant it remained unapproached until Jack Nicklaus came along. But two more seconds followed, one of them a play-off loss to Sam Snead. Still Ben remained polite, if not cordial, and continued to hit hundreds of practice balls.

Both Jones and Roberts admired Hogan's doggedness, his dignity, and his capacity for suffering. Someone once asked Bobby that stock question regarding who he'd like to have hit a shot or a putt for all the tea in China. "That's not hard for me to answer—Hogan," he said. "Hogan had the intangible assets—the spiritual." Roberts and Hogan were superficially similar, in that both turned a cold shoulder to most of the world but were regarded as pretty good guys by their small circle of friends. Perhaps Cliff knew that, like him, Ben had lost a parent to suicide. Ben may have known about

Cliff's years in Texas. Hardly a Calcutta went by that Roberts's "Greek Syndicate" didn't buy Hogan.

Sarazen's double eagle in 1935 showed what wonderful things Augusta National could inspire. And he presented such a lively, quotable presence for so long that he became as much a part of the Masters tableau as the dogwoods. AN OLD FAMILIAR FIGURE read the photo caption. "No Masters Tournament would be complete without Gene Sarazen in the field," the *Augusta Chronicle*, April 2, 1947. Just before attending another Masters half a century later, Sarazen leaned back in his chair. "I remember going out for drinks with Roberts one evening and I told him that number sixteen is a *terrible* hole. One hundred yards over a ditch. 'Now go get Trent Jones,' I said." And it came to pass: the club hired architect Robert Trent Jones to redo the sixteenth.

Nelson was gracious, Hogan was admirable. Sarazen was feisty and ageless. Patton charmed everyone. But neither personality nor golf skill alone secured each his favored seat at the Masters table. They all contained a third crucial qualification—appropriate behavior and diplomatic speech. They were gentlemen, in short, in the Augusta National sense. Gentlemanliness had been the very basis of the tournament founder's life and of his golf; Cliff, the keen assistant, picked up on the boss's strict standards of behavior, his love of honor. Roberts amplified Jones. Together, they made a fetish out of monitoring the behavior of everyone in or near their tournament.

For example: as Freddie Haas prepared to putt on the eighth green during the third round in 1947, someone in the following group hit his ball onto the green, a severe breach of etiquette and of safety. Haas finished putting, teed off on the ninth, and returned to the eighth green to address Johnny Bulla, the offending party. "I wasn't mad," Haas recalls. "I stopped about forty yards away from him and said, 'Hey man, you hit into me. Someone could have gotten hurt.'" Roberts summoned Haas to his office in the clubhouse after the round. "Fred," Cliff said, "we don't tolerate that kind of attitude around here. If you will write a letter of apology, we might have you back again." Apologize to who, for what? Although he seemed more sinned against than sinning, the Haas faux pas had been raising his voice above a conversational level and allowing a customer to hear it. It was more important to be correct than to be right at Augusta National; any scene offended the club. Haas wrote the letter. Roberts and Jones invited him back.

Certain guys they liked, certain guys they didn't. Keiser's victory in the Masters might have been memorialized as an inspirational upset, but the dark-horse champion fell so far out of favor that the club chairman accused him of stealing his own green jacket. Jimmy Demaret won the tournament three times, more than Sarazen, Nelson, or Hogan. No bridges bear his name, however. "I can't even get an outhouse named for me," he joked. He was always joking. One ill-considered comment earned him a written rebuke from Jones that, in the words of his best friend, "just crushed him."

Frank Stranahan, an amateur, finished second in a Masters soon after the war, and given Jones's reverence for amateurism, he might have taken his place next to Byron, Ben, and Gene. But the next year Cliff and Bob threw the defending runner-up out of the tournament before it even started.

* * * * * * * * * * *

"Five dollars, five dollars, five dollars."
Clifford Roberts stood on the front porch of the clubhouse, watching the cars stream up Magnolia Lane. He'd recently fought for, and won, an increase in Masters ticket prices from three bucks to five. As a member of the tournament improvements committee, Byron Nelson remembers the impassioned speech Cliff delivered when the subject of admission revenue came up: "We went to New York recently to watch Beau Jack fight. We had ringside seats to watch just two men fight. Here, you've got a field of the best golfers in the world, and the people are paying just three dollars while we paid fifty dollars for those ringside seats. That's ridiculous." When Byron came out onto the veranda and stood nearby, Chairman Roberts gave him a little smile and continued counting cars.

The blessings of solvency arrived at Augusta National with the war's end. The club paid its bills, on time and in full. The tournament purse doubled to $10,000 in 1946, and Arkell and Monroe no longer had to fish the first- and second-place money from their own wallets. Jones announced his participation in the construction of a new Atlanta Athletic Club course, which caused some Augustans to fear the loss of the Masters. But after a dozen years of financial struggle, the steady stream of five dollars, five dollars promised that the club's moneymaker wasn't going anywhere. Roberts already had plans for every penny.

The first Masters in four years exuded a strange air of giddiness and aberration. Calcutta parties sprung up like spring flowers, answering the pent-up demand for fun, games, and gambling. The *Chronicle* covered the auction at the Bon Air, but far more money was wagered at the private Calcuttas at Augusta National and, after 1949 (when Calcuttas were officially frowned upon by the USGA), at the Jewish Community Center.

But betting was still big, and still acceptable, in 1946. Bookies patrolled hotel lobbies as well as the golf course, never neglecting their best clients, the golfers themselves. One of their steadiest customers had been Herman Keiser, a long-faced, long-legged man from Missouri. He'd spent his final summer in the Navy sharpening his handsy swing at the driving range at the base in Norfolk, Virginia. He'd played very well early in the year, so he bet twenty dollars on himself, on the nose. But the smart money was on Hogan.

The natural order seemed amiss when the lightly regarded Keiser shot 69 and 68 in the first two rounds to lead the highly regarded Hogan by seven shots. Things became even more bizarre when Keiser discovered—he thought—a plot to keep him from winning. A bookie waylaid him by the eighteenth green after the second round to quietly inform him that two well-known Augusta National members had bet $50,000 each on Hogan, a mind-boggling sum. Herm started to see conspiracy. First, the club refused to replace his limping caddie, a young man whose feet were so sore he could barely walk from tee to green. Then, the next day, according to Keiser, he almost missed his third round starting time due to an unannounced change. Finally, Grantland Rice came out on the course to threaten him with a slow play penalty. Keiser's suspicions were confirmed.

Keiser talked about the situation with Hogan before the final round. Ben, Keiser says, was sympathetic, "a real gentleman about it." But other players like Art Wall and Fred Hawkins dismissed Herman's conspiracy theory as mere paranoia or a fantasy plot hatched by the bookies, who'd make a bundle if an underdog won. Whether the forces allied against him were concrete or imaginary, they were real to Keiser; so it was a considerable accomplishment when the Missouri Mortician hung on to beat the mighty Hogan by one. Both players blew the tournament, in a way, since both three-putted the slippery final green. First Keiser, from about thirty feet; then, an hour later, from twelve feet above the hole, Hogan.

Keiser drinks Busch beer and reminisces in the dim interior of his driving range in Copley, Ohio, near Akron. "When we walked up the hill to eighteen, Byron says to me, 'You haven't three-putted all day. That's wonderful.' And I said, 'Well, Byron, I've got one more to go!'" Keiser cackles at the end of this anecdote, his head and shoulders bobbing up and down. He wears a flannel shirt and big leather boots; the hunting dogs he keeps in a kennel out beyond the 300-yard markers are his life now, not golf. Practically his only contact with the game comes from his annual pilgrimage to Augusta for the Champions Dinner. His ritual calls for a Monday drive to Columbia, South Carolina, usually with one of his three sons. He leaves the Holiday Inn on Tuesday and glides his Cadillac sixty miles east to the Washington Road exit on I-20 in Augusta. He attends the dinner, chats with the other old pros, collects his $1,500 honorarium, and leaves.

Someone at the range asks for the identities of the two Augusta National members, the ones who didn't want him to win. "It wouldn't do either of us any good to tell you," Keiser replies. He excuses himself to get something from his apartment upstairs, while a visitor looks at a picture taken many Aprils ago. The hand-tinted photo hangs on the dark pine-paneled wall to the left of the men's room. There's Keiser, in the center of the oval frame, looking slightly dazed. Hogan, the perfect sportsman, stands to Herm's left, showing two rows of perfect teeth. On Keiser's right, Bobby Jones regards the new champion without expression.

Herman Keiser returns with his flannel shirt buttoned to the neck and over it a green sports coat. Single breast, single vent, two brass buttons on each sleeve, two buttons in front, circular logo on the left chest. "Sure, try it on," he says. The 1946 Masters champion holds it open, and you slide your hands and arms through the silk-and-rayon lining and into the green jacket.

****

Would the Masters return to normal in 1947? Could it, when one of the favorites was Jimmy Demaret?

"Not too many people know we used to wear shorts on the tour, on occasion," recalls Freddie Haas. "In fact, I won the Memphis Open [in 1945] in shorts. Anyway, it was really hot one year at the tournament in Chicago, so we all decided we'd wear shorts the next day. Everyone wore sort of longish Bermudas. But Demaret comes out in what looked like a very short, very tight bathing suit. Every color of the rainbow! The next day the word came down: no more shorts."

In an era when not wearing a tie with your gray tweed trousers cut the fashion edge, Demaret usually appeared at the first tee in salmon pink or lavender or brick red or pumpkin. With matching golf shoes. He topped his ensembles with a tam as big and snappy as an hors d'oeuvre tray of jalapeño peppers. All this—and more—on a squatty body that resembled Fred Mertz more than Mark Spitz. Sunny Jim grinned merrily at the astonishment he caused. "Sam Snead and Vic Ghezzi would kid him, but that was water under his wheels, exactly what he wanted," Paul Runyan says. "He was the life spirit of our tour. An attention-getter of the first order. He was everybody's friend and extremely popular with his peers."

Demaret had a simple explanation for why, out of the robin's-egg blue, he decided to colorize the pro golf tour. His father back in

Houston had been a housepainter and had let little Jimmy help him
mix his paints. The colors, he said, had fascinated him. But his motivation for founding the Loud Plaid School of golf clothing had to
have been a little deeper. Some recessive gene, perhaps? Probably
birth order and family size played a part: as the fourth of nine children, Jimmy must have felt he never got noticed enough.

Certainly no one could ignore his golf game, which was only
a notch behind Nelson, Hogan, and Snead. He won the Masters and
five other tournaments in 1940. In the eleven events before the
1947 Masters, Demaret won three times and won the most money,
$10,600. If his clothes or his golf didn't cause enough of a stir, if he
couldn't buy you another drink, or if you'd heard his joke before,
Jimmy had another way to make you pay attention. He sang.

Demaret discovered how wonderful his voice sounded
through a microphone at about age twenty-two. He worked as the
head professional at the Galveston muni course during the day and
at night frequented the beachfront cabarets and casinos on the redneck Riviera. Along the way Sunny Jim befriended Sam Maceo, who
owned several Galveston Beach nightclubs, and bandleader Ben
Bernie. With the cooperation of both, he occasionally got in front of
the band to croon some standard tunes—"Stardust," for example, or
"My Blue Heaven." His soft tenor was pleasant, better than Skinnay
Ennis's, not as good as Merv Griffin's. Jimmy so loved the stage, the
spotlight, and the music that he briefly considered making singing
his career, but Maceo and Bernie, witnesses to both Demaret's skills,
persuaded him to stick with golf.

The familiar urge to be seen and heard hit Demaret again on
Tuesday night of Masters week in 1947. He rose from the audience
and stood in front of the band in the gently decaying Bon Air ballroom. "I've got my l-l-love to keep me warm," Jimmy sang sweetly
into the mike. All the golfers in attendance had listened to their favorite ham sing before, but none of them seemed to resent his showmanship. "He was very poised," recalls Runyan. "Particularly if he
was around [bandleader] Phil Harris. But Jimmy would have been
a much better player if he'd never met Phil Harris." In other words,
Phil and Jimmy drank a little bit and stayed out late.

But the funny thing about Demaret was not the funny things about Demaret. It was his warm and serious side. He assumed a second-father role for three younger pros—Dave Marr, Jack Burke, Jr., and Don Cherry—Texas boys whose fathers had died young. "There was a lot of substance underneath the surface," says Dave Marr. And though he often pressed a fifty on a caddie or a pro to help get him to the next event, "He was a very smart guy, really good with money. He invested very well; he bought stock in AT&T when telephones were black and had rotary dials. Left [his wife] Idella a fat estate. And, of course, there was Champions." With Burke, the golf pro son of a golf pro he had worked for, Demaret founded Champions Golf Club in north Houston. Jimmy's and Jack's course has hosted a Ryder Cup, a U.S. Open, a U.S. Amateur, and two Tour Championships.

"Jimmy would come down to Memorial Park [a Houston muni course] and say hello to the mayor in the pro shop, then go to the caddie pen and play tonk with the black guys," Marr said, not long before he died. "Charlie Price, the writer, told me once, 'I never could get Jimmy Demaret down on paper.'"

Seven of the eight men who had won the Masters posed for a picture the afternoon after Jimmy's concert (only Ralph Guldahl, the shy 1939 champion, didn't attend). If the photo shoot had been a post parade at the racetrack, you'd have had no trouble picking the most confident horse: Demaret. On body language alone, he looked most likely to succeed. He stood in the center of the green-jacketed group on the practice tee looking so enormously pleased you'd think he'd already won. Only Jimmy maintained the correct one-leg-forward stance for a full-figure photograph. In fact, only Demaret and one other champion, Byron Nelson, remembered to look at the camera and smile.

Byron had been raising hogs and fixing fences for the previous eight months. He'd quit the tour in 1946, to the shock of many, and he and Louise bought 630 acres near Fort Worth. But Byron would always accept an invitation to share the love at the Masters. The Nelsons arrived in Augusta two weeks before the tournament so Byron could practice. They stayed at the Richmond Hotel, which was quieter than the Bon Air—the Nelsons didn't drink or dance— and had better breakfasts. "I can still remember the hot biscuits and country ham you could get there every morning," recalls the pork aficionado. "I didn't have the ham a lot because it was too salty, but it sure was good."

In the end, the 1947 Masters came down to a three-horse race between Nelson, Demaret, and an extraordinary amateur golfer, Frank Stranahan. Byron hid his competitiveness behind his pure country goodness, and Jimmy clothed his ambition in coats of many colors. But Frankie didn't possess the knack of disguising how badly he wanted to win.

He and Byron went way back. In 1940, Robert A. Stranahan signed up his seventeen-year-old son Frank for a series of lessons with Nelson, the new pro at their club (Inverness, in Toledo). "Well, I soon found out this young man wouldn't listen to anything I had to say," wrote Byron in his autobiography, *How I Played the Game.* "He just wanted me to watch him hit balls, and he wouldn't change anything or take any of my suggestions seriously." After a few weeks of this, Byron quit as his instructor, telling the teenager, "You're wasting my time and your father's money." The father intervened, a truce was reached, and Frank attended to the pro's advice a *little* more in subsequent lessons. He worked extremely hard, and his game advanced impressively.

A few years later, Frankie marched into the golf shop with two other young members and, as usual, asked the pro to make the fourth. And, as usual, Byron turned him down. But Stranahan had become somebody in the golf world since his first lessons with Byron; he'd won the Inverness club championship twice, the Ohio Amateur, and a dozen other worthwhile events. So when Nelson declined and Frank implied that his refusal was based more on a fear of losing than on the need to inventory sweaters, he'd hit the pro's hot button. "Okay, Frankie, I'll play you. Not only will I play you, but I'll throw in your two buddies and play all three of you, right now, best ball!" The Masters and U.S. Open champion shot a course-record 63, beat the rich kids, "and Frankie never bothered me again."

Demaret's relationship with Stranahan also involved putting him in his place. Jimmy was a kidder, and Frankie provided an irresistible target. Frank's inherited wealth allowed him to turn down prize money and remain an amateur. That the muscles on his arms and chest bulged from lifting weights was almost as unusual as the hours he put in on the practice tee. He practiced as much, in fact, as the champion practicer, Hogan (*"More,"* Stranahan insists). And Frank was such a handsome devil that young women pressed their phone numbers into his hand. "Jimmy just ate him alive teasing him about the weights, the practice, the girls," Marr recalls.

"Demaret was like a clown, with the tam and all the colors," says Stranahan without rancor. "Yeah, Jimmy kidded with me all the time. But I don't care for people who are always joking. I prefer someone who makes a lot of enemies and a lot of friends."

* * * * * * * * * * *

Jimmy and Byron played together in the first round of that 1947 Masters, and both shot 69s, the best scores of the day. Demaret and Cary Middlecoff led after thirty-six holes, with halfway totals of 140, four under par. Byron held second a shot back. Stranahan stood at 145, but with heavy hitters like Sam Snead, Ben Hogan, and Lawson Little, Jr., between him and the lead. In the third round, Jimmy hit the ball from tee to tree but saved his uncharacteristically wild day by one-putting ten times. The most spectacular of the ten was a four-footer on fifteen, since the shot that preceded it was a spectacular explosion from the water and mud from the edge of the pond in front of the green. Demaret's 70 gave him a three-shot lead over Byron and five over Frankie. Who would win tomorrow? Masters customers wondered. And what would Demaret wear?

Jimmy chose head-to-toe canary yellow. "If you're going to be in the limelight, you might as well dress like it," he said. He teed off at one-eighteen, Byron started a half hour later, and Frankie a half hour after that.

Nelson caught Demaret, then fell back with three-putt bogies on nine and ten. Something felt wrong to Byron, something was missing. "There wasn't one particular hole where I could say, 'That's where I lost it,' " he recalled. "The fact was, I really didn't care anymore . . . [the Masters] in '47 showed me once again that I was definitely through with the tour." Byron eventually shot 70 and tied for second.

Stranahan suffered no such drop in competitive fire. Even though it was his first Masters, "I didn't feel any pressure," he says. "Winning didn't scare me. And I'd beaten those guys before." His 68 was the lowest round of the day, but it was not enough. The winner shot 71, two shots clear of Byron and Frank. Bowman handed him a jacket and Jones handed him a check for $2,500. Masters green complemented Demaret's canary yellow.

****

GOLFDOM'S ELITE AWAITS MASTERS MEET THURSDAY
by Charles Bartlett, *Chicago Sunday Tribune* (April 4, 1948)

Golf's smartest boys are shining up their sharpest shots and best manners these days for next Thursday's opening of the fanciest fairway shindig of the year—the 12th annual Masters tournament at the Augusta National Golf Club . . .

As had become traditional, Bobby Jones teed off in the first round of the 1948 tournament with the defending champion. Demaret shot 73; Jones's play was barely adequate, a 76. But he played dismally in the subsequent rounds: 81, 79, and 79. After play each day, in what turned out to be his final Masters, he'd head for an upholstered chair in the locker room and sit down heavily in it. Within seconds a white-jacketed, black-skinned attendant would gently slip off Mr. Jones's shoes and replace them with slip-ons, while another solicitous employee placed an old-fashioned at his right hand. "They treated him like a god," recalls Vern Tietjen, a newspaper writer from Oregon. "I mean the players, too. Lloyd Mangrum says, 'Can I have a game sometime, Mr. Jones?' Lloyd Mangrum!" (Mangrum, a twice-wounded World War II veteran, often hit shots with a burning cigarette in his mouth—a tough guy.)

Bobby seemed weary. He'd lost some of his vigor and had been complaining of a sore back and a crick in his neck. The strain of age, perhaps. Or the stress of dealing with Frank Stranahan.

Jones and Roberts had bungled the Stranahan situation horribly, and they knew it. And in their bungling they revealed far more than they wanted about themselves and about the club.

Before he became a situation, Stranahan began his Masters week in the usual way. On Monday, he docked his Cadillac convertible under the porte cochere at the Bon Air. As usual, neighborhood kids on bicycles buzzed around as he disembarked, staring at the face they'd seen in the newspapers come to life. And girls, there were always girls. "Frank, remember me?" America's Most Eligible Bachelor of 1948 smiled—but rarely signed autographs. "[Henry] Cotton and Snead didn't sign, so I didn't either," he says. Photographic evidence proves, however, that he often wrote *something* on paper for the young women in orbit around him.

Aging black bellboys in faded blue uniforms staggered as they hoisted the suitcases from the Caddy's trunk. This was Strannie's running gag. He traveled with 365 pounds of weights—"a full Olympic set"—and sometimes with other paraphernalia of the bodybuilder's art. Watching hotel porters nudge his steel-laden bags to the elevator was a once-a-week-laugh. Frank stayed on the road as many as forty-five weeks a year and credited weight training for his endurance.

After finishing second in the previous Masters, the best amateur since Bobby Jones traveled to England for the British Open at Hoylake. And just as he did at Augusta, Stranahan finished a spectacular second. Spectacular because he knew if he could hole his second shot on the final hole, a par four, he could tie for first. He almost did. Twice he walked from his ball to the green; then, from 165 yards, his downwind nine iron lipped the cup and stopped three inches away. He won the Fort Worth Invitational later in the year, against Hogan and Nelson, on the course they'd grown up on as caddies.

"Every week, I had the biggest crowds you can imagine," Stranahan recalls. "Fred Corcoran always paired me in the first round with whoever had won the previous tournament." The tour commissioner understood that Frank was a draw. A rich kid; as everybody knew, his father founded Champion Spark Plugs. Good looking. Didn't take a dime in prize money. Long hitter. Sharp dresser.

He was also the athlete many people loved to hate. "As a golfer, Stranahan is the most egocentric, monomaniacal character who ever swung a niblick," wrote Tom Siler in a September 1947 article in *Collier's* entitled "Golf's Bad Boy." "Frankie walks ramrod-straight, taking long, deliberate steps, something between a strut and a swagger . . . his solid-colored polo shirts fit him as tight as Mabel's girdle." Stranahan Senior reacted badly to the gossipy article and canceled $300,000 in advertising.

Frank registered at the Bon Air, in obvious decline now that it had lost its affiliation with the Vanderbilt chain. Then he got in his Caddy and retraced the path of the original members to Augusta National for a practice round. Up the hill, past the arsenal, right on Highland-Berckmans, right on Washington, and through the magnolias.

He checked in, got a locker and a caddie, and went to the pro shop, where he had a very strange conversation with the pro, Ed Dudley: "As soon as I got there, Dudley told me I was going to be thrown off the property this week," Stranahan says. The pro also warned him against hitting a second ball to the green during his practice rounds. Only one ball per player per green was allowed. Frank had violated the rule the previous year.

Stranahan teed off, accompanied only by his caddie. But unwelcome company appeared twice during the first few holes, when course superintendent Marion I. Luke came out to remind him yet again about the regulations regarding practice on the course. The second conversation, Frank recalls, "got really nasty." The super accused Frank of violating the one-ball rule; according to Strannie, however, all he'd done was drop several extra balls to practice his putting. They called each other sons of bitches, and Superintendent Luke stormed off to tell Mr. Roberts about it.

A delegation of Augusta National members stood waiting for

Stranahan as he came over the hill to the eighth green. "We're taking away your permission to play," their spokesman said. "Your invitation has been withdrawn. Please leave the golf course."

"When I heard about that, I said, 'Jesus Christ!' " recalls Gene Sarazen. "None of us could believe it." Stranahan was equally dumbstruck.

"I called Dad, and I called Tommy Armour, and I asked them what to do. 'Go see Jones,' my father said. 'He's the greatest sportsman of his era.' They were certain he'd listen to my side." When Jones did not make himself available for two days, Frank bought a ticket, watched, "and talked to everybody." He knew, of course, that was the last thing Roberts expected or wanted. But all present concur that Stranahan behaved impeccably while he waited for Bobby. Although at first he threatened "repercussions" for the Augusta National "high hats," he also apologized in writing and asked for a hearing. The incident was closed, Roberts replied. No hearing.

No one got behind Frank. No players walked out or held a candlelight vigil. Golf's bureaucracies also stood in Cliff's corner. The Professional Golf Association might have been expected to back Stranahan, except that Frank was an amateur and thus not a member. Also, the president of the PGA, Ed Dudley, was the head pro at Augusta National. The United States Golf Association might have raised a hand in protest; Frank belonged to the USGA. But the president of the USGA, Fielding Wallace, belonged to Augusta National. "It's none of my business. I don't know who is right." Maynard "Scotty" Fessenden, the president of the Western Golf Association and chairman of the Advisors to the PGA Tournament Committee, seemed to express the bureaucrats' mood. "The incident will probably do Frankie a lot of good," he said. "It never hurts anyone to have his ears pinned back once in a while."

The Masters did not fall under the jurisdiction of the PGA, the USGA, or the WGA, of course, so it is debatable what effect a protest from them might have had. The Masters was the Masters and went its own way.

O. B. Keeler, of all people, broke the story in the *Atlanta Journal*. Jones's long-time collaborator apparently was not under

Roberts's thumb, and Bobby had not yet arrived in Augusta. But the club still announced nothing, Stranahan decided to keep quiet and hope for a good result from his meeting with Jones, and Superintendent Luke had no comment. The writers wondered what the hell was going on. Finally, Roberts invited the newspapermen to his suite. In a vintage performance, Cliff confirmed Stranahan's dismissal, declined to say why the previous year's runner-up had been disinvited, and said that the club would appreciate it very much if the press would downplay their coverage of the incident.

That many writers did indeed soft-sell the story was testament to Cliff's clout and manipulative skill. The key guys, to Roberts, were the men from the wire services, Associated Press, United Press, and International News Service. Hundreds of papers, without a writer of their own at the Masters, depended on their reports. The wire service reporters toed Cliff's line, but their editors and rewrite men at headquarters in New York were beyond the Roberts reach and gave the story the play it deserved, under headlines like POLITICS PREVAIL AS STARS AWAIT START OF MASTERS.

At last, on the day before the tournament started, Stranahan got to see Jones. "I went down to his cottage and asked him to reinstate me. And he says, 'I let Cliff run the tournament.'

" 'Well, that's about the cheapest thing I ever heard of,' I said."

Frank Stranahan sighs lightly. "I haven't talked this much in fifteen years," he says. He had opened the door to his white house in West Palm Beach wearing a black Speedo bathing suit and a tight black tank top with GOLD'S GYM in gold across the chest. The startlingly white man pads barefoot across the white carpet. Except for a bed and a tiny kitchen table, his house contains no furniture. An assortment of fifty-year-old free weights and a lifting bench preside in the nominal living and dining rooms. No pictures or mementos adorn the white walls; scrapbooks in boxes and framed black-and-white photographs lean together in casual disarray on the floor. Frank appears in one shot in a heroic pose, a heel lifted to bring one leg in front of the other, head back, his shirtless torso rippling with smooth muscle. Another picture is a head-and-shoulders shot of

Frank inscribed to his father, urging him to observe healthful habits of exercise and diet "until a cure can be found."

Were you disappointed, a visitor asks, that the other players didn't protest when Roberts suspended you?

"That's not true. A lot of them took my side, a good percentage. No, I can't remember who they were off the top of my head. And sixty percent to seventy percent of the writers backed me afterward."

Stranahan has deep-set blue eyes, most of his hair (it's gray), and perhaps one cubic centimeter of body fat. He's incapable of slouching. He has the trim physique and stagy presence of Patrick Stewart, a Shakespearean actor better known as Captain Jean-Luc Picard on *Star Trek*. His monk's life begins each day at three-thirty A.M., when he flips on the TV, presses PLAY on the VCR, and watches the biography he's taped from The History Channel or A&E the previous night. He works out while he's watching, this man who was seventy-five in August 1997, and drinks some carrot juice or eats a raw sweet potato or half a dozen eggs. That is, if he's not fasting. One day a week, and ten consecutive days four times a year, nothing passes his lips but mineral water. Every morning he leaves the sterile luxury of his gated golf-course community before dawn in a leased black Lincoln Town Car for another workout. He returns from the gym before the sun peeks over the ocean; Florida sunshine, he knows, is no good for his skin. He says he's never had a drink or a smoke or a cup of coffee in his life. He'll be in bed by 7:30. His bed has no pillow, just a thin white towel folded precisely in half.

"I'm into longevity," he says. "You will be, too, but by then it will be too late." How does he plan to achieve his target age of 120 or 140? By drinking lots of milk? "I think milk is the worst food in the whole world. So I can see you don't know much about nutrition." A pause, then: "Have you noticed how they're advertising milk now? With athletes?" He holds equal disdain for doctors, who, he is certain, consistently order unneeded "six-thousand-dollar CT scans" for indigent patients, thereby making themselves rich at taxpayers' expense. He believes that physicians, the Food and Drug Administration, and the big drug companies are in league to thwart the growth of natural medicine. "Doctors," he says disgustedly. "What the hell can they cure? Drugs can't cure anything."

Doctors couldn't cure his father. Or his son, Frank Junior, who died at age eleven from cancer. They couldn't save his wife from cancer, either. Ann Stranahan died at age forty-five. Drugs killed his second son. Jimmy, a student at a Houston prep school, overdosed in his apartment at age nineteen. Dave Marr's mother, who ran the apartment building, found the body.

Frank Stranahan turned pro in 1954 and won the Los Angeles Open in 1958. Ten invitations to the Masters followed the brouhaha in 1947, but his best finishes in this period were ties for fourteenth in 1950 and 1953. He quit golf in the sixties to concentrate on business. He took up running in 1970, at age forty-eight; six months later he ran in the Boston Marathon, the first of 102 twenty-six-mile races he's run. He deadlifted 505 pounds once, squatted 425. He weighed 176 "and didn't wear a lifting belt." Lately he enters and routinely wins seniors' bodybuilding competitions. He gives talks from time to time, which end with him taking off most of his clothes, "to show what a guy my age can do."

Frank Stranahan lives this life and thinks these thoughts and makes plans for his 120th birthday. A little incident in a golf tournament more than half a century ago is hardly a blip on his radar screen.

But for the things the incident seems to imply, you want to know *why* it occurred. Was it simply delayed, oversevere punishment for breaching a little rule a year before? Stranahan doesn't think so. "Tim Rosaforte [a golf writer and Frank's West Palm Beach neighbor] took me down to the Masters last year. And there's Greg Norman and Tiger Woods and everybody else hitting two balls to the green during the practice rounds."

The rumor persists, as *Golf World* magazine wrote in 1948, "that Frankie had 'dated' a blond who was palsy with a club member; that this made said member jealous and the greenkeeper incident presented an opportunity to chastise Stranahan for his winning ways with the ladies." The rumor within the rumor was that the affronted member was Himself, Clifford Roberts, and that the blonde was his secretary.

"I don't want to go into that," Stranahan says.

But the cause of the banishment matters less than the conduct of the banishers. Jones, a lawyer, understood due process as well as anyone but stood by while Stranahan was denied a hearing. "I let Cliff run the tournament" was his only comment, a U.S. and British Open champion acquiescing to a man whose most important competition had been in the A flight at the Blind Brook club championship.

When Roberts booted Stranahan from the Masters, he dominated not only one player—the least little dictator might do that. Cliff also cowed the entire field, the golf organizations, the press, and Bob Jones. In a gym or a boxing ring, Frank could have crushed him like a bug. At Augusta National, however, Roberts kicked sand in the muscleman's face.

But Cliff kicked only with the full faith and cooperation of the other members. When they decided to stonewall inquiries into the conflict, no one broke the silence, revealing both the personality of Augusta National's leaders and the membership's remarkable loyalty to the office of the chairman—and perhaps to the chairman himself. The decision to boot Stranahan without a trial and then to not talk about it also revealed a breathtaking institutional arrogance.

Cliff's exact role in the affair remains difficult to pin down— was he the offended party in a matter of the heart or the point man for another member or an unflinching defender of the one-practice-ball rule? Jones's part, however, is much clearer. Despite his stature in golf generally and in Augusta in particular, he avoided the conflict and fell in step with the others. He supported an indefensible course of action.

Indefensible because the Masters was not the member-guest at Boston Hills Country Club. From its first staging in 1934, the

Masters ranked as one of the ten most important golf tournaments on earth (some of the others, according to Sam Snead, were the Metropolitan Open, the North and South, the Western Open, the World Championship, the PGA, and the U.S. Open). By 1948, due to the wonderful design by Mackenzie, and to the brilliance of Roberts's and Jones's administration, the tournament had moved into the first tier of the big ten. Officials at lesser events might yield to pettiness or caprice, but administrators of championships must hew to higher standards; something as vital as a disqualification should not be handled like an assassination in Russia under Stalin.

The Stranahan affair illustrated Augusta National's enduring dilemma: how could the club remain very private while at the same time hosting a tournament everyone in golf wanted a piece of?

****

An old man in a dark business suit sits crookedly in his wheel-chair, smoking a cigarette in a long black holder. Around his neck are two long loops of string; a lighter is attached to one, and to the other, a pen. He is not a clean-desk man. Manila file folders, a telephone, an intercom, and a huge glass ashtray crowd the glass top of the brown wood desk. On the wall to his left are pictures of his father smoking a pipe; his wife, Mary, in her prime; paintings of Eisenhower and Cliff Roberts; and a framed letter from Ike. Jean Marshall, his secretary, perches in a chair to his right, her pencil hovering above a yellow legal pad. "Dear Mister Bigga," the old man drawls.

In his April 19, 1965, letter to Gordon G. Biggar of the Shell Oil Company, Jones proclaimed himself to be a dedicated fan of Shell's *Wonderful World of Golf*, a TV travelogue/golf match filmed in exotic locales around the world. But the announcing on the shows had been bothering him to distraction, Jones wrote force-fully. He felt Sarazen was being severely underutilized in favor of the smooth but less-than-expert George Rodgers: "Rodgers's some-times breathless commentary would be better suited to a horse race or a prize fight than to a leisurely contest at golf."

"Rodgers liked to hold the microphone in his right hand," remembers Sarazen with a laugh. "I always stood on his left side."

Rodgers was fired. Shell hired Jimmy Demaret to replace him.

* * * * * * * * * * *

Jones again showed the range of his emotions in a letter to Demaret written two years later.

In the April 15, 1967, *Houston Post,* Demaret was quoted as saying: "There was something missing at this year's Masters, and I believe it was the lack of enthusiasm of crowds because of the limited ticket sale. Crowds were off all week, even for the practice rounds. . . . Why do you have to limit crowds at golf tournaments? It's unnecessary. You could put 40,000 people out on a course like the Masters and lose them."

Jimmy's quotes infuriated Jones and Roberts, who revealed thin skins when it came to criticism of their baby. Jones wrote to Jimmy, asking pointedly how a three-time Masters champion could minimize the prestige of the tournament to a newspaper reporter. "I have known you for a long time as a person with a ready wit and facile tongue, and I always thought you were a pretty savvy guy. This last, I am now beginning to doubt."

Jones's letter was something of a collaboration with Roberts, who wrote in suggestions on Jones's first draft. Cliff wanted to include Burke in the stern admonition to treat the Masters with more respect. But Jones ignored or overruled that, and virtually all Cliff's marginal advice. The letter was Jones's own. And, according to Burke, "it just crushed Jimmy."

Disease tightened its grip on Jones. He wrote to his doctors, "I am getting pretty fed up with this 'relatively good prognosis.' My life day and night is about as miserable as one could imagine." In another note to his personal physician, Dr. Ralph Murphy, he wrote, "I have a very real horror of spending my final years lying paralyzed or in twisted agony."

Years later, his worst fears gradually coming true, Jones reflected on the emotional debate over who would control the professional golf tour (read: TV money), the PGA or the players. "We live in an idiotic society," Jones wrote to Cliff. "Frankly, if I knew any more profitable ways of taking advantage of the idiots, I would exploit them. This is no time for idealism." Later, he apologized for the severity of this remark.

CHAPTER FIVE

•

Dead Game

James Brown at the unveiling of the sign renaming
a portion of Ninth Street in his honor.

Ben Hogan, 1951 . . . Sam Snead, 1952 . . . Ben Hogan, 1953 . . . Sam Snead, 1954 . . . Cary Middlecoff, 1955 . . . Jack Burke, Jr., 1956 . . . Doug Ford, 1957 . . . Arnold Palmer, 1958 . . . Art Wall, Jr., 1959

James Brown's boss held up a tire iron and prepared to smash his employee's stupid head.

The State of Georgia had paroled the future Godfather of Soul a few months earlier, in June 1952, after three years and a day of incarceration. The terms of his release stipulated that he attend church regularly, get a job immediately, and stay away from Augusta. The job James found wasn't much—washing and greasing cars at Lawson Motors in Toccoa, in northeast Georgia, where the prison was located. And the work was made worse by the taunts of his superior, who apparently wanted to provoke a fight that would send him back to the slammer. One day the boss looked at the 1950 Ford Brown had just carefully washed and waxed. "Do it over," he said. So James decided to get a little dust on the car before doing the work again. When no one was looking he backed the car off the lot and drove out to the prison, honking the horn and waving and hollering to friends still behind the barbed wire. But he drove too fast on his way back to work and slid the Ford into a ditch. His boss and the car's owner were waiting for him when he returned with the wobbling, misaligned vehicle much later, and James narrowly escaped death by tire iron. "One way or another, my troubles always seemed to involve cars," he observed.

Brown refocused his attention on music, his third love after boxing and baseball. He and the Ever Ready Gospel Singers recorded "His Eye Is on the Sparrow," but the local radio stations wouldn't play it; James's raw, powerful voice wasn't quite right for gospel or close harmonies. His next band, the Flames—a.k.a. the Famous Flames—played rhythm and blues, a more suitable genre. "Race music," they called it back then. James hit his stride: at halftime of an intramural basketball game at whites-only Stephens County High School, he slid across the floor with a dust mop and danced with it, while his band played and the kids went wild. Hundreds of one-nighters followed. The Flames played Livonia, Hartwell, Cornelia, Cleveland, and Kingsville, and in Seneca and Greenville in South Carolina. Clemson, Austin Peay, and the University of Georgia booked the band, too. But they stayed away from Augusta.

As James rose, Beau Jack fell. Early in a 1947 fight at Madison Square Garden with Tony Janiro, Beau threw a left hook that missed and caused him to tumble to the canvas awkwardly. He fought on for a couple of rounds, hopping around the ring on one leg while the knee on his opposite leg throbbed. Beau's brave stand revealed what his flamboyant style often hid: he was "dead game," an old sportswriter's phrase, meaning undaunted, or full of pluck. But after a round or two the referee tired of the spectacle of a one-legged fighter versus a bipedal one and stopped the bout in the fourth. Janiro whooped and celebrated as if he'd won by knockout instead of by accident, an unseemly display. Beau went to the hospital for his broken kneecap and didn't fight for nine months, but he beat Janiro in a rematch in May 1948. Dead game.

He was more than just a fighter. As the best-known and most popular Augustan of the forties and early fifties, Beau provided a rare link between poor black and rich white in Augusta's stratified society. Beau Jack enthralled both the members of Augusta National, who "owned" him, and those who owned him in the "he's one of us" sense. One group sat ringside, the other gathered around the Philco and just listened. Neither faction thought about the disappointment of the other when Beau lost to Kid Portuguez or Kid Gavilan or Fritzie Pruden. When he knocked out former lightweight champion Lew Jenkins in 1950, Cliff Roberts didn't drive down to the Terry and buy a round of beer for the house. But Beau Jack fought 112 times, so on 112 nights over a dozen years, Augusta and Augusta National dreamed the same dream.

* * * * * * * * * * *

The National's off-campus headquarters lost its cachet like the tycoon in *The Great Gatsby* lost his fortune—gradually, then suddenly. Fat William Howard Taft wrote his inaugural address in his room at the Bon Air, relaxing between bouts with pen and paper in a cavernous, specially built bathtub or on the hotel's ninety-acre, nine-hole, sand-greens golf course. But Alfred Bourne, the Singer Sewing Machine magnate who wintered in Augusta, bought the course and built a house on it. With the loss of the Bon Air golf course, vacationing Northerners had still another reason not to detrain in Augusta on their way to Florida. Increasingly, empty beds gave the Vanderbilt hotel chain all the reason needed to unload the aging Bon Air. When light fixtures or doorknobs broke after the divestiture, thick brass was replaced with thin, shiny steel. The Bon Air was a woman in a ball gown with a patch on the seat.

Augusta National members hated what the Bon Air had become. They were men of means, unaccustomed to bad food in dingy hotels. "The Augusta National was doomed unless the club provide[d] living quarters on the grounds," Roberts wrote in his club history. "This was something we did not at all want to do." Did not at all want to do because the club still had no money. But a member named Eddie Barber, of the Barber Steam Ship Lines in New York, sailed to the rescue. In 1945 the cleft-chinned, bushy-browed Mr. Barber offered Cliff $25,000 for whatever quarters the club might build for him; not that he'd *own* the room or apartment, he'd just have the right of first refusal when he was in town. At other times, the club could rent it to another member. Roberts, who knew that the best capital belongs to someone else, heartily approved of the personal-bed license idea. The other terms of Barber's proposal included a $100,000 loan to get the East Wing Expansion underway and his pledge to liquidate the debt upon his death, which he did when he died eight years later. Barber's will also included a gift to the club of an additional $200,000. As Cliff had been aware for twenty-five years, the rich have pleasing ways.

The Barber bequest gave Cliff a potentially big idea. At the conclusion of the annual report to the members—a rundown on the club's big events, new members, improvements, policies, and financials—a new category appeared:

BEQUESTS

Because our Club and the Masters Tournament have become firmly established as institutions of considerable importance to the game of golf, we feel justified in suggesting that members consider making provisions in their wills for a bequest to the Club . . . Stipulations in wills should read as follows:

"I hereby give to my golf club, The Augusta National, a corporation organized under the laws of the State of Georgia, and known as the Augusta National Golf Club, the sum of _____ dollars."

Barber was given his choice of the five East Wing suites. Roberts picked second and selected the quarters at the end of the building, the only suite with a fireplace. (It's the closest suite to Eisenhower's cabin, the one on the far right as you face the clubhouse from the putting green.) No one who ever uttered the phrase "Isn't that darling!" was allowed a hand in the interior decoration. This was a men's club through and through, and the golf prints, muted colors (dark green carpets and off-white walls predominate), and overall simplicity of the decor reflected a Real Man's taste. With the help of a $200,000 bond sale to the members, increased revenue from club operations, more personal-bed license money, cash gifts, and probably, a boost from the Masters, nine club-owned cabins were eventually built to the left of the tenth tee (the club used the plantation-era designation "cabin" for any structure, no matter how large, that was not the Big House).

With the completion of the Jackson T. Stephens Cabin in

1969 and including the suites (now known at the club as the Roberts Suites) and rooms in the clubhouse, the Augusta National Hotel had ninety-four beds. Providing sleeping quarters at the golf course wasn't a new idea; back when country clubs really were in the country, many of them provided dorm space. The beds at the club symbolized the character of the place—cooperative living and planned giving—and increased the club feeling.

While the investment in hostelry also represented a significant withdrawal from the community, the National wasn't the only one giving Augusta the brush. First, Vanderbilt left the Bon Air, then Owen Cheatham, a local lumberman (and a National member), merged his pine company with a spruce business in the Northwest and put the headquarters of Georgia Pacific in Atlanta. The Forrest Ricker, converted to a hospital during the war, never reopened as a hotel. The Richmond Hotel and Union Station faced a wrecking ball. The federal government closed down the arsenal. And the Titleholders, a major women's tournament held in the fall at Augusta Country Club, began to wither.

"We started out as an amateur tournament basically. The founder, Mrs. Dorothy Jean Manice, paid everyone's expenses," says historian Eileen Stulb. The *Chronicle*'s coverage of the first Titleholders in 1937 revealed that perhaps Augusta was not quite ready for women's golf: "As the darlings returned clubward, officials heard more than one complaint that 'the course is too hard.' " But the tournament grew alongside the Masters, just more slowly. "Augusta did support us, with donations, and buying program ads, and tickets," Stulb says. "But we didn't have the industry we have now. We had no sponsors."

Still, the Titleholders assumed real importance in women's golf. "The Titleholders was always a highlight for us, just as the Masters was for the men," says Mickey Wright, who won it in 1961 and 1962. "But the old hotels on our tour, like the Bon Air, the Cloisters in Hot Springs, Virginia, and the Miami Biltmore were always sort of scary and somewhat disappointing in the accommodations. Seedy. But that aura of old wealth permeated."

Beanie Morris, a former bellboy at the Forrest-Ricker Hotel, gives you chapter and verse about the Masters, but can recall only this from a Titleholders week: "Some women up in one of the rooms called for a boy, so I went up there and it was Louise Suggs [who won the Titleholders three times in the 1950s] and a few others. And they're all gigglin'. They'd messed up the cork in a real good bottle of champagne. So I had to push the cork through, and when they poured it into glasses they strained it through one of their stockings."

Augusta's wealth was too old to support both a men's and a women's tournament, and the Titleholders would be gone after 1966. The city lost population during the 1950s, and thus tax base. White flight accelerated the decay of downtown. The Masters got a little bigger every year, however, and that was something to rally around.

****

"We got free tickets in those days," recalls Larry Jon Wilson, a musician and a native son. "Someone from the club would come around to the schools to give away practice-round tickets, trying to increase interest in the tournament. On Wednesday, there'd be Paul Hahn, the trick-shot artist, and a driving contest, which George Bayer always won, and an archer shooting coins out of the air. But it wasn't really a carnival atmosphere.

"Augusta National was a smaller part of things here than people realize. Like music is in Nashville."

The club and the Masters prospered together in the afterglow of World War II, even if the town didn't. Prize money skipped from $12,000 in 1950 (which was about average on the tour that year; the 1950 Fort Wayne Open paid $15,000) to a magnificent $74,700 in 1959—the biggest purse in professional golf; the PGA Championship, the second richest event, paid $51,175). The field grew from sixty-four in 1950 to eighty-six in 1959. Attendance increases may be assumed, although Roberts never made any exact numbers available. He counted cars instead and didn't reveal that number either. Was this one of his seemingly innocuous quirks? Or was he trying to obscure tournament income?

More intimate details of Augusta National's progress can be found in the annual reports to the members that Cliff sent out every September and in the letters from Roberts—and to a lesser extent, Jones—to Eisenhower. The documents, which are preserved in the Eisenhower Library in Abilene, Kansas, reveal Roberts's personality thoroughly. His intelligence, his second-in-command usefulness, and his tendency to be as subordinate as possible shine through both in his words and in the sheer volume of the missives Cliff posted to Ike—about two thousand pages.

But the newsletters and letters often raise as many questions as they answer. For example, this announcement in September 1953—"Major W. H. Corlett is resigning as the Secretary of the Royal Birkdale Golf Club of Southport, England, to become the Manager of the Augusta National"—was followed by this one in November 1954—"Mr. Peter S. Fithian has been appointed and is now serving this Club as its Manager," which was followed by *this* announcement in September 1955: "Mr. John Pottle of Linville, North Carolina, has been engaged to serve the Club as Manager." By remaining at his post for two years, Pottle outdistanced about a dozen other postwar managers who each stayed four months or less. Why the turnover?

"Roberts wanted a flunky," says one of the disgruntled dozen, who asked not to be identified. "He actually did all the managing when he was there. He was pretty impossible to work with. . . . I'd sit for two or three hours at a time with Roberts and Jones, and they'd say, 'We're getting older now, and we really need your help.' Then Roberts would go and do whatever he wanted.

"He was a ruthless man."

Bowman Milligan presented another intractable problem for the club manager. "In the letter inviting me to take the job, Cliff wrote that 'certain employees have proven to be indispensable,' " the former manager says. This, he discovered, meant Bowman. "He had tremendous power. All the clubhouse employees reported to him, all of them black. A prodigious worker, coming in at six A.M. and staying until nine or twelve P.M., seven days a week (his wife worked in the Augusta National kitchen). He came across to the Southern members as arrogant and pushy and demanding of the tip policy. He managed Beau Jack, you know, and he was able to talk to all these CEOs at the club. He liked to go out to Daniel Field and meet their private planes. The airport manager told me it didn't look right, a black man shaking hands with those men like that, and he was thinking of banning him from the airport. . . . Bowman loved his importance, and he bragged about it.

"And he loved Mr. Roberts like a father."

Milligan's unusual clout percolated up past his alleged superiors and bubbled down to the waiters, busboys, shoeshine boys, and locker-room attendants. He controlled their life blood: tip money. "We suggest the simplest and most equitable procedure is to give Bowman, the Club's Steward, for distribution, anything which you feel has been earned," wrote Roberts regularly in the annual report. "He will follow your instructions with regard to those who are principally responsible for extra services rendered."

At some point after the suites were built, Cliff made Bowman his gentleman's gentleman, which, naturally, increased their closeness. During the three to four months a year when Roberts was in residence, the black man awakened the white man in the morning, helped him into his clothes, and assisted him into bed at night.

The other mainstay in the Augusta National clubhouse was club secretary Mrs. Helen Harris, wife of the local Western Union man. "She worshipped Mr. Roberts as much as Bowman did," according to the former manager. "I remember that from about late February to a week after the Masters in early April she came to work at nine A.M. and left at nine P.M., six or seven days a week, eating her meals in her little windowless office. I tried to get her a raise, but Mr. Roberts turned her down, even though he knew Bowman and Ed Dudley were taking in plenty of cash that wouldn't be taxed."

Mrs. Harris and Milligan stayed through the decades, but

managers—and members—came and went. Thirty-nine original and early members had gone to glory by 1951, including Bartlett Arkell and Jay Monroe, donators of early prize money; Thomas Barrett, Jr., the Augustan who'd told Roberts about the Fruitlands property; and Louis Berckmans, the Belgian whose father had started the nursery that became Augusta National. Other members quit or were dismissed. Five resigned (or were shown the door) in 1950, one in 1951, three in 1953, two more in 1954, two in 1955, and two in 1957. That's a high turnover. Several dropouts a year is not unusual for the typical private golf club, but Augusta National took far more than the usual care in selection and recruitment; potential members were approved *before* they were asked to consider joining the club. Perhaps the men who left had been expecting to join Bob Jones's club and were disappointed to discover instead the pervasiveness of Charles de Clifford Roberts, Chairman.

Not that Augusta National had any trouble attracting new blood—far from it. With the influx of fifteen initiates in 1950, the roster totalled 170, "within five of the authorized limit of 175." The club raised the maximum membership to 200 in 1951 (today it's 300). Of the 183 members on the books in 1951, New Yorkers outnumbered Georgians forty-seven to forty-six; thirty were from Augusta. The club's status as a Manhattan golf club was lessening.

An unusual new man, Freeman Gosden, joined the scant handful of Augusta National members who were not lawyers or businessmen (Grantland Rice and former heavyweight champion Gene Tunney were two of the others). Gosden was in show business. As the costar and cocreator of *Amos 'n' Andy*, the most successful radio program in history, Gosden pulled down $100,000 a year in the days when a new Ford cost $900. Six days a week, from 1928 until 1943 (after 1943 the show aired weekly), Gosden (Amos) and Charles Correll (Andy) riveted America. Dinnertimes, factory shifts, church services, and movie intermissions were juggled so people could hear the fifteen-minute comedy show. Gosden and Correll wore blackface for a 1930 Amos 'n' Andy movie, *Check and Double Check*. The show had a brief run on TV in 1951 and

1952 with black actors; reruns played until 1966, when the
NAACP's protests that *Amos 'n' Andy* demeaned blacks convinced
CBS to withdraw it.

"The wonder is not that America in the 1960s had no place
for Gosden and Correll," wrote Melvin Patrick Ely in *The Adventures of Amos 'n' Andy*, "but rather that, during 35 years of profound social change, a radio and TV series with roots in
nineteenth-century minstrel shows had given Americans their most
pervasive, sustained picture of what purported to be black life and
personality."

During the 1951 tournament, Gosden climbed the tower by
the eighteenth green to comment on the Masters for CBS Radio—in
character. Gosden did two voices: "Say, dat's a pretty good shot
dere, Amos, by Mister Mangrum." "Sho is, Kingfish." "And we'd like
all our friends out dere to come see dis here Masters." "We sho do."
Like millions of other Americans, Cliff found the two white men
lampooning country blacks in the big city to be hilarious. Gosden
became a popular member and part of Cliff's inner circle.

Like the information on the evolving membership—"We welcome Mr. Freeman Gosden of Beverly Hills, California. . . . We report with great sorrow the passing of James T. Greene of Greenville,
South Carolina"—most items in the annual reports were straightforward. A guard had to be posted at the gate in 1953; too many
tourists were wandering up Magnolia Lane. The club's barber shop
lost $1,615 in its first year. Green coats could be bought for $28.50
from Brooks Uniform Company in New York or for $50 from Cul-
lum's (Henry C. Cullum was a member of the club) in Augusta, "for
those wishing to obtain a better tailored coat of a little lighter weight
material . . . made [from] a fine gabardine bolt of cloth exactly the
same shade of green used in the old coats." Green fees were increased from $5 to $10, annual dues were raised to $400, and the
initiation fee was increased to $2,000. But it's hard to give much
credence to the profit-and-loss numbers, because Cliff quite obviously began playing accounting hide-and-seek with the Masters
money.

Tournament receipts in 1949, according to the report, were $60,081. Expenses totaled $54,283, yielding a profit of $5,798. The numbers were almost identical the next year. But starting in 1951, the annual report no longer showed revenue or expense, only a single line, net profit. Roberts had the means, motive, and opportunity to reject generally accepted accounting practices by redistributing money from a profitable enterprise (the Masters) to a loser (the club's huge and grossly overstocked wine cellar, for instance). This is an important point, because the Masters was a corporation separate and distinct from Augusta National, Incorporated. Each entity had its own mandatory IRS reporting requirements. The reporting should never have been mixed.

A telegram from Roberts to Eisenhower dated April 7, 1952, hinted at what was going on: "The big winds blew the scores sky-high but didn't blow away any of the Tournament Receipts," Cliff crowed. The $110,000 gross for the 1952 Masters was, according to Roberts, the best-ever gate for a golf tournament, and a hefty $21,000 increase over the previous year's take.

Despite the record income, the club newsletter reported that 1952 Masters profits were only $6,868, slightly more than in 1948, when tournament income was a mere $60,000. Cliff could squeeze only $1,000 more profit out of an extra $50,000? That makes no sense at all.

Roberts mentioned in the oral history that Masters income by the late 1950s had reached $250,000, "quite remarkable for a little tank town like Augusta." But the annual reports to the members continued to show net profits of only eight thousand to nine thousand dollars.

****

With the exception of Roberts, no Augusta National member had a greater impact on the postwar history of the club than Bill Robinson. A sales and advertising man from Providence who rose through the ranks at the *New York Herald Tribune*, he convinced Eisenhower to write his memoirs shortly after their first meeting in 1944. He handled the publishing details, including excerpting the book in his paper. After another crucial meeting with Robinson seven years later, Ike announced his willingness to run for president.

"One day [in the spring of 1948] Robinson mentioned to me that the General was planning a long-awaited vacation but could not decide where to go," Roberts wrote. "I suggested to Bill that he let [Ike and Mamie] know they would be welcome at Augusta National." Despite his dispassionate tone, Cliff must have been as giddy as a schoolgirl at the prospect of the most popular man in the country blessing the club with his presence. Roberts suspended guest privileges and called the Pinkerton National Detective Agency, the uniforms and guns he always hired for the Masters.

Ike, then about to take his first civilian job as president of Columbia University in New York, arrived soon after the 1948 Masters. *And stayed eleven days.* The general had found golf heaven: Augusta National in April, a comfortable house by the tenth tee— Bobby Jones's house!—and penny-a-point bridge games at night (the usual stakes were halved to suit his modest budget). Roberts proved to be an attentive host, as well as a pleasing companion on the golf course and at the card table. Mamie, a delicate flower who rarely rose before noon, fell in love with the place, too. She responded immediately to the Old South atmosphere of beauty and courtesy, or as Roberts phrased it, "she liked the organization we had there, practically all of which is colored help. She became quite devoted to Bowman." Mamie's thumbs-up would have been crucial in Ike's mind; despite her fear of flying, she almost always accompanied her husband on vacation trips.

At the end of his stay, Ike stood near the eighteenth green and had his picture taken in a borrowed green jacket. He sent inscribed copies of the photo to Jones ("Mr. Jones"; he knew Bob not at all) and to Cliff—"who did so much to make our visit to Augusta National the most delightful vacation of our lives." Did he have to hold up a sign? The general was obviously dying to be asked to join the club.

When both returned home to New York, Cliff included Eisenhower in his New York social whirl.

On June 17, 1948, Roberts composed a letter in his office at the Reynolds Company proposing a day of play "at Deepdale on Wednesday, June 23rd. We shall meet there at 12 o'clock noon for luncheon and remain there through dinner . . . after which some of the party are going to the Louis-Wolcott fight and the balance of us are returning to the city to see the fight televised." The invited guests were Eisenhower and Augusta National members Thomas Butler, whose bucks built the Butler Cabin at Augusta National, the one with a TV studio in the basement; Pete Jones, who, through Cliff, would offer Ike $1 million for his 1952 campaign for president; R. T. "Bob" Jones, Jr.; Joseph King; Charles McAdam; Bill Robinson, Ike and Cliff's mutual friend; Clarence "Schooie" Schoo; E. D. "Slats" Slater; and R. W. Woodruff, the King of Coca-Cola.

For the next dozen years, this band of golfing Augusta Nationalists interacted again and again with General, then candidate, then President Eisenhower. Ike started to refer to them as the Gang, whose core members included Roberts, Jones, Robinson, Slater, Bob Woodruff, Bud (washing machines) Maytag, Albert (General Motors) Bradley, Alfred S. (Singer Sewing Machines) Bourne, Pete Jones, and George Humphrey (the secretary of the treasury).

Ike wired Roberts at year's end: THE BEST THING THAT HAPPENED TO MAMIE AND ME DURING 1948 WAS THE NEW AND WONDERFUL FRIENDSHIPS WE WERE PRIVILEGED TO MAKE. AMONG THESE FRIENDS YOU HAVE A VERY SPECIAL AND WARM SPOT IN OUR HEARTS. [WE] HOPE THAT 1949 WILL PERMIT US TO SEE YOU WITH MAXIMUM FREQUENCY AND GROWING INTIMACY.

Cliff's memorandum setting up the first or second Gang meeting begs several questions:

Who won the fight? Joe Louis knocked out Jersey Joe Wolcott in eleven.

Did any of the Gang members possess any qualifications for advising the leader of the Free World? Yes. Foremost among their talents was success in and understanding of capitalism.

Did they expect, or get, favorable treatment for the cardboard box, liquor, and soft drink industries in return for conceding Ike's three-footers? None of the gang were shy about suggesting cabinet officers or ideas—even the text—for speeches, but bringing up a specific political question violated the spirit of the membership. Ike went to Augusta to get away from just that sort of pressure.

Inevitably, of course, one hand washed the other. For example: when Eisenhower administration officials traveled to South America, a standard part of their assignment was to check on American foreign policy interests in the local Coca-Cola bottling plants. The Ike—Coke—Augusta National connection began through Bill Robinson, who'd introduced Ike to Cliff. Robinson got an important new client for his public relations firm in 1954: Coca-Cola. Bob Woodruff went a step further when he made Robinson president of Coca-Cola in 1955. Three years later, when that job didn't work out, the Boss kicked Bill upstairs and made him chairman of the board.

Another question suggested by that early Gang meeting: what was Bob Jones of Atlanta doing in town? It could have been a happy coincidence; since 1939 he'd owned a Coca-Cola bottling plant in western Massachusetts. But sometime during the summer of 1948 Jones made a special trip to the big city to visit Cliff. They talked in Cliff's apartment on Park Avenue. Jones told Roberts he was considering a delicate surgery to the back of his neck; paralysis was possible if the surgeon's scalpel slipped, which would of course affect his ability to earn a living. He had some questions for Cliff regarding his estate. Roberts could hardly believe what he was hearing.

Did the horrible irony of the situation occur to either of them? Just as Eisenhower and Augusta National began a glorious coalition and just as the Masters had finally achieved a plateau of profitability to match its status, Jones's life fell into a tailspin.

He had recently endured a disturbing six-week period of double vision of distant objects; one golf ball but two greens. In May

1948, according to a physician's notes, "patient noticed difficulty in the use of his right hand and began stubbing his right foot." At East Lake, his home course in Atlanta, Jones played in a farewell round for an assistant pro who was leaving the club. "On the eighth hole, he duck-hooked his tee shot into the woods," recalled East Lake club champ Tommy Barnes in a 1995 interview with writer Furman Bisher. "And he just started walking straight ahead. Didn't say a thing, just started walking. I had no idea until I saw a headline in the paper a day later, 'Jones Enters Emory Hospital for Tests.' " Except for some desultory efforts at Augusta National in later years, Bobby Jones never played golf again.

He entered Emory Hospital in Atlanta in November, and had the surgery. The pain returned, however, and spread, and his spasticity increased; since he couldn't dorsiflex (lift the toes upward) his right foot, he had to raise his knee high to take a step, which brought the foot down with some force. "Slap gait," doctors call it. His decline was inexplicable. He had a second surgery, at the Lahey Clinic in Boston, sixteen months after the first one. Cliff wrote to the Gang after the operation in May 1950: "I feel compelled to tell you in strict confidence, of course, that the doctors have made a very frank report to Bob and the net of it is that no great amount of improvement is expected."

The doctors were right. Sometimes Jones forgot the lighted cigarette in his hand; the butt burned into his flesh, but he felt nothing. He used a cane, added a leg brace, another cane, a second brace, and finally, in the mid- to late fifties, a wheelchair. His hands withered and twisted like an old olive tree. The club bought him a three-wheeled golf cart with a big piece of green sheet metal wrapped around the front and a tiller instead of a steering wheel. It looked like an old amusement park ride. Jones would watch his friends play a few holes, then return to his cabin to listen to classical music and opera.

The tragedy of a magnificent athlete cut down by a wasting disease reminded his friends of baseball slugger Lou Gehrig. Jones did not have Lou Gehrig's disease, amyotrophic lateral sclerosis, but an equally rare neurological disease called syringomyelia. Vertical, cylindrical holes were pocking his spinal cord, disrupting or short-circuiting the messages from his brain to his arms and legs. The protecting bone, the vertebrae, were not affected; the problem was with that shiny, white tube that has all the nerves, the spinal cord. No one knew then or now what caused it or how to cure it.

Jones bore it all with dignity and courage, and kept his despair private. During Masters practice rounds, he hobbled into his green golf cart to tour the course and greet every contestant by name—he had a great memory for names. He presided over the various dinners and the closing ceremony with good humor. Cliff always sat at Jones's right hand—in the cart, at the dinners, and at the championship presentation. Bob Jones, the greatest golfer of his era, had to take up bridge so he could play *something* with his old cronies. But even that eventually became a trial. He couldn't shuffle, deal, or hold the cards. Ike, an amateur artist, gave Bob some paints and brushes after one of his surgeries, an unintentionally cruel gift.

Back home in Atlanta, Jones continued to work and to write, although his gradual crippling made his customary longhand composition impossible. He had to dictate the new sections of this third and final book, *Bobby Jones on Golf* (1966), yet still he expressed himself beautifully. "The words in our language that we must use to describe feel are necessarily vague and susceptible to varying interpretations," he said in the introduction. "No one can describe the feel of a muscular action with assurance that the description will be readily and inevitably understood by another. . . . Be aware of the differences between mannerisms and fundamentals . . . no two fine golfers will present precisely the same appearance any more than two human faces."

Although his physical self deteriorated like the picture of Dorian Gray between 1948 and his death in 1971, Jones did not give up on life. Even compared to the period when he was winning golf tournaments or when he volunteered to do his part during World War II, this may have been Bob Jones's finest hour.

And Cliff Roberts's worst.

****

Roberts, his ego engorged by his affiliation with Eisenhower and by the growing success of the Masters, quickly expanded his authority to fill the leadership void at the club caused by Jones's illness. Cliff encouraged the pro, Ed Dudley, to resign, without Jones's knowledge or consent. Jones himself had made friendly, toothy Ed the club's first pro twenty-seven years before. "I think Cliff was jealous of Dudley, who was president of the PGA, because people would come out just to see him sometimes," says a former club employee. Easy Ed had been a great pro; he was frequently a high finisher in the Masters and Eisenhower's favorite golf instructor. When Jones found out that Dudley had decided to quit in favor of a job at Dorado Beach and Golf Club in Puerto Rico, "he was very upset."

The situation repeated with Dudley's successor, Gene Stout. "Cliff didn't always fire people, he'd just make it so continuing to work there became intolerable," the former employee says. Stout, who'd been Dudley's assistant pro, already occupied Cliff's doghouse. Stout and three amateurs—only one of whom belonged to Augusta National—won the International Four-Ball in Ireland one year, and Stout apparently allowed the team to be listed as being from Augusta National. This enraged Cliff, who made Stout send the championship cup back. When Stout later resigned, Jones, again "very upset," made a point of inviting the golf pro to come back to the club anytime he wanted, and even to bring guests. Which he did.

Another incident, this one involving amateur golf champion Bill Hyndman, showed how completely and quickly Chairman Roberts grabbed power from the increasingly weak and absent President Jones.

Hyndman now lives in a spacious house with grounds on a leafy street in suburban Philadelphia. His square, pleasant face, the view from his picture window, the pair of retrievers who usually lie vigilantly at his feet all suggest that commercial insurance has been very, very good to him. The mementoes on his office and living room walls reveal a long period of championship-level golf that enriched him as well.

That enviable life at the top of amateur golf included the Masters. "Twelve invitations, ten appearances," Hyndman says with pride. "I'd come down a week early and stay in one of the member's rooms. The rent was three bucks a night!" In 1959, Hyndman made a hole-in-one on the twelfth, the most frightening par-three in golf. There was a lot of tension on that tee; Hyndman's playing partner was Tommy Bolt, and terrible-tempered Tommy had just three-putted eleven. "I'd taken out a seven iron, but my caddie, First Baseman, said, 'No, Mr. Bill, you can't make it with a seven. Hit a cut with a six.'" When First Baseman had first introduced himself, Hyndman told him thanks, but he preferred his usual caddie, P-Man. "No you don't, Mr. Hyndman," First Baseman replied. "P-Man dead." He'd been stabbed in a bar fight.

Hyndman played practice and tournament rounds at Augusta with Hogan. "In a locker room once, he crooked his finger at me. We were at the U.S. Open, and we were paired for the next day's round. 'Come over here, Billy,' he says. 'I just want to apologize. I didn't talk to you at Augusta. And I won't talk to you tomorrow, either.'"

An important part of Hyndman's Masters ritual included a visit with Jones in his cabin. "I had a great relationship with Bob Jones," says Hyndman. "There was nobody else like him. He never complained. Everything was all right with him." They'd become friends during the World Amateur Team Match at St. Andrews in 1958, when Jones captained the American side and—knowing he'd never cross the pond again given his health—bid a dramatic farewell to Scotland. Hyndman was the star of the U.S. team; Jones described Bill's final match four iron to the green at the Road Hole as "the finest shot I've ever seen." Thereafter, on Wednesday mornings at exactly ten-fifteen during the first week of April in Augusta, Mr. and Mrs. Hyndman called on Mr. and Mrs. Jones. All four hit it off. "Mary Jones reminded me of [former First Lady] Barbara Bush," says Mrs. Hyndman. "Not physically, but with her enthusiasm and friendliness."

In short, the Masters had for years been a joyously anticipated annual event for Hyndman, a sort of Christmas in April. So
when he opened the mail one day and found a letter from Jones
inviting him to join Augusta National, he was pleasantly shocked.
Hyndman could easily afford the initiation fee and dues, "but we
had young children, and I'd just joined another club, so I wrote and
asked if I could pay half now and half later." And based, apparently,
on that faint whiff of hesitation on Hyndman's part, Roberts never
responded to the request, effectively withdrawing the invitation. A
pocket veto by the chief executive. "It would have been *perfect* for
me," Hyndman says from the couch, with more amazement than
sadness.

But Roberts's friend Charley Yates saw Roberts in a different
light. Yates, an Atlantan and a member since 1940, began a long
stint as club secretary in the late forties. An honorary title, he con-
cedes: "At the governor's party one year [one of the two big member get-togethers annually], Roberts says to me, 'What's on the
agenda, Mr. Secretary?' Well, I didn't even have an agenda. So Cliff
moved we adjourn, and Ike says, 'Damn, if I couldn't be in more
meetings like this!' " Yates, immobile with age and a recently broken leg, leans back in his recliner and chuckles silently.

"Cliff Roberts. The benevolent dictator, a man of great depth,
thinkin' all the time. He did everything for this tournament. . . . He
sure was good to me. No, he didn't harbor a grudge."

Like Yates, most Masters contestants respected Roberts. They
knew who was primarily responsible for the cleanest, most courteous, and best-run tournament they played in all year, on the best,
or almost the best, golf course. *Hello, Mr. Roberts*, they said, and got
a nod in return; the brave ones, like Skee Riegel, called him Cliff.
A few players got to know him fairly well. Most often they were the
best players: Nelson, Hogan, and Arnold Palmer; probably, no coincidence.

"I considered Cliff Roberts one of my closest friends," Palmer
says. "But you really had to get to know him for a while before he'd
warm up to you, as if he wanted to give himself the benefit of really
seeing what you were like before he got on your bandwagon."

Palmer's bandwagon would have been a pleasure for Roberts to board. Masters income and popularity skyrocketed with the ascension of Arnie, who won the tournament four times. The Masters made Palmer a god; Palmer gilded the stage for Nicklaus, Player, Watson, Faldo, and Woods. But even as Augusta National, starring Arnold Palmer, debuted on TV, looking more each year like *Gone With the Wind* under glass, Cliff's treatment of Bob Jones might put you in mind of another movie: *What Ever Happened to Baby Jane?*

****

"**W**ell, I haven't thought about that in a long time," says Arnold Palmer, recalling the triple bogey on the twelfth hole in the final round of the 1959 Masters that cost him the lead. He sighs, then plunges in: "First, I knocked it in the water with a seven iron; the pin was back right. Then I blew it over the green. Chipped back. Two putts." Six. Every shot makes somebody happy, as they say, but who would benefit from Arnie's disaster? He had started the day tied with Stan Leonard for the lead, with Cary Middlecoff one shot back. Where the heck were they?

"Palmer went off two hours ahead of Middlecoff and Leonard, who teed off dead last," says Art Wall, Jr. (It wasn't until 1968 that highest scoring players teed off first, lowest last.) The Lords of Augusta and the Georgia golf fans adored Ahno Pomma and they wanted him to win the Masters every year, but the best player in golf had an Achilles heel: he was capable of having a really bad hole at just the wrong time. Arnie hit a home run or he struck out swinging. Wall was a singles hitter. He wore glasses. Writers always pegged him as looking like an accountant.

Today, the younger players on the tour don't even know the name Art Wall. But everyone knew his name that Sunday evening in April 1959. "I was packing my car that morning at the Bon Air," says Wall, his voice soothing, almost hypnotic. He is eating something light (he had a triple heart bypass in 1996) in an anonymous hotel restaurant in Tucson, but for the moment he's forgotten about lunch. "Gene Sarazen walks by and says, 'Go out and have a good finish.' The next year we played nine holes in practice and I asked him if he remembered that, and he said, 'How could I forget!' "

After twelve holes, Wall stood one over par for the tournament, going nowhere. Then two funny things happened. First, Bobby Jones drove out to the thirteenth tee in his tunnel-of-love golf cart to watch Wall and Julius Boros finish up. Jones piloted his three-wheeler inside the ropes and up to Wall. "Young man," he said, "I understand you're a very good putta." The second funny thing—maybe it's the same funny thing—was how right Jones suddenly was.

On thirteen, after a chip from eighty feet, a ten-foot putt "*just* fell in. On fourteen, I made [another] ten footer, from behind the hole. On fifteen, I hit a four wood to twenty-five feet, the pin was back center. And the putt [for eagle] went all the way around the hole and lipped out." Wall's third consecutive birdie took him to two under, tied with Arnie, who was at that moment about to putt from four feet for a birdie on the final hole.

The defending champion had fought back after his triple bogey at the twelfth, with birdies at the two par fives. But on seventeen, he'd lipped out a two-foot putt for par. His head shot quickly up, his eyes clenched shut, and his mouth formed into an O, the posture of a man passing a kidney stone. His large gallery and millions of TV viewers felt his pain. And they felt it again when Palmer missed a four footer on eighteen.

Wall still had three to play. At some point—Wall doesn't know when—Jones left the scene. "The pin on sixteen was back left," he says. "I aimed right." He hit a good shot to ten feet, but missed the putt. The spell, apparently, was broken. But on the seventeenth tee, Boros said in his smoker's baritone, "Art, if you make three here, you'll win." Again Wall responded to suggestion and knocked it in from twenty-five feet. With one hole to go, he was three under par, one ahead of Arnold.

As Wall and Boros walked up the hill on eighteen, they heard the roar of the crowd reacting to Middlecoff's eagle on fifteen. Suddenly, Cary had also moved to three under. But Wall was outside himself, beyond himself. A notoriously short hitter, he smoked his drive over 300 yards, then feathered a nine iron just over the blindingly white sand of the front bunker, leaving an uphill ten footer to win.

He made it, dead center. He'd birdied five of the final six holes to win by a shot, if not the best finish in Masters history, then damn close to Sarazen in 1935, Player in 1978, and Nicklaus in 1986.

"A guy like me gets only one or two chances in a lifetime to win a major," Wall says, in that soft Mr. Rogers voice, with a little smile.

Two years later, Palmer imploded again. He led the 1961 Masters by a shot with one hole to play, but overplayed a punch-fade seven iron from the middle of the eighteenth fairway into the bunker on the right. From a half-buried lie, he tried another short follow-through shot. But the ball zinged out of the sand with startling speed, a fastball when everyone expected a lob. Arnie, furious, did not look up to see his ball bounce once on the green, scurry down the bank, and stop between the thighs of a woman in an orange windbreaker and a wide straw hat.

Palmer putted up the bank, too strong. Charlie Coe, a wiry amateur from Oklahoma, missed a long putt for a birdie to tie Player. Arnie's bogey putt from about ten feet didn't come particularly close and elicited no dramatic body language.

The beneficiary of Palmer's collapse was Frank Stranahan's protégé, Gary Player. ("After his first tournament in the U.S., at Seminole, I took him to the gym," says Stranahan. "I lent him my car when I was flying to a tournament. And I taught him how to dress. Wear all black or all white, not like Arnold Palmer and all these other guys with no class.") The perpetually keyed-up South African had staggered in, with a double bogey on thirteen and a bogey on fifteen, holes the leading men usually birdied. He'd lost a four-shot lead over Arnie and six over Coe. But he made a clutch couple of shots, getting up and down from a good lie in the same bunker that had buried Arnie's hopes. The first foreign-born Masters winner repeatedly combed and palmed his pomaded black hair into place as he walked to the TV studio in the basement of the Butler Cabin. And there Palmer, the devastated defending champion, smiled bravely and helped Gary Player into a green jacket.

****

Most Masters disasters occurred more slowly than Arnold's collapses. Wind, fast hilly greens, and simple, suffocating pressure sometimes made even great players doubt themselves, and on Sunday, that nervous first-tee feeling could return anywhere on the back nine. Breath, sweat, and thought come too quickly on the final day of the Masters, too thickly. Suddenly, the ball refuses to stay hit.

The same thing can occur in any big tournament, of course, but a two-hour death on the back nine at Augusta is a nightmare shared on worldwide TV. Routine tasks like chipping or putting become impossible, as in bad dreams, and the familiar becomes grotesque. And what's more familiar than holes ten through eighteen at Augusta National? You don't need to be clairvoyant to feel what Ken Venturi felt in 1956, or Palmer in 1961, Ed Sneed in 1979, Scott Hoch in 1989, or Greg Norman in 1996.

Or Jim Ferrier in 1950. Poor Jim endured a Masters nightmare as horrifying as any ever suffered. A strapping Australian born in Sydney in 1915, Ferrier stood six feet four and looked a bit heavier than the 192 pounds he claimed. He was a white socks and brown shoes kind of guy: as the years went by and his weight increased, Ferrier hiked his pants upward, stopping at last at the midpoint between his belly button and his chest. He dipped violently at the ball and limped slightly, both quirks caused by a soccer injury to his left knee suffered in his youth. A great putter, he practiced constantly with his ancient blade, until the chrome on the sweet spot wore through. But perhaps the most unusual thing about this unusual man was his wife. Norma Ferrier ducked under the ropes (gallery ropes had debuted at Augusta in 1949) after every one of her husband's tee shots, handed him a drink, and chatted with him as they walked to his ball, at which point they parted, only to meet again after he putted out. Eighteen repetitions a round. "Don't you get tired?" someone asked her once. "I have been doing this for Jim since 1932 and it's never bothered me," she responded.

Ferrier's big win before 1950 had been in the 1947 PGA, when he beat hometown hero Chick Harbert in the finals at Plum Hollow Country Club in Detroit. Fearing fan interference, Jim had hired two policemen to prevent his ball from being kicked behind a tree and Harbert's from being nudged into better lies. And though his wild tee balls and second shots hit seven of the spectators he distrusted, Ferrier won, 2 and 1.

He repeated that great putting almost to the end of the 1950 Masters. The key word is: *almost*. Up to the final six holes, the tournament had been notable both for the quality of the players Ferrier was holding at bay—Snead, Hogan, Nelson, and Demaret—and for the qualities of Jimmy D's clothing. He'd featured these items and colors during the week: green suede shoes; lavender, pink, and chartreuse pants; a salmon pink sweater; an old rose shirt; and a red dickey. But Demaret's play merited attention, too; he shot 283, five under par. Good enough for second, apparently. With six holes to play, Ferrier led by three.

Big Jim had birdied the par-five thirteenth twice in the previous rounds, but now he quick-hooked his drive into the creek and made six. Still two ahead, though, nothing to worry about. Then he three-putted the maddening fourteenth green, a relief map of Switzerland, and the lead fell to one. Still nothing to worry about, fifteen was a birdie hole. But Ferrier could only manage a par. What did Norma say as he limped toward the sixteenth green? The wrong thing, apparently: Jim three-putted. Tied now with Demaret, two to play, and plenty to worry about. A bad second shot fell into the bunker on seventeen; another bogey. He needed a birdie now on eighteen just to tie. But Big Jim didn't do much with his second shot, and once more, he three-putted.

Demaret sang at the presentation ceremony on the practice

green, and he dedicated the song to himself. A little tune called "Do You Know How Lucky You Are?"

Ferrier must have felt like strangling him with his little red dickey.

****

Jack Burke, Jr., didn't burst into song like his mentor when he won the Masters in 1956, but his win depended just as much on an unlucky opponent's sudden utter ruin. Ken Venturi was cast in the role of tragic hero this time, a part he was destined to play again in 1958 and 1960. But 1956 was the worst of these by far, a figurative death. He shot 80 when 78 would have won. And through the magic of television and an accident of golf history, Venturi had to watch himself die yet again, forty years later.

Greg Norman's debacle in 1996 seemed so eerily similar to his own. Both Ken in 1956 and Greg in 1996 shot final-round back nines in the forties, when thirty-*anything* might have saved their days. Two men, almost completely dissimilar, yet with one identical fate.

Venturi was twenty-four, darkly handsome, and, praise be to Bobby Jones, an amateur. He'd played on a Walker Cup team, then served a two-year stretch in the army. He returned to his native San Francisco in October 1955 after being sprung from the service to take a job selling cars at Lowery Lincoln-Mercury. Ben Hogan became a god to him; he wore the same flat white cap and practiced almost as much as the King of the Range. He also drew close to another of his heroes, Byron Nelson. His boss, golf gadabout Eddie Lowery, arranged for Byron to give young Ken lessons after he got out of the army; Byron, in turn, led the charge to get his talented student an invitation to the 1956 Masters. While Venturi loved Hogan and Nelson, and told them so, he absolutely adored his dad, the pro at Harding Park Municipal Golf Course in San Francisco. The son still quotes the father constantly: " 'Don't bother telling anyone how good you are,' he always said. 'When you're really good, *they'll* tell *you.*' " In fact, "Hogan always said" or "Byron says" or "My dad said" form the preamble to many Venturi remarks.

Warmed by the approval of his father, Ken Venturi wore his heart on his sleeve. Greg Norman's emotions lay coiled inside him like a rope. His father, an unaffectionate parent, disapproved of golf as a career for his son, preferring instead that he follow him into engineering. But Norman's lack of interest in school combined with early success in golf compelled him to go against his father's wishes. He turned pro in 1976, at age twenty-one. He won New South Wales Opens and Sydney Opens and Australian Opens by the handful, but his father would not deign to watch him play. Greg won in Europe, he won on the PGA Tour, he was always winning, winning, winning. But he was never really happy because of the tense and hostile relationship with his father. Not until 1986 would Norman Senior agree to watch his son play golf; not until 1992 would Greg ask his father why he had never hugged him. The big chill thawed a little, then. And Norman won the British Open in 1993.

Norman's is a vivid, unmistakable personality, amplified by the most apt sports nickname since Mordecai "Three Finger" Brown pitched in the National League. The albino hair, the obvious tension in his body, and his implacable blue eyes give him the eye-catching look of a predator. He doesn't have a lot of friends on the Tour; a little jealousy on one side, some standoffishness on the other. The Great White Shark swims alone.

And he stood alone in April 1996 in Augusta, just as Venturi did in 1956. After three rounds, Ken led by four, with sharply ascending scores of 66-69-75. Norman's similarly stair-stepping 63-69-71 gave him a six-shot lead.

The worst wind in Masters history arrived on Friday, April 6, 1956, and stayed for the weekend. The scoreboard near the eighteenth green blew down like the Second Little Pig's house. Sam Snead hit a driver and a one iron to the first green—and came up short. At the same time, Bob Rosburg struck a four iron to the 155-yard twelfth, but the gale in his face vanished, and his ball sailed majestically over the trees onto the ninth fairway of the neighboring

Augusta Country Club. A fifty-mile-per-hour gust collapsed a concession tent between the seventh green and the eighth tee. Ms. Helen Boshears of Augusta and R. M. Fleming of Shelbyville, Indiana, were treated by a nurse at the scene—possibly for pimiento cheese impactions—and were allowed to return to the gallery.

Ken and Conni Venturi had dinner in the clubhouse on Saturday night with Byron and Louise Nelson. Roberts walked by; he had just taken the final round pairings into Mrs. Harris to be typed up. As had become traditional, Nelson was paired with the leader going into the final round. But Cliff saw a problem; Byron was the tournament leader's instructor. "Roberts said, 'We don't want to have an amateur win and have it tainted in any way.' So I was asked who I wanted, and I picked Snead. I said, 'I'm gonna win and I'm gonna walk up the fairway with one of the three greatest players in the game.' Everyone wrote that Sam didn't talk to me and that it hurt me. But *I* picked Sam. He knew I was nervous and just left me alone."

Venturi reminisces from a golf cart under a tree outside the CBS TV trailer at Colonial Country Club in Fort Worth. Back home in Florida, his second wife, Beau, is dying. But Venturi leaves her bedside and goes to work as a commentator and answers questions on a difficult subject ("Tell me again how you lost the Masters"). He does it because he knows that Hogan never missed a day and that Byron never blew off a writer.

"The wind made the greens as hard as rocks," Venturi says. "And the *Poa annua* made them so hard to read." *Poa annua* is a stiff, white-topped, thick-stalked grass that makes greens bumpy and indecipherable. Hard, fast greens with slopes and bumps, and a strong wind? Add pressure, a big gallery, the first-ever TV cameras at Augusta National, a twenty-four-year-old leader, and you get . . . 80.

Venturi's tumble did not resemble Norman's, except on the card. Ken hit the first nine greens in regulation, but putted like he had a cattle prod in his pocket. "I was hittin' it close, just on the wrong side of the hole," he says. "It was inexperience. And nerves, strictly nerves. I'm not afraid to admit it." Despite his travails, Venturi had an eighteen-foot putt on the final hole for a birdie to tie Jack Burke, Jr., but as he had all day, he missed.

Forty years later, despite perfect weather for round four, tournament leader Greg Norman looked uncomfortable in his own skin. You could see it with his first swing, a hook into the trees that led to a bogey. The tendons on his arms jumped as he prepared to putt. He stood three or four extra seconds over his full shots, obviously fighting some sort of internal battle. The Shark missed little putts on nine, ten, and eleven, just as Venturi had forty years earlier. His lead over Nick Faldo disappeared as if, well, as if being devoured by a shark.

Disappointingly, there was no direct on-air reference to Venturi's déjà vu. "I related to it. I felt for him," Ken says. "But run it into the ground? No, I would never do that."

Norman doubled the nerve-wracking twelfth, taking a five, fought back with birdies on the par fives, then finally cracked like a set of cheap dentures with a yank into the water on sixteen. For the fifth time, Norman had lost the Masters as much as the other guy had won. The question immediately afterward was: *how would he react?*

Faldo hugged him on the final green, and both normally stoic men teared up. He shook the necessary hands, accepted the necessary condolences, met the press, expressed no bitterness, and took all the blame. With his good grace standing in stark contrast to the appalling, global collapse of sportsmanship at the Atlanta Olympics two months later, Shark stock shot through the roof. The Masters hadn't brought out his best golf, but it brought out the best in Greg Norman.

* * * * * * * * * * *

Venturi believes that if he'd won the windswept Masters of 1956, he would not have turned pro, would not have gone into television, and would not have won the U.S. Open in 1964, an accomplishment he justifiably treasures. A tough bargain, he says, but not a bad one. In a speech once, his friend Jack Whitaker considered Ken's early heartbreak and eventual glory. Whitaker quoted Alexander Pope: "As the twig is bent, the tree's inclined."

Venturi says it again. "As the twig is bent . . ." He loves that one.

CHAPTER SIX

•

Opera

Doug Ford, 1957 champion, assists Arnold Palmer in 1958.

**Arnold Palmer, 1960 . . . Gary Player, 1961 . . .
Arnold Palmer, 1962 . . . Jack Nicklaus, 1963 . . .
Arnold Palmer, 1964 . . . Jack Nicklaus, 1965 . . .
Jack Nicklaus, 1966 . . . Gay Brewer, Jr., 1967 . . .
Bob Goalby, 1968 . . . George Archer, 1969**

It was an emergency. The delegate from Virginia was switching his vote to Robert Taft. Cliff Roberts sprang into action.

"I had called a friend of mine in Los Angeles, name of Freeman Gosden, who's a member of the famous Amos 'n' Andy team," Roberts recalled. "I remembered that Freeman was born in Virginia, and I knew he was very popular and had lots of friends in Virginia, and I knew he was most enthusiastic about seeing the General nominated. So Freeman got busy . . . and there was such a wagonload of these telegrams that [the delegate] realized . . . that he had really had made a mistake in switching to Taft. So he said, 'I'm ready to go back into the Eisenhower camp, that I'm going to stick with him this time, you can count on me.'"

Ike got the nomination. The conventions of 1952 were the last ones not stage-managed by the political parties, and Roberts met with the eventual nominee several times a day during that exciting and historic week in Chicago. At the convention's behind-the-scenes climax, Ike looked exhausted; Cliff hid him in an unused hotel room for a nap. When he decided the time was right, Cliff revealed the general's location to anxious minions. Moments later, Taft conceded the nomination and Ike gave a speech. After the convention Cliff accompanied the general on a campaign speaking tour from New York to Augusta, during which Eisenhower became ill: ". . . when he finally reached his car and he and I got in the backseat, he literally collapsed, and I held him in my arms all the way to the golf club."

You might hear a muted fanfare when you read Roberts's tales of the glory years, as if the theme from a Mighty Mouse cartoon is playing on a distant TV: "Heeeere I come to save the day." Most oral histories sound similarly self-serving, however; it's the nature of the beast. Cliff was too secure in his own status and abilities to be dismissed as a mere braggart. As a resourceful, well-connected spear-carrier for the leader of the Free World, he assumed real importance in the life of Ike and thus in history. And not just because Eisenhower loved golf and Cliff held the keys to Augusta National, although, of course, that was a big part of it.

After supersalesman Bill Robinson persuaded Ike to record his wartime reminiscences in a book, Robinson supervised the selection of Douglas Black of Doubleday as publisher; Doug was also a member of Augusta National. When Cliff took on the responsibility of investing the general's half-a-million-dollar advance—and then made the new author a member-in-waiting—the whole project stayed neatly in the brotherhood.

These relationships clicked from the start. These men with money impressed Eisenhower. Until he sold his war memoir, he'd never had any; when he and Mamie paid cash for a Chrysler after the war it had required virtually every cent they had. For their part, Roberts and the others held Eisenhower in an almost religious awe. He was the architect of the invasion of Normandy, the man who beat Hitler. World War II was the turning point of the twentieth century, and Ike had planned and executed the turning point of the war. You'd have to go back to Grant and Lee or to Douglas MacArthur to find a similar-sized military hero.

Roberts and Robinson handled another Eisenhower book deal just before the 1952 convention. Kay Summersby, who in 1948 implied a wartime romance in *Eisenhower Was My Boss*, surprised Cliff by calling on him at his office in New York. "She told me a lot about her troubles which were principally financial . . . that now she was working as a sales girl at Bergdorf-Goodman's for a very small salary, and living in a tiny one-room apartment, and how the work was ruining her health, how she had recently been approached several times about writing [another] story and what should she do about it?" Cliff sent her to Bill, who gave her $2,000 to satisfy her creative urge by writing a play, using "some of the cash that one of my good friends had given him to promote Ike politically." When that ruse ran its course—she took the money but didn't write the play—Summersby asked for a job on the Eisenhower campaign. According to Cliff, "Bill then promptly got her an office job working for the American Express Company, using Ralph Reed, the president, whom Bill had met through me." Reed was—surprise!—a member of Augusta National. Not another peep was heard from Miss Summersby during the campaign.

After two years on the job, Ike quit as the president of Columbia. How he had hated meeting with alumni groups and department heads and liberal academics! President Truman bailed him out of academia by asking him to move to France to command the communism-containing and NATO-restoring Supreme Headquarters of the Allied Powers in Europe (SHAPE). Ike missed the Gang as soon as he got to Marnes-La-Coquette, near Paris, but he didn't have to miss them long. Robinson, Slater, and Roberts came over within months. Roberts returned several times to the scene of his World War I conquests during Ike's posting there. When Roberts's doctor diagnosed a gastric ulcer in the summer of 1951, Ike invited his pal to rehab his tummy in France. Cliff stayed two months. Eisenhower told him things: for example, how disappointed he was with his conferences with Winston Churchill, who still thought of Britain as an empire; the prime minister wouldn't wear a hearing aid, so Ike had to slt next to him and shout into his ear. And Cliff observed things: the general's three-to-five-pack-a-day smoking jones, and how he liked to put his steak directly into the glowing coals of an outdoor fire, then brush off the ashes and eat.

The two out-of-country Augusta National members dined and dealt each other cards at night, and played golf at Saint-Germain on Mondays. During eight sittings lasting twenty to thirty minutes each, Ike painted his first live subject—Cliff Roberts.

Back home, Eisenhower's popularity and reluctance to run

were making him irresistible to the electorate. When he won the New Hampshire primary over the nominal favorite, Taft, Mamie was mad as hell—at Cliff. "She said some pretty unkind things to me," Roberts recalled. But he'd never urged Ike to run, Cliff explained, only kept him informed, "let him know what the score was, and kept him from falling into some trap or some mistake that would put a blemish on his great military accomplishments." On the other hand, Roberts admitted in the oral history that he'd hired drivers to take likely Eisenhower voters in the Granite State to the polls. And he further confessed that "from all of us, [Ike] had been told repeatedly that he was the only one that had a chance of beating Taft." The Gang worried that Taft might not be able to beat the opposition's nominee. *Another* tax-and-spend Democrat in the White House? Estes Goddamn Kefauver or Adlai Flipping Stevenson? Either of those men with the word "president" in front of his name was terrible even to contemplate.

"For heaven's sake, if there's any chance on earth of getting that man to run, try your best to talk him into it," Pete (Cities Service) Jones told Cliff, according to Roberts's recollection in the oral history. "Moreover, I don't want you to ever leave anything undone that money can do. . . . You can call on me for any amount up to a million dollars." At least ten times, Cliff picked up $25,000 at Pete Jones's office, "then I'd have to figure out how I could get it into the treasury of one of the various committees that were working for General Eisenhower's election. . . . But my technique was to use the money that Pete gave me. . . . I'd have to go and get a friend of mine that I knew I could trust, and I'd say, 'Here's a thousand dollars that somebody gave me, he wants to contribute but he doesn't want to contribute in his own name. Will you take this thousand and put with it whatever additional amount you want to give, then give me your check, say, for two thousand dollars?' "

Cliff became a bag man, Pete Jones distributed money like it was cents-off coupons for tooth powder, and both broke the law. But their candidate didn't share their fervor or their fear of Adlai. Ike was an apolitical man, who voted for the first time in 1948 (in Kansas, for Dewey, and for the repeal of the state's law prohibiting liquor sales). He didn't even know he was a Republican until shortly before the GOP nominated him for president. "Soon I shall be coming home [from France] and I really dread—for the first time—the prospect of coming back to my own country," Ike wrote to Cliff in May 1952. Eisenhower felt with considerable justification that he'd already done his duty. When his country and the Gang insisted, Ike ran and won. But he got something in return for his sacrifice. The leader of the Free World played golf about eight hundred times during his two terms, got a house next to Bobby Jones's and his own fish pond, and two shots a side (Roberts secretly inflated the presidential handicap).

Ike flew to Augusta National the day after the 1952 election.

* * * * * * * * * * *

This man ushered the president to his pew—fifth from the front, left side—at Reid Memorial Presbyterian Church. This photographer shot miles of film of the arriving or departing (but never golf-ball-hitting) chief executive and even had a few friendly words with him once, outside the gate at the National. This woman watched his plane land and applauded when, with a wave, he got out of the *Columbine* and into a Ford Galaxie. This man's father drove the car.

"One time someone thrust a copy of Ike's book through the window for an autograph and it fell in," recalls Stovall Walker, whose father owned Walker Ford in Augusta. "An agent sat on it, made my father drive to a field, and the agent threw it out. Afraid it was a bomb. Dad didn't drive Ike no more after that."

There were no bombs, of course. Not in Augusta. Augusta liked Ike. "Southerners seem to like military men," reflects Larry Jon Wilson, the songwriter. "And we were a typical Southern city." Local citizens lined his route from Daniel Field to Augusta National. Augusta liked Ike because he'd won the war, because he seemed such a polite, benign man, and because his presence was good for business. A local company, for example, got a contract to enclose the 365-acre Augusta National grounds with twelve-feet-tall metal storm fence with three strands of inward-slanting barbed wire at the top. Ike made twenty-nine trips to town during his presidency (Cliff counted), and he traveled with twenty or thirty aides and that many more security people, and they all needed hotel rooms, and eggs and grits, and dry cleaning.

"I asked my mother who she voted for," says a second-generation Augustan. " 'Why, Eisenhower!' she said. 'He comes here to play golf.' "

Ike's relationship with the city would coincide with the National's polite but distant interaction. On the plane to Augusta after the election, Roberts recalled that he "explained [to the president-elect] that if he ever accepted a single invitation outside the club grounds he would be swamped more than ever and in the end the Augusta National would cease to be a retreat or a haven and would therefore become useless to him. I suggested that he make a firm compact with me that whenever he came to Augusta he would never leave the club grounds except to go to church." Ike promised.

Two incidents—one trifling, the other profound—marred the Eisenhower years in Augusta. The trifle involved the Chamber of Commerce–run Masters Week Parade, which lumbered noisily east along Broad Street, parallel to the river, during the mid-1950s to the mid-1960s. The floats were better and more elaborate than you might expect for a little tank town, because a Rose Bowl Parade float engineer named Bob Ship hammered them together (he'd married a local girl). Augustans who've been around for a while can still see the whole thing: the bunting on the buildings and the huge painted plywood golfers propped up at the corners of Fourteenth and Fifth Streets, the two ends of the parade route. A giant scoreboard by the Confederate Monument. Miss Golf Augusta, in clouds of taffeta, waving from a crepe-papered float. Befezzed Shriners buzzing around in their go-carts. High school bands providing the sound track, the blare and snap of horns and drums echoing down Broad. The all-black Lucy Laney Pride of Augusta Marching Band pacing the hot pavement in ornate red and gray; the Purple Pride Musketeers of all-white Richmond Academy strutting in purple and gold. Nineteen-fifties supermodel Virginia Jinx Falkenberg graced the event once, but the real stars were the Masters golfers. They sat like royalty in white Oldsmobile 88 convertibles. "Two or three per car, in no particular order," recalls Chuck Ballas, Sr., whose Luigi's Restaurant marked the parade's home stretch. "Yeah, Ben Hogan rode in the parade. Sam Snead didn't want to do it, until Mr. Roberts made him."

One year a papier-mâché figure on a float depicted a smiling bald man swinging a golf club: Ike. Roberts raised a fuss with the Chamber. "Had I known anything about it I most assuredly would have vetoed the thing," sniffed Cliff. "I didn't think it was in too good taste to elaborate on one of the general's hobbies in order to attract a little attention to the city of Augusta."

A second problem dwarfed the first. Eisenhower's 1957 ordering of federal troops into Little Rock to protect nine black students attempting to integrate Central High School completely alienated the South, including Augusta. Every states-rights politician in the land took bitter shots at this symbolic recreation of the North's Civil War invasion. The governor and both Georgia senators took their shots at the president. Even the *Augusta Chronicle* blasted Ike, disparaging the president for running the country from a country club. Ouch. Cliff's counterattack included a reminder that "when [the *Chronicle*] found fault with the club's most prominent member, they were hurting the Augusta National, and when they hurt the club, they damaged the Masters Tournament, the principal asset in many respects that the city of Augusta possessed."

The *Chronicle*'s critical editorials stopped. Through Jim Hull, a local member, Cliff organized a welcoming committee at the airport for Ike's visit in November. Roberts referred to them with magnificent condescension as "a dozen or more of the bigwigs of the village. . . . Also I was very happy that the son of the owner of the newspaper made his appearance." But the crowds along the route to the club were sullen and sparse, and Mamie felt their hostility; she canceled her plans to do some Christmas shopping in Augusta. That week Ike played uncharacteristically bad bridge and lost repeatedly. The big crowds didn't return until December 1959, two years later.

In earlier, happier times, the just-elected president had asked

Cliff not to set up any sort of office for him. Roberts ignored the request and put a desk, table, chairs, phone lines, and a potted plant in a room above Ed Dudley's pro shop. "Ike liked to come downstairs and take little half-swings with the new clubs," recalls Brien Charter, then the assistant pro. "One time I heard him say to himself, 'I used to think I had a brain.' I think he was working on his state of the union address.

"Cliff Roberts had everything to do with everything. Yes, including what we stocked in the pro shop. He even told the president who he was playing golf with. And if a member brought in a guest, Cliff's rule was that they [the member and his friend] couldn't play together a second day. . . . A few members made it a point not to be at the club when Roberts was."

The staff stayed on its collective toes during one of Ike's visits, but then again, the place stayed spotless and efficient every day of the year. As usual, the kitchen remained open from six A.M. to midnight, "open all the time for anything" in a former manager's words, breakfast at night or dinner in the morning. "Colored cooks and colored cooking," he says. "The food was plain; everyone ate steak and roast beef back in those days. Remember, it was a men's club." The cooks could do justice to a rural Southern dish like ham hocks in beans or ham hocks in pea soup, and at times members requested such old-fashioned comfort food. But Mr. Roberts, showing how thoroughly he dominated club life, wouldn't permit it. Possibly he did not find the ankle joints of the pig to be healthy. As a result of his ulcer or of the mild heart attack he suffered in 1956, Cliff took a great deal of care about what he (and everyone else) ate. He gave up scotch except for special occasions. French fries *non*, French wine *oui*, Cliff decreed; he took the former off the menu and encouraged the consumption of the latter. In the early years, Cliff had made coconut ice cream the official club dessert. Then one day he decided he liked peaches. Canned peaches. Soon the floor of the National pantry groaned under the weight of boxes of #10 cans of the state fruit, and not ordering boiled peaches for dessert became a faux pas on the order of calling the chairman "Cliffie."

"He was very nice, but he was a strange man," recalls Evelyn

Stout, who worked as a secretary at the club in 1955. "The absolute king. When he spoke, everyone jumped, even the members. I remember going out on the golf course with him, taking notes while he made suggestions. And the greens committee would be there, too. It was like a parade."

Roberts's rigid style reminded you that he had Fort Hancock and World War I in his background. Ike, too, was businesslike about his fun and parceled out his time at the club with military precision. After his manservant, Sergeant John Moaney, cooked him breakfast in his cabin, the president arrived, shaved, in his little office at 0800 and worked for an hour to an hour and a half. Then to the driving range with the pro, Ed Dudley, then to the practice green (he needed the work; Ike had the putting touch of a piano mover). His group teed off at ten; a thin, mournful little man named Cemetery carried the clubs. Most days, Dudley was Ike's partner; they rode in a cart together. Often the other two or three in his group were guests who had contributed heavily to the Republican party. The president grew tired of this arrangement eventually, and told Roberts to henceforth assign his friends to his foursome.

The odd-looking golfers in the groups immediately in front of and behind the president didn't use caddies. They carried their own bags, but instead of clubs in the bags, they had machine guns.

Ike played quickly, but poorly, and for modest stakes. An old football knee injury caused a falling-backward swing, which caused a slice, just the wrong curve for Augusta National. His congenital lack of finesse with short clubs resulted in some horrid scores on the par threes, especially on the twelfth. "How many, Mr. President?" Slater or Robinson or Schoo would have to ask. "Six," Ike would have to answer (once he took a twelve on number twelve). He was competitive, and he had a temper, so these would not have been happy moments.

Just before or just after golf, depending on the light and the state of the world, Ike returned to his cabin to paint, in the little north-facing studio next to his bedroom. At precisely 1600 hours, the first bridge game began, also in Ike's cabin. This warm-up match with three companions lasted two hours. Dinner at seven, just Ike and Mamie, in the cabin; only once during a one-week stay would the president dine in the Trophy Room with everyone else. At eight, fifteen serious bridge players would convene in the top floor of Ike's white, three-story house. Meanwhile, whatever wives Cliff had been able to order (through their husbands) to Augusta sat downstairs with the sedentary first lady and her cigarette smoke for a game of canasta or Bolivia or Scrabble. Finding company for Mamie was a real problem but one Cliff never delegated. The card game broke up at midnight. You could set your watch.

Roberts was on hand in every activity, of course; in all Ike's trips to Augusta, Cliff missed greeting him in a green jacket at the airport only once, in 1958, when he was on his honeymoon in Europe with Letitia, his second wife. (He stayed in touch by letter, however; he wrote to Ike of his admiration for the buildings constructed in Italy under Mussolini: "No one but a dictator could have done such a fine job.")

Slats Slater often stood at the gate by Cliff's side. No one was closer to both Roberts and Eisenhower, and Cliff stocked the National's gargantuan wine cellar with the help of and discounts from the dignified and highly moral whiskey executive. Bill Robinson, the heavy, hearty newspaperman turned Coca-Cola executive, drank all day and still won at bridge. Pete Jones, the Eisenhower campaign's secret money man, seemed to show up at the club only when Ike was there. He'd been a poor boy once upon a time, and the huge wads of cash he carried—always including at least one $10,000 bill—seemed to ease his remembered pain. He liked to throw out a $1,000 bill on the first tee and ask who wanted to play for it. No denomination under a twenty made it into his wallet, and he liked to tip. Clubhouse employees swarmed around him like happy bees.

When Pete Jones died in a plane crash in 1962, he had $60,000 in his wallet.

("There were really two cliques at Augusta National," an ex-employee observes. "The Northerners and the Southerners. The Southerners felt pushed out. They didn't like those big tippers, who got better service and more attention. When Bobby Jones died, a lot of the Atlanta boys left the club.")

Less wealthy but better-known personages came to town when Ike did, men like John Foster Dulles or Robert Taft. But the Second Golfer, Vice President Richard Nixon, never got an invitation. It was a curious omission, since Augusta National remained, even after Ike, such a high-level Republican playground. Nixon played the game: he loved it, in fact, only slightly less than his boss did. Bush, Quayle, and Reagan teed it up in later years at Augusta, but no RMN. Why the snub? The Gang had mixed feelings about him, for one thing; a few of them even urged Ike to dump Dick in 1956. Eisenhower admitted no great enthusiasm for the vice president as a person, but decided against replacing him. Then Dick went and lost the 1960 election to Kennedy, after having spurned the president's offer to help with the campaign. He also turned down the money Cliff offered. "Here is $50,000 from fifty people, and within a week or two, $50,000 more," Roberts recalled saying to Nixon. "Well, this is the biggest defeat of my life," Ike told Slater.

To top it off, Nixon had committed an unforgiveable sin: he'd identified himself with Pepsi. Augusta National, the home course of Robert Woodruff and of Joroberts, was Coca-Cola.

Photographers frequently snapped Ike during the White House years drinking a bottle of Coke through a straw. Great, Woodruff told him, but lose the straw. Looks sissy. No, Ike replied, proving himself a master marketer, "when I tip up a bottle of Coca-Cola for a good drink, it only lasts a few seconds. With a straw, a lot of talking and more walking, I [am] able to contact more photographers and newspaper correspondents."

Nixon and Pepsi-Cola produced a similar public relations master stroke at the American International Exposition in Moscow in 1959. Donald Kendall, Pepsi's overseas man, arranged for the vice president (who was already running for president) to lead Soviet leader Nikita Khrushchev into the Pepsi booth after their contrived "debate" in a model kitchen. Dick seemed very firm in this discussion with the head of the communist monolith, a performance he used as the centerpiece of his 1960 campaign. In truth, however, "it was ridiculous," recalled Elliott Erwitt, one of the photographers on the scene. "Nixon was saying, 'We're richer than you are' and Khrushchev would say, 'We are catching up and we will surpass you.' That was the level of the debate.

"At one point Nixon was getting so irritating I thought I heard Khrushchev say [in Russian], 'Go fuck my grandmother.'" Erwitt caught the eye of Harrison Salisbury of *The New York Times*, one of the few other Westerners present who spoke Russian, to see if he'd heard the same thing. He had.

The clash of worldviews apparently made Comrade K. thirsty; the world press recorded every gulp of the seven Pepsis he drank. And from that point on, any stroll Richard Nixon might take on the verdant slopes of Augusta National would come only over the dead body of Robert Winship Woodruff.

****

Bobby Jones didn't really care about the Coke versus Pepsi controversy. Deeper thoughts and more profound issues than soft drinks and Dick Nixon occupied his mind.

Mary Jones couldn't look at him without thinking about his immortal soul. *Please consider this, dear,* she pleaded time after time. Mary belonged to the Roman Catholic church, and she wanted her husband to convert. But Jones, never a religious man, resisted.

He was sixty-two in 1964, the fifteenth year of syringomyelia's stranglehold on his spine and on his life, but he looked eighty-two. And not a good eighty-two; smoke, pain, codeine, cortisone, and whiskey had puffed and etched his face, and his muscleless right hand collapsed around his black cigarette holder like a mechanical claw. He had by then read the literature of neurological disease so thoroughly that certain medical phrases echoed from one text to the next: "Dissociated sensory loss . . . multisegmental weakness, wasting and areflexia in the upper extremities . . . no proven or definitive therapy." Jones searched for escape from the trap of his own body. Dictating business and personal letters and his final book into a machine or to his secretary was a distraction, but the pleasure of hitting a golf ball was a distant memory. And he couldn't hold a pen to write or hold a book to read, an ironic and cruel punishment for a man in love with language. He found respite only in music.

At home on Tuxedo Road in Atlanta or in his cabin at Augusta, Jones frequently sat in a dim room while a turntable spun under a phonograph needle. How much can be read into the fact that one of the several albums he played over and over was Giuseppe Verdi's *Rigoletto?* The original title of the typically melodramatic, lachrymose opera had been *La Maledizione (The Curse)*. Life has cursed the title character with a deformity—a hunchback—making him fit for no other job but that of the court jester to a tenor, the profligate Duke of Mantua. But providence has also blessed him with a lovely daughter, Gilda. Rigoletto, enraged at the budding romance between Gilda and the duke, plots in baritone to kill him. At midnight, the hitman Sparafucile (a bass) hands Rigoletto a body in a bag. Just as he's about to throw it in the river, he discovers he's the butt of another cosmic joke: his daughter is in the bag. With her dying breath, she says she's happy to die for her lover. Rigoletto shakes his fist at heaven, and sobs *"Ah! la maledizione!"* Curtain.

Jones may have thought himself to be a tragic figure during these musical interludes, but he showed a stoic face to the world. As he listened, he may have thought about life and death or of the relationship between the hard wiring of the spine to consciousness or of the face of God, but he did not become formally religious as his wife desperately wished. When visitors called at his cabin, Jones received them graciously and kept things light. He treasured his friends, and they him. Charley Yates. Charlie Nicklaus and his son, a pretty fair young golfer named Jack. Charlie Price, the writer. Sarazen. Bill Hyndman and his wife. Gordon Brand, a USGA guy. George Cobb, the golf course architect.

Outside the Jones cabin door, the crowds around the putting green and the tenth tee swelled and hollowed like the sea. What had brought the ocean of humanity? The short answer was that the Masters opera had a new tenor named Arnold Palmer. But a walk around the grounds in April 1964 showed other changes almost as profound as the growing popularity.

The course itself evolved subtly year to year, but if viewed through the time-lapse photography of age, the changes would have been dramatic. Trees grew up, greens changed shape, bunkers were added or deleted, and the sand in the bunkers bleached from off-white to pure cane sugar. "On number ten, the tee was near eighteen green, and the green was next to where that fairway bunker is now. Easy hole." Charley Yates, a member since 1940, has given this speech a thousand times. He sticks to the back nine because that's what people know, from TV. "The tee on eleven was up on the hill [behind the present tenth green], makin' it a dogleg right. No pond, just a creek. Also easy. Twelve, thirteen, and fourteen are unchanged [but hardly untouched; Mackenzie certainly didn't install the heating and cooling pipes under the surface of the problematic twelfth and thirteenth greens]. The pond was expanded on fifteen [and a concrete bridge over it destroyed]. There were mounds to the right of that green, and you took great comfort in hittin' at those mounds. Cliff bulldozed them. Sixteen you know about [in 1948, architect Robert Trent Jones moved the tee from the right of fifteen green to the left, and added a pond, and rebuilt the green]. On seventeen, I'll never forget, Cliff called up a bunch of us, and we went down in Jack Stephens's plane so he could ask us what would we think about some mounds off to the side. 'But Cliff, you've already put the mounds in.' 'I know,' he said. 'I just wanted someone to blame it on if people don't like them.' "

As Jones faded and Eisenhower neared the end of his time in office, Roberts's attention turned to the service and exaltation of a third great being. The most casual observer could see it; the micromaintenance of Augusta National was taking it where no golf course had gone before. Roberts and Masters money were beginning to turn the place into a giant terrarium, an awe-inspiring and unprecedented weed-and-pinecone-and-fallen-branch-and-gopher-hole-free perfection.

An important part of the continual tweaking took place the

day after the Masters, when a group of experts convened to inspect the golf course and offer suggestions. "We all got into a big van by the first tee, greens committee guys, Roberts, a few executives, like the man from Toro, and me," recalls golf architect John LaFoy. LaFoy began his career as an assistant to George Cobb, the club's consulting architect from the 1950s to the 1970s. "Cliff said, 'If anyone has anything to say, say it to the whole group. Otherwise, no talking.' Sure enough, halfway up the fairway someone in the back whispers to someone else, and Cliff says, 'Stop this van!' The driver threw it in park. And Cliff turned around and shouted at us, using every expletive in the book. You could hear a pin drop."

Of all the changes to the golf ground at Augusta National since it opened in 1934, one project dwarfed the rest. Roberts introduced it in a typically cunning letter to the members in April 1958. "Enclosed is a map of a proposed Par 3 Golf Course," he wrote (the course was not really "proposed"—it was *already laid out*). "We have a drainage problem, also a muddy water problem in Ike's Pond. The one proper solution is another pond above the present one [*there are no alternatives*]. It will be [*not "would be"*] about 3¼ acres in size and the area surrounding it is a most inviting place to locate nine Par 3 golf holes." Cliff estimated the cost for the damn, pond, and course at $67,500. Subscription forms enclosed.

George Cobb was officially the architect of the Par 3, but Cliff rode herd on the project to the point that he deserves a codesigner credit. "The main course was Jones and Mackenzie, but with Mackenzie dead and Jones sick, Roberts thought of the Par 3 as his," says LaFoy. During a daily construction conference "there'd be eight people on the first green and just two on the second. Cobb and Roberts arguing." Although a course built along the edges of two ponds wouldn't be expected to have a problem with standing water, Cliff wanted the same network of underground drainage tile as on the big course. He got it. He also wished to have each green on the Par 3 replicate the slopes and curves of a particular green on the big course. Cobb, the architect of such gems as the Sharon Club in Ohio and Cleghorn Plantation in North Carolina, patiently explained that this was impractical, if not impossible. The little-course surfaces were just too small for much steepness; there'd be no place flat enough to cut a cup. Cobb prevailed, but Roberts put in his two cents on a hundred other issues.

The Par 3 succeeded completely. The finished course was a perfect little world, a glass globe with greens and tees perched on the edges of mirror lakes and sheltering pines on the perimeter accentuating the coziness. Starting in 1960, a nine-hole tournament on the Cobb-Roberts course replaced the Wednesday grab bag of driving contests and bow-and-arrow exhibitions. Gene Sarazen, a forthright man, declared it the best par-three course in the world, and he was right. Cliff loved it.

"Roberts and I were playing the Par 3, and we were all even going into the ninth hole," recalls Bob Craft, a member since 1966. "My caddie was Willie Peterson, Nicklaus's caddie. Characteristically, the caddie just handed you a club, and you'd hit it. So I hit but it's about twenty-five yards too long. And I said hey, Willie, what's this? 'Mr. Craft, I knowed it was too much,' Willie said. 'But Mr. Roberts don't like to lose.'"

* * * * * * * * * * *

Many of the other changes in Augusta related to the transforming popularity of the Masters. Tickets became scarce, then valuable, then heirlooms, like mother's good china. In 1972, the club started a waiting list—The List—and closed it in 1978, when it became impossibly long. "I helped out selling souvenirs, towels and things, in a tent outside the pro shop," recalls Mrs. Brien Charter, the assistant pro's wife. "One year we ran out of *everything*. Those people wanted to buy something so bad that someone offered to buy the green rope around the tent."

Those people also wanted shelter so badly that they were willing to endure the rusty water and lumpy beds at the now thoroughly decrepit Bon Air. Augusta, wrote Dan Jenkins in *Sports Illustrated* in 1964, is "Where Georgia Retaliates for Sherman's

March." He poked fun at the old army town ambience and at the rattletrap Bon Air, "whose whitewashed face looks into the almost always dry cavern of its own swimming pool . . . [and whose] ancient waiters tumble drowsily into the dining room" and take half an hour to refill your coffee cup.

"We admit to imperfections," the *Chronicle* responded editorially and humorlessly. But "Augusta, while deeply proud of the Masters Tournament and Masters Week, is not dependent on them for its economy as Jenkins implied. By acquisition of some $200 million of industry in the past seven years, Augusta has almost the greatest industrial growth of almost any city in the Southeast." Augusta Country Club sold one of its two courses to a residential developer, who built Country Club Hills. National Hills shopping center and scores of other businesses sprung up on Washington Road.

The city's expansion did not include enough good hotel rooms, however, which led to one of the pillars of the Masters experience, the rental house. Something about a house induced a rare relaxation in the Augusta pilgrim. Was it the pine-tree-enclosed backyards, the proximity to the National (most of the houses were within three miles of the club), the presence of friends, the familiar hum of a refrigerator compressor, or the fact that Arnold Palmer was also having a drink and a steak on a nearby deck? House renters lived a buddy movie or a bacchanalia every April, and they wanted it again the next year and the one after that.

Possibly the only group enjoying the Masters more were the scholars from Athens, Georgia, who convened on the bank below the sixth tee and to the left of the sixteenth green. The University of Georgia–to–Augusta trip required less than two hours by Volkswagen. Greek letters, depictions of bulldogs, and the color red decorated the students' torsos. Vodka and pull-top Pabst Blue Ribbon beer jammed their coolers.

"My first tournament was in 1964," says Stovall Walker, Class of '67. "What a party. . . . The only golfers we got really quiet for were Arnold Palmer and Jack Nicklaus." After one of Walker's happy classmates jumped into the lake during play and another forged enough tickets for all the sisters of Delta Delta Delta to gain admittance, security forces tightened around the Bulldog Bash.

Augustans also joined in the revelry, of course, and scores of parties, Calcutta-based and otherwise, became annual rites. But ambiguity clouded the picture. Like parents whose babies grow up to become teenagers, many Augustans didn't like what was happening to the tournament they'd nurtured so long. They hardly recognized a *crowded* Masters. "The first time I was impressed with 'I don't like this' was in 1961 or 1962," recalls an Augusta woman of a certain age. She goes back to the days of $5.50 season tickets, which "was also about what you paid a servant for a week. You saw all Augusta people back then. You knew everybody.

"You're writing about the club and the town and the tournament? Well, the three are getting more and more distinct."

Other disaffected Augustans say what many leave unspoken. "About then, in the mid-sixties, was when I stopped going to the Masters," says Larry Jon Wilson. "Too many blue tags." Blue tags? "License plates on cars from the North. New York, Pennsylvania, Michigan. They all had dark backgrounds." Yankees, in other words. Yankees, those pushy, grasping, impolite sons-a-bitches who kicked great-great-grandaddy's ass in the War of Secession. In the battle between the Southerner's instinctive and historic dislike for Yankees and his better nature, better nature usually won. Especially if there was money in it.

Some Augustans left town to avoid the influx, and some financed their trips by renting out their houses. But most Augustans stuck around for the big show and sold the visitors a shady place to park or food or drink or a room to stay in. And everyone in town found common ground in their enthusiasm for a Pennsylvania golfer named Ahno Pomma. Northerners incorrectly hardened the consonants to Ar Nold Palm Er, but who cared? Palmer belonged to the whole country, and the Masters belonged to him. For six out of seven years he either won the tournament or should have. The one exception to the run was 1963, when a rival arrived, a hard-to-like fat kid from Ohio who stole the tournament away. Now *there* was a Yankee.

Jack Nicklaus sharpened Augusta's love for Arnie.

* * * * * * * * * * *

So, too, did Ben Hogan, the man Palmer replaced as the best in the game. Arnie for Hogan was like Kennedy for Eisenhower; they were young guys with hair and pheromones in exchange for moody brooders and your grandpa. People instantly liked Palmer's style. Elvis had entered the building.

"I was always very conscious of my appearance," the King recalls. He's sitting in his office in Latrobe, Pennsylvania, gray hair contrasting handsomely with brown skin. Golf clothes (for a game this afternoon), fingers twice the diameter of normal digits, and a handshake that's so enveloping you feel like a child meeting an adult. "My pants always had a crease and my shoes were immaculately shined. My father always said you can tell a person's character from his shoes. . . .

"I *did* think I could win the Masters the first time I played in it [in 1955]. Yes, I did, without question. I was always very confident I could do well at Augusta.

"After walking on that golf course after playing the winter tour, well, we played a lot of public courses back then. Played off a lot of dirt; not to pick on Brackenridge Park, but at San Antonio the mud on your shoes made you an inch taller. . . . I'd played most of my amateur golf in better conditions, on pretty good courses around Cleveland and Pittsburgh."

The Palmer era began in 1958, when Arnold first won and three other players narrowly lost. Venturi, unnerved by what he thought was an incorrect imbedded-ball ruling in Arnie's favor on the twelfth, three-putted fourteen and fifteen and finished tied for fourth. Doug Ford missed a four footer on the second-to-last hole and finished second by a shot. Fred Hawkins, needing two birdies to tie, got the first on seventeen, then hit a six iron just past the flag on the final hole. "I remember that the cameras were noisy as hell," says Hawkins, "and that I lipped out." In 1959 and 1961, Palmer contrived to lose to Art Wall and Gary Player with some poor but spectacular play on the final holes. Venturi might have won for a third time in 1960, but Arnie snatched it away with a lucky two-putt on sixteen, an even luckier thirty-five-foot birdie putt on seventeen, and a godlike three on the final hole. In 1962, Palmer finished birdie-birdie-par just to shoot 75 and make a play-off with Player and Dow Finsterwald. Another fast finish on the TV holes in over-time gave Arnie a third Masters win (Palmer 68, Player 71, Finster-wald 77). Ahno Pomma exhausted his galleries, but he never disappointed them. He became a phenomenon. The first celebrity pitchman. Richer than God, bigger than golf, and worshipped like a deity.

But Nicklaus interrupted Palmer's Augusta glory in 1963.

Volumes have been written about the Meaning of Arnie. Could the nearly simultaneous success of Palmer, TV, and the Mas-ters be considered separately, or were they all part of the same meringue? Did he represent the dawn of a new age, or did the new age of the mass-media Masters make him? The Meaning of Arnie discourse took on a rich, full-bodied flavor in the inevitable com-parisons with his bête noire, Nicklaus. Arnold played a ski-jump hook or a defensive block-out and swung ferociously at all times. His follow-through terminated—at his waist, above his head, or in the vicinity of his left shoulder—abruptly, not smoothly as ortho-doxy demanded, as if his club had suddenly hit frozen air. His tech-nique made every good shot seem like a happy accident, a seeming randomness that increased his solidarity with his fans, who'd seen variations of Arnie's stroke in their own foursomes. And his smiles, winks, waves, and nose wrinkles in acknowledgment of their shouts linked athlete and spectator still further. The charm and excite-ment of Arnold radiated through the ether, too, as clear on TV as in person.

Nicklaus, twenty-four in 1964, ten years Arnie's junior, was not lovable. He possessed hips that made you hope he wasn't seated next to you in coach, and the Vitalis on his lank blond hair made it look like he had no hair at all. Jack played a high, biting fade and hit like a kicking mule; you could admire his scientific and awesome game but you couldn't identify with it. Masters fans didn't like him much. Some even openly rooted against him, which infuriated Jones to the point that he wrote a two-paragraph essay on comportment that has been printed on every Masters ticket since:

MOST DISTRESSING TO THOSE WHO LOVE THE GAME OF GOLF IS THE APPLAUDING OR CHEERING OF MISPLAYS OR MISFORTUNES OF A PLAYER. SUCH OCCURRENCES HAVE BEEN RARE AT THE MASTERS BUT WE MUST ELIMINATE THEM ENTIRELY IF OUR PATRONS ARE TO CONTINUE TO MERIT THEIR REPUTATION AS THE MOST KNOWLEDGEABLE IN THE WORLD.

"I had a lot of respect for the way he handled that," said Dave Marr. "Jack always said, 'I never heard anything,' but I guarantee you [his wife] Barbara did."

Such things rarely pan out in a ninety-six-man field, but people expected a showdown between the two best players in the world in the 1964 Masters. Nicklaus had defeated Palmer in a playoff for the 1962 U.S. Open and had won the 1963 Masters. Arnold had won the coveted green jacket in the previous three even-numbered years, but he hadn't won a tournament in six months.

He'd also been four months and nine days without a cigarette. "January first, 1964," Palmer says. "A lot of peple said, 'You've just ended your career,' and I had serious thoughts about that. Actually, I'd quit smoking on the golf course in 1962. Just closet or bar smoking after that. A lot of people said it was a bad example, and I took it to heart." And to waist. Without appetite-suppressing nicotine in his diet, Arnie's weight quickly skipped from 175 to 188.

But his victory total stayed unchanged. A deep inhalation of the fine tobaccos of an L&M had been as much a part of his preshot routine as pulling a club out of the bag. He'd had an endorsement contract with Liggett & Myers Tobacco Company since shortly after his dramatic and smoky victories in the 1960 Masters and U.S. Open. Could Arnie win without the weed?

Tuesday morning: The Parris Island Marine Band leads the Masters Week Parade under clearing skies. Fifty units march or roll this year, the most ever. The marching bands include, as usual, Lucy Laney High, Richmond Academy, and Strom Thurmond High from across the river in South Carolina. Augusta Coca-Cola, E-Z GO Golf Carts, Continental Can, McDonald's Hamburger, and Lily Tulip Corporation float floats, as do the City of Augusta, the Augusta Merchants Association, and the Titleholders. Various queens wave and smile. Golfers do the same from the backs of the big white convertibles.

Thursday: Palmer, one of the strongest men in golf, causes a stir among his huge, adhesive gallery by standing in the center of the fifteenth fairway and taking the cover off his three wood. "He's going for it!" someone yells. He slashes, the ball clears the hazard, and he shoots 69, tied for the lead. "Bracketed with the bronzed king of the fairways," the *Chronicle* reported, "were 1961 Masters champion Gary Player, Australian Kel Nagle, Bob Goalby, and an unknown club pro from Charlotte, N.C., Davis Love, Jr." Nicklaus has a thirteen-foot putt for birdie on the last hole. He holds his head way back and his hands way forward, as if in a particularly uncomfortable yoga stance. He three-putts for 71. In the press building afterward he complains about his putting.

Friday: Again on fifteen, the bronzed king of the fairways has cleared the pond in two. In the clear blue air overhead, a droning single-engine plane circles the National trailing a banner that reads GO ARNIE GO. Arnie fluffs his third shot, leaving a thirty-five-foot putt for birdie. Which he makes, to the absolute delight of his fans, who resemble the mob of extras in a Cecil B. DeMille epic. Jones is part of the pandemonium. As Arnold passes by his cart on his way to the sixteenth tee, Jones pats him on the rear end with his right claw.

Palmer shoots 68 and leads Player by four. Nicklaus shoots 73 and complains about his putting.

Saturday: Arnie's 69 and ten-under-par total lead by five over Bruce Devlin and by six over "freshly scrubbed New Yorker" Dave Marr, a Texan working under Claude Harmon at Winged Foot in New York. Nicklaus, with a 71, is tied with Ben Hogan (67) at one under. The *Chronicle* uses seventeen military references in its tournament stories, apropos of "Arnie's Army."

Sunday: Nicklaus begins the day nine shots behind, but he's charging. Jones and Roberts roll their cart under the ropes and park their cart to the right of the twelfth tee to watch Jack attempt the rooftop-to-rooftop par-three twelfth, the only tee shot at Augusta National with almost no room for error. What a setting: the defending champion, desperate to make up ground on his biggest rival; the tournament founder among the silent, watchful throng; Nicklaus gazing down at the green, a skinny plateau above reclaimed swampland; wide, muddy Rae's Creek in front, a bunker and a thousand bad lies behind. Silence as he prepares to hit an eight iron. Shank.

The worst shot of Jack's career ends up in the thirteenth fairway, 110 yards from the green, only 40 yards closer to the green than whence he started. "I put it almost over Roberts's and Jones's heads," Nicklaus recalls. "No, I didn't make any comments to them. I was too embarrassed." He pitched on to eight feet but missed the putt. Despite that bogey, Jack closed fast with a 67.

Sunday, the closet in the bedroom in Arnie's rented one-story red brick house: Miss America contestants wear something in the evening gown competition that will go with a rhinestone tiara. Do potential Masters champions select clothing that might look good with an Augusta National club blazer? "I won't deny that from time to time I gave that some thought," Palmer says. But on this morning he steps into purplish-blue pants, a bold color statement in its own right, and not a pleasing complement to green.

Arnie needs a 67 to break Hogan's tournament record, but he won't get it. Instead Nicklaus shoots the 67, five-under, the best round of the day. Marr, Arnie's playing partner, also supplies a little heat.

Angry after missing an eight footer for birdie on the ninth, Palmer swings extra hard at his tee shot on ten and takes off down the hill like a race walker. His caddie, Nathaniel "Ironman" Avery, struggles to keep up. Ironman must have really known those greens, hey Arnold? "No, I never asked him to read a putt." Yardage, then, he must have known to the inch how far your ball was to the hole? "No, I did most of that myself. Sometimes I'd check to see if he had the same distance I did." A great coach? Did Ironman calm you down or pump you up, as appropriate? No again. "One of the great things about him was that he didn't talk unless he was spoken to." But when Arnie three-putts the tenth, pulling Marr to within four with eight to play, Ironman breaks his customary silence. He hands his boss his driver by the tenth green and shocks Palmer and Marr with what he says:

"Boss, is you chokin'?"

Marr's threat effectively ends on the twelfth hole. "I needed a perfect eight iron, but I hit it *just* fat, and it rolled back into the water. Made a good four from there." Marr gets a four wood across the pond in front of the fifteenth, which the setting sun has turned into a blinding mirror. Arnie, keyed up, slashes a three iron; he squints into the glare but cannot see his ball. "Did it get over, Dave, did it get over?" he asks anxiously.

"Shit, Arnold, your divot got over," Marr told him.

Palmer's 70 gave him a a six-shot win over the runners-up, Nicklaus and Marr. His fourth win was the most in tournament history. He was thirty-four, theoretically the prime of a golfer's life. But the strangest thing happened, or didn't happen: Arnie never won another major tournament.

Did the world of commerce deprive him of a longer run at the top? Arnold thought so; he'd become the hub of an unbelievably large and profitable corporate wheel. "I've just got to get rid of all this business involvement so I can concentrate on nothing but my golf," he told his agent, Mark McCormack, during a depressing slump in 1965. "I never used to think about all these business things. Now I'm worrying about the Arnold Palmer Golf Company and the inserts in the woods and if the shirts are shrinking and why some guy in New York doesn't have his laundry back and that somebody's upset in Georgia because his putting course isn't making enough money. I'm sick of it. I used to blot these things out when I got on a golf course, but now they follow me around."

McCormack listened as an agent must, but he disagreed. As he recalled in his book, *Arnie*, "I have a different theory. . . . His concentration was being destroyed not by the intrusion of business thoughts but by his inability to smoke when his system most needed a cigarette."

Palmer smoked again on the golf course from time to time in the sixties before quitting for good. While his golf remained slightly below its previous heights, the business opportunities continued to pour in. He pitched for Coca-Cola for a while in the early seventies, but that seems to have been a trifle for both parties. Much more important were his relationships with Pennzoil, Hertz, and the Cadillac Motor Division of General Motors. Arnold owns three Caddy dealerships. And the company hired Arnie as the lead dog in its "Team Cadillac," a collection of Senior PGA Tour players who wear the logo on their shirts and who star in the commercials.

Cadillac sponsors the Masters on TV; Palmer's identification with the Masters is immutable. Thus Cadillac, Arnie, and the Masters intertwine like wisteria vines, each augmenting the other, the Holy Trinity of luxury car advertising.

* * * * * * * * * * *

The most valuable piece of art on Arnold Palmer's living room wall is an oil painting of a pastoral scene given to him by the artist, Dwight Eisenhower, at a surprise birthday party in 1966. Ike devoted himself to painting, writing, charity, and staying warm after Kennedy's inauguration in January 1961. He spent his winters in Palm Springs in the Southern California desert, where each year a dozen or so of his cronies from Augusta National would visit. Freeman Gosden was the ringmaster at these outings. The format never changed: golf during the day, bridge at night, no wives.

Ike visited Augusta eleven times after his presidency. Roberts organized several elaborate parties in his honor during this period. In May 1961, forty members who'd paid to build Ike's Cabin (known to some as Mamie's Cabin) convened at the club to accept the general's thanks. In October 1965, eighty-six of his friends gathered to give him and Mamie an intricately carved, eighty-four-ounce gold bowl commemorating their fiftieth wedding anniversary. Bob and Mary Jones drove in from Atlanta—Bob was to serve as toastmaster—but the trip wore him out so badly he had to stay in bed.

Eisenhower, enfeebled by two heart attacks, visited Augusta National for the last time in 1967.

* * * * * * * * * * *

Slats Slater opened his diary on April 1, 1969. He would never forget, he wrote, the sight of the afternoon sun coming through the cathedral's stained glass windows. Or the baby-blue uniform and regal bearing of the president of France, Charles de Gaulle. And what a tall man, six feet six if he was an inch. De Gaulle marched down the center aisle of the Washington National Cathedral, his monumental nose in the air. He took his seat in the front row, near President Nixon, to the left of the flag-covered steel casket.

On the right sat the family. The widow sobbed uncontrollably, and her son John tried to comfort her. Behind them were Cliff Roberts and the others from Augusta National, Ike's old Gang, together for the final time.

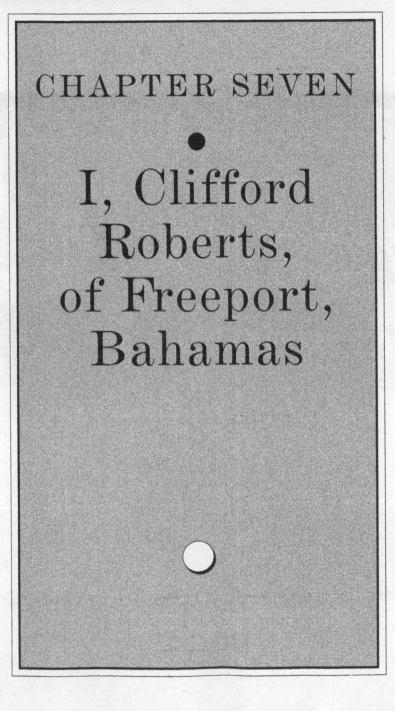

CHAPTER SEVEN

•

I, Clifford Roberts, of Freeport, Bahamas

Jack Nicklaus wins his fifth Masters.

**Billy Casper, 1970 . . . Charles Coody, 1971 . . .
Jack Nicklaus, 1972 . . . Tommy Aaron, 1973 . . .
Gary Player, 1974 . . . Jack Nicklaus, 1975 . . .
Raymond Floyd, 1976 . . . Tom Watson, 1977 . . .
Gary Player, 1978 . . . Fuzzy Zoeller, 1979**

B obo absently taps the empty can on the table. Yes, he would like another beer.

Hey, Gene, a couple more, you say. You are drinking the sixteen-ounce container of Schlitz Malt Liquor, the Bull. A buck sixty each. You are buying. You drink, sinfully, in the middle of a January afternoon. A sunny afternoon, as you are reminded each time the door to Hill's Pool Room creaks open and you squint against the sudden light.

"They don't care nothin' about seniority out there, that's what dehydrates me," Bobo continues, stubbing out another Kool. You nod while trying to avert your nose, for this Augusta National caddie (ret.) breathes mentholated breath so bilious you think it might actually be green. "I played hooky to caddie there when I was fifteen. Since 1973. Thirty years. Now the best bag I ever had in the Masters was Larry Nelson, he . . ."

Bobo bitches and tells stories and time-travels and slurs his words like Foster Brooks, the pretend-drunk comedian. After a while his memory stalls and he starts to eye you like you're an ATM machine. Bobo has remembered that he doesn't have a job and notices that, apparently, you do. He would appreciate a small payment, he says, in exchange for his continued observations on the caddie's life. *How about another beer?* you reply. Bobo crosses his arms and looks away, pouting.

Eugene Andrews solemnly observes this spectacle from behind the bar. The owner of the joint is backlit by a signboard that lists three potent but economically priced beers, in three sizes. The thirty-two-ounce Bull is the most expensive item on the menu, $2.85. On the walls are posters of sultry black women in tight dresses caressing huge bottles of Budweiser. On the floor by the door are two functional but tired-looking pool tables. In the back is the men's room, whose awesomely stained fixtures and bare CD-grade plywood walls with black Magic Marker illustrations remind you of the facilities in a caddie shack you knew long ago and far away.

Hill's Pool Room is not in the Terry, Augusta's ghetto, as you might expect. It's in a black enclave on the Hill, only a mile or so from the National, less than that from the Country Club, at the corner of Wheeler Road and Monte Sano (pronounced "Monna Sanna"). To get there from the Bobby Jones Expressway you go east on Wheeler, past scores of beautifully situated Georgia colonials, and past the leafy, curving entrance to the Westminster School. The houses get gradually smaller, the road narrower. Two hundred yards after you see a dark blue four-door Ford Falcon on cinder blocks in a front yard, you're there. Jim Dent, the Senior PGA Tour star and former caddie at the National, lived in that two-story brick. A whorehouse known as the Oak used to service the needs of a varied clientele over there, where that basketball court is. No Oak anymore, and no nets on the rims. Hill's does not advertise its existence, but you know you're on the right corner when you see the mural on an exterior wall of a boarded-up diner called the Stockbroker's Grill. The painting depicts black men in white coveralls carrying golf bags. A sign near it says NO WETTING.

"Jim Jamieson, Tom Purtzer, Andy Bean." Bobo is back at the Masters. "But Bean, he had a temper mental thing. He'd throw his club and make you feel like a dog for goin' to pick it up.

"Cliff Roberts, now. A real man. Took no shit from nobody. When Lee Trevino complained about things, Roberts said, 'You don't like our rules, there's the road out.' We *loved* him." Not for his exorbitant tipping, that's for sure. Bobo shrugs. "Pay ya twelve-fifty,

fifteen dollars, and tell his guest to pay you the same if you're carrying double." Not for his charm; everyone remembers how Cliff
was always scanning the ground for trash or pinecones and barking
at his caddie, "Go pick that up!" But at Christmas he gave all the
permanent loopers fifteen dollars, and his loyalty to them did not
waver. "I wish he was still alive," says Bobo. "He believed in black
people *serving him.*"

What about Bill Lane, Cliff's successor as chairman at the National? Thumbs up: "Back in 1974, when the rate was twelve-fifty,
you know what Bill Lane pay a caddie? Fifty dollars!" But of Hord
Hardin, the man who succeeded Lane, the old caddie only mumbles
"that old no-good ass." Better change the subject. Yes, another beer.

Bobo admits that he liked to caddie, even in the Masters, with
a little buzz. No, he didn't drink on the course. "You prepare yourself before, you know, with a little g-i-i-n. It makes you looser, gives
you better advice. I was more than a caddie. I was a coach." Again,
Bobo asks for money, begging this time. Embarrassed, you shove a
couple of bills in his hand and get up to go to the men's. When you
return, Bobo is gone.

Lisa joins your table and declares after two twelve-ounce
Magnums that you are the rare white man "who doesn't look too
bad. Sorta like *Third Rock from the Sun.*" So who is a particularly
good-looking black man? Augusta's own James Brown? Lisa makes
a face. "I saw James right when he was getting out of jail the last
time and nobody did his hair for a long time. Man looked like
Planet of the Apes."

Lisa tells you Bobo's real name. Most Augusta caddie nicknames were bestowed by Willie Mason, the caddie master at the
Country Club; the light traffic at the National compelled most caddies to work at both courses. Nubbins lost most of a couple of fingers in a meat grinder. Leven was the 'leventh child in his family.
Stovepipe, Sarazen's caddie, had the hat. Nathaniel Avery was Ironman "because he always pulled out the right iron, man," in Bobo's
version of the etymology. Cigarette, Cemetery, Rat, Jap, Pokie,
Pappy, 8-Ball . . .

The basic elements of the ever-circulating library of caddie stories are the colorful but trivializing nicknames, rustic humor, and failure to achieve agreement between subject and verb. "Them others is all green numbers," Willie Peterson told Jack Nicklaus, who is colorblind between red and green and couldn't decipher the eighteenth-hole scoreboard in 1963. Gardner Dickinson took pains to get a caddie who could really read the bumps and slopes of the National's greens. But instead of the seer he hoped for, caddie master Freddie Bennett gave him Reindeer, who was dyslexic. Former assistant caddie master Thomas "Porky" Paquette recalls the time pro Bert Yancey made the mistake of lending his car to his caddie. "Well, he doesn't show up for the first round, and Yancey's clubs are in the trunk, and he's frantic. So I go down to the Oak and sure enough, there's Yancey's Grand Prix out front. 'I'll be there, man,' the caddie says, scratchin' himself. And he was, but he'd sold every damn ball out of that bag the night before."

A lot of the guys with funny names died young, poorly educated, often with bad teeth and exhausted livers. Ironman, for example, who carried Arnie's bag to four wins, didn't make it to age fifty. The others died a figurative death in 1983, when Augusta National chairman Hord Hardin acceded to the pros' wishes and allowed them to bring their own caddies to the Masters. Those of us outside the ropes imagined a romanticized Masters player and caddie kinship, a team, like Rocky Balboa, the fictional heavyweight, and Mick, the trainer who cajoled and inspired him to the championship. Sometimes it happened: in 1979, Jariah Beard told Frank Urban Zoeller to aim at that tree, hit this club, putt it right there. Fuzzy had never played in a Masters before, and barely seen the course before. As with abstract art or James Joyce, players invariably needed a few attempts to understand Augusta National. Zoeller's win, Beard's win, defined the high point of the caddie's art.

The low point is described by an old pro who talks quietly about how in the old days the caddies helped you cheat. The greens were not fast every year, this Masters veteran reminds you, but a down-grain, downhill putt always gave you the willies. When his shot finished above the hole on the marbleized sixth or ninth greens, for example, the in-cahoots player and caddie exchanged meaningful looks or a certain phrase. And the simple scam began: the contestant marks his ball and hands it to his caddie for cleaning. The caddie spits on it, rubs it with a towel, hands it back. "It's loaded, boss," he says under his breath; he has not wiped the saliva off. And the tiny gob of water and protein retards the ball's speed just enough, in theory, for the dirty cheater to two-putt.

Nothing Augusta caddies could do—or were allegedly willing to do—could save their jobs at the Masters. "If you ever smelled his breath, you'd know why I didn't ask for his advice much," says one Masters champion of his hired hand. But sobriety was not the key issue and neither was the ability of the locals to decrypt the National's greens. Dave Marr found the mark when he asked, "Would *you* want to play Carnegie Hall without your own band?" The modern professional golfer worked with one caddie week after week; they really were a team. But columnists and fans railed against the demise of the tradition of the ebony man in ivory overalls, an idiot savant where this course was concerned, striding next to his employer on a sea of green.

The caddies lost a huge part of their income when the Tour caddies came in, but it was worse than that. In Jaime Diaz's award-winning article "The Men the Masters Forgot" (*Golf Digest*, April 1993), Jariah Beard pointed to his dark face. "In golf, you don't see any more of this. Players or caddies. The Monday of the Masters, I was somebody in this community."

"They brought it on themselves," says Paquette. " 'What's your name?' a player would ask, and the caddie says 'Jumpin' Raisin' or whatever, and right away he says, 'What are you gonna pay me? Can I get fifty up front?' "

Fifty up front. So different from the old days, when Ike Washington and his brother Henry Son looped at the National. Ike had the thrill of carrying Ty Cobb's bag one day in the late thirties—Cobb wintered in Augusta—and a second thrill when the baseball star handed him a dollar and said "Keep the change, sonny." The rate was only sixty-five cents! Ike remembers, too, that he and the other caddies would put a hand on the small of the back of aged or out-of-shape golfers and push them up the hills.

That image hangs in your mind for a long minute, and the
beer and the hypnotic click-roll-clack of a pool game keep it there.
Until Bobo unexpectedly reappears and reseats himself. He leans in,
exhaling poison air, and you hold your breath and lean back. "I tell
you somethin' you really want to know," he says conspiratorially.
"Cost you. About Roberts. He didn't kill hisself. Murder." Lisa tells
you later that Bobo's been smoking that crack cocaine.

****

White people applied for jobs in the Augusta National clubhouse and caddie yard over the years, but Roberts kept them
out. "Now *that's* discrimination," laughs Ike Washington. Did having only blacks on one side and whites on the other appeal to Cliff's
sense of order or achieve a continuity with his youth in South
Texas? Did he care that it enhanced that *Gone With the Wind* atmosphere of masters and slaves?

As for admitting a black *member*, that would have been completely preposterous. First of all, why should they, other than to con-
form with some liberal's idea of correctness? The National was a
family, after all, a white family, and disinclined toward black in-laws.
It was not a high school. Cliff told nigger jokes (and passed them
along in writing to President Eisenhower), yet he loved and respected Bowman Milligan, a black man, without apparent conflict.

He did not think of himself as a racist. His view on the subject bears repeating: "I'm talking about the members of Augusta National who lived in Augusta, Atlanta, and various other Southern
states," said Roberts in the oral history. "Almost to a man they just
said, 'Integration means one thing. It means mixed marriages.' I
don't mind admitting to you that those people were a lot more right
about it than I thought they were at the time." Based on his work in
the melting pot of Brazil for Joroberts, Cliff ranked the races thus:
white, black, mixed. "The mixed are the worst," he said. "They are
the most worthless of all in every respect."

Roberts was watching, of course, when in September 1957

Ike had to call in the 101st Airborne so that nine black children could enroll in a high school in Little Rock, the worst constitutional crisis since the Civil War. Arkansas governor Orval Faubus simply closed down the town's public schools the next year rather than submit to any more of the federal government's intrusion into his state's affairs. Faubus and *Brown* v. *Board of Education* kept the country in an uproar over integration and civil rights. The chairman suddenly realized the potential public relations disaster for Eisenhower if a black man applied for membership to the National and was turned down. "So we had to get busy in a hurry and change our procedure around entirely, so that no one was ever turned down," he said. *Race* was the reason for the invitation-only new-member policy, not the enduring popularity of Bobby Jones. In the oral history, Cliff recalled his pride at being able to keep any listing of the ethnic makeup of his members out of the press. Once a writer asked, " 'Well, do you have any Jewish members at this time?' I said, 'I can't answer that question because that is not one of the questions that an invitee is expected to tell us about.' "

The interviewer for the oral history asked, "So you were completely in the clear, in terms of membership requirements?"

Roberts replied: "We were completely in the clear to our own satisfaction, put it that way."

Cliff couldn't be quite so coy on the more public issue of a black player in the Masters. Every other major sport and every other major golf tournament had integrated long before. Through the civil rights cauldron of the 1950s and 1960s, the bus boycotts and lunch counter sit-ins, no black man teed off in the Masters. King, Kennedy, and Malcolm X were killed, the Mets won the pennant, a man walked on the moon, a war was fought in Vietnam, and still no black man played in the Masters.

Veteran golf writer Al Barkow recalls the scene at his first Masters, in 1968, "when Roberts walks into the press building preceded by all these old men in green jackets. And all the writers get very quiet, like the Pope's walked in.

"The next year, I had written a piece that really blasted them, for a lot of things, especially the blacks. I was in the TV truck, watching [producer] Frank Chirkinian, and Roberts comes in. Frank introduces us, and Roberts says, 'Are you the one who wrote that *article?*' And he's nudging Frank; he wants me out of there. But Frank says, 'Nah, let him stay.' " Barkow stayed; Roberts glared.

The era of the groveling press was beginning to end. Jim Murray of the *Los Angeles Times* wrote a column in April 1969 under a headline that read AS WHITE AS THE KU KLUX KLAN:

> The circumstances are well known, but I will recount them briefly here, to the accompaniment of the *Battle Hymn of the Republic* and a recitation of the Gettysburg Address.
>
> Charlie Sifford is a golfer, an American, a gentleman. He is not, however, a Caucasian. Until 1961, this seriously interfered with his life, liberty, and pursuit of happiness, to say nothing of his occupation—because golf was a "Members Only" club till then. . . . Charlie was almost 40 years old before he got to play with the big boys. You can make book Arnold Palmer couldn't have overcome a handicap like that. . . . [Sifford] won two important tournaments, the Hartford [in 1967] and the Los Angeles [in 1969].
>
> Now, one way you can get in the Masters is by winning the championship of Formosa or making a good showing at Kuala Lumpur. Plus, you can be invited by a vote of former champions.
>
> As a two-time tour winner, a guy who had been a victim of 20 years of injustice, and a surrogate for his people who have been victims of 200 years of same, it occurred to me, a sense of shame might have directed that vote to Charlie Sifford this year. Charlie is not any black man, and this would not be tokenism, he is a tour winner under circumstances as adverse as for any athlete who ever lived.
>
> Art Wall, Jr.—and let's hear it for him—voted for Charlie Sifford. As far as I know, the other guys voted for Bob Murphy.

But Murphy had already qualified under another category, so the champions nomination for 1969 was wasted. Once again, no Charlie.

According to Augusta National member Bob Craft, there was no particular pressure to get Sifford an invitation. Even after the one thousandth column echoing Murray, and even after a grand-standing group of congressmen led by Herman Badillo (D., N.Y.) sent Cliff a telegram urging him to invite a black man to compete in the 1973 Masters. "Roberts had no doubts," says Craft. "There were obvious rules and we abided by those rules. Sifford didn't meet the qualifications."

Sifford shot 67 to lead the Canadian Open in '62. Shortly thereafter, according to Charlie, someone from Augusta called the clubhouse at Royal Montreal Golf Club. A sign was immediately posted on a bulletin board: "The Masters golf tournament has announced that it will not offer an automatic invitation to the winner of this year's Canadian Open," which it had in the past. The Royal Canadian Golf Association could not confirm Sifford's charge.

In *Just Let Me Play*, a disturbing account of his trials, Sifford quotes Roberts as saying, "As long as I live, there will be nothing at the Masters besides black caddies and white players." But that does not ring true; Cliff was not a man to show his hand. "Charlie forgets," says Dave Marr. "There were a lot of us on his side, trying to get him to be the first black in the Masters. He deserved it."

While walking in the gallery following Tom Kite and Ben Crenshaw in a 1996 made-for-TV match in Houston, his adopted hometown, Sifford talks about those painful times. A bow-legged man, age seventy-five, Sifford wears lavender pants and matching shirt, sunglasses with two-tone black-and-white lenses, and shoes that match the shades. He speaks with Marine Corps–quality profanity and a slowly burning double Corona in the right corner of his mouth.

"People ask me if I asked Jack Nicklaus and Arnold Palmer for help getting in the Masters," Sifford says. "Shit, I'm stronger than either of them. If they'd been through what I've been through. I didn't *want* any help. All I wanted was a chance to play. Them motherfuckers [in Augusta] kept me out."

Yes, Charlie says, he eventually stopped caring. No, he never met Clifford Roberts. *Fuck* him.

Sifford is silent for a minute, as he walks in the rough by the sixth hole at Champions Golf Club. He has a rolling gait, like a cartoon sailor. "But I'll tell you one thing," he says, with a sudden smile. "I outlived most of those sons-a-bitches."

He never played in the Masters. "With Charlie and Roberts, you had a negative going up against a negative," says Jim Thorpe, the second black man (after Lee Elder in 1975) to compete at Augusta National. "It just wasn't going to work."

****

Court-ordered integration sounds like a dismal thing, but Augusta experienced a fierce excitement from it, even joy. Joy, that is, if your high school football team beat the other guys, who, for a change, really looked like other guys.

The black Lucy Laney Wildcats versus the white Aquinas Shamrocks in 1967. Laney versus the Richmond Academy Musketeers in 1968. Under the lights on Friday night, with the air so charged you could hardly breathe. To those who played or watched, those first integrated high school football games in Augusta deserved the slow-motion camera work and voice-of-God narration of an NFL Films production. "Scholars by day, tape and pads and raw emotion transform these fresh-faced sons of Augusta into Friday night warriors. The fondest hopes and dreams of a city are joined in football's savage ballet."

"Biggest games in Augusta history," says David DuPree, Laney's head coach from 1958 to 1984. "You couldn't even get in the stadium." DuPree's 1966 team averaged fifty-four points a game, while Aquinas coach Tom McDevitt admitted his Catholic boys were "painfully slow." "So he [McDevitt] asked me to hold the score down," says DuPree. When you shook hands before the game? "No, when he scheduled it the year before." Laney beat Aquinas 30 to 0.

"Everyone was amazed afterward that there was no extracurricular activities, no incidents," recalls *Chronicle* sportswriter Bill Baab. "Maybe that's because it was forty-two degrees and rain-ing," says Mike Rucker, a hard-hitting 150-pound defensive back for the losing squad.

The Richmond Academy players joked nervously before their big game with Laney in 1968 about how some of their opponents were twenty, twenty-one years old, with wives and children in the stands and service records. And criminal records. Truth is the first casualty when middle-aged men recall their high school athletic glory, of course. One beer-bellied guy with his hand around a Bud recalled a dozen incidents from the big game, but turns out not to have even been on the team. But another Augustan, long beyond his playing weight, who really did participate remembers the adrenaline gushing into his bloodstream as the Purple Pride Musketeers Marching Band played the National Anthem. And he remembers running downfield on the opening kickoff in the October night, "and I hit that boy with the ball harder than I ever hit anyone in my life. He went one way and the ball went the other way." Richmond Academy 21, Lucy Laney 7. Dancing in the streets on the Hill.

And plenty of dancing in Bell Auditorium, which James Brown integrated in 1964. The celebration at the Bell had nothing to do with sports. It had everything to do with the rise of a superstar entertainer.

In an era when black groups often featured top hats and canes and close harmonies, James Brown was a raspy-voiced dervish, an electrified man in a bright red ripcord suit. "I look like someone you would pay to see," he said, and he was. And his voice! In his percussive shrieks and rhythmic grunts, music critic Bruce Tucker heard history: "ring shouts, work songs and field cries . . . one of the unique sounds in American singing." After his *Live at the Apollo* album in 1962, white kids began attending his concerts in increasing numbers, which was a problem in Augusta and other Southern cities. The awkwardness inherent in segregated seating was worsened by the fact that a James Brown crowd liked to get up and do the Mashed Potato or the Camel Walk. How could you just sit there when James played his chart-topping showstopper, "Please Please Please"?

He'd been back to his hometown a couple of times before 1964, but it hadn't been pleasant. As a parolee, a twenty-four-hour pass from the district attorney had at first been required, and the police escorted him across the bridge into South Carolina immediately after the show. Even the performances hadn't felt right. Blacks sat on one side of the municipal auditorium and whites on the other, with a stage in the middle. Brown hated turning his back on half of his fans to play for the other, so he requested open seating for his second show at the Bell. A Macon audience of blacks and whites together had recently watched James without a problem, so city officials allowed it. And the mingled races in Augusta also experienced the James Brown Revue peacefully. Several months later, President Johnson signed legislation that made segregated public facilities illegal.

James made the cover of *Look* magazine in 1969, and the cover story asked, "Is this the most important black man in America?" Maybe he was. With the fortune that followed his fame, he bought (among other things) three radio stations, one in Knoxville, another in Baltimore, and WRDW in Augusta. He entertained in Vietnam and at Nixon's inaugural party. He filled Yankee Stadium for a concert and basked in the warmth of homecoming and acceptance when Augusta held a James Brown Day. But trouble loomed.

When James bought a house at 3560 Walton Way in one of Augusta's nicest and whitest neighborhoods, his new neighbors offered him double the purchase price to move out. He refused, and at Christmas decorated his big front yard with, oh Lord, black-skinned Santas. In May 1970, a month after Billy Casper won the Masters and a week after the Ohio National Guard killed four students at Kent State, a riot erupted in Augusta. Someone—police or other inmates—beat a sixteen-year old-black kid to death in his jail cell. Then another someone burned a Georgia flag at the culmination of a protest march, police moved in, rocks were thrown, and the violent cycle of fires and looting lasted for days. Brown walked the streets of the Terry telling people to go home and broadcast appeals for calm on his radio station. He met with Governor Lester Maddox at the WRDW studio on Eisenhower Drive. He helped all he could.

****

James Brown and athletics made a modest start at healing the wounds caused by white flight and history. Augusta National had no role whatsoever. But let's not talk about it. Augustans will chat all night about golf and politics and Jesus and other controversies, but race is the elephant in the corner. It's a big subject, but not a proper one for someone whose accent doesn't come from south of the Mason-Dixon line. "I'll tell you this," says stockbroker Jerry Matheis from a French Market Grille barstool. "When Augusta had to change, it made more of an effort than *Boston* did."

Touchiness on racial issues is understandable in any American city. More mystifying, however, is the undying now-who-was-your-momma? contest among white Augustans. Efforts to be or appear more Augusta-than-thou cause one woman to hide her roots in Charlotte like a bottle blonde hides her roots in brunette. Another woman hesitatingly admits she once dated a boy from *North* Augusta. The shame.

A recurring scenario: a frequent visitor to the Garden City of the South is introduced to a group in a social setting. "Tell them where you're from," the introducer urges.

"Dallas."

"No, where you're really from."

"Well, Dallas for the last seventeen years."

"Before that."

"Let's see, Chattanooga, Charleston, Columbia, Atlanta . . ."

"No, tell them where you're *really* from."

The visitor is aware of being checked for Yankee. And finds himself tempted to describe the Civil War musket and army discharge papers that hung above his great-grandfather's bed. In *Chicago*. From the *Union* Army.

Why the impulse to peg? "Of course, we're provincial," an Augustan says. "This is one of the few cities in the United States with a sense of place. . . . My daughter-in-law calls me from New York and asks, 'How are things in the center of the universe?' " Augustans are uniquely gracious and hospitable, but their need to know a stranger's background is acute.

William Lowndes Yancey of Columbus, Georgia, big-pictured the situation in 1855. The Creator, he wrote,

> has made the North and the South; the one the region of frost, ribbed with ice and granite; the other baring its generous bosom to the sun and ever smiling under its influence. . . . Those who occupy the one are cool, calculating, enterprising, selfish and grasping; the inhabitants of the other are ardent, brave, and magnanimous, more disposed to give than to accumulate, to enjoy ease rather than to labor.

Jack Nicklaus of Columbus, Ohio, was ribbed with ice and granite. Augusta didn't like him.

* * * * * * * * * *

Not at first, anyway. The main reason for the disaffection was simple and obvious: Jack beat Arnie. The biggest factor in his redemption, which began in 1965, was equally simple: Jack beat Arnie. And everybody else. Simple excellence was the basis for his appeal.

In the way they swung golf clubs, Nicklaus looped around Palmer to connect with Hogan. Arnie's stroke looked like a punch in a bar fight, but Fat Jack and the Hawk possessed the balanced and precise violence of martial artists. Jack should have worn a *gi* instead of a too-tight polo shirt when he won his second Masters, in 1965. Golf's only black belt shot a godlike 64 in the third round, ten pars and eight birdies. He hit the 485-yard thirteenth and 500-yard fifteenth greens in two with five-iron second shots. His MacGregor driver had a wooden head and a steel shaft, remember, and his Tourney golf ball flew only 90 percent as far as the modern ball, if that. His 67-71-64-69 beat Hogan's scoring record by three shots and Arnie and Gary Player, the runners-up, by nine.

Nicklaus rated the Masters the fourth most important tournament in the world, but the one he wanted to win the most. His admiration for the course and the tournament were so profound, in fact, that he decided to try to more or less duplicate both near his hometown. A transplanted Englishman named Desmond Muirhead would be Nicklaus's Alister Mackenzie. Like Mac, Muirhead had been educated at Cambridge, disliked rough, and had some novel ideas about golf architecture. Pandel Savic, an old friend and Ohio State football hero, would fill the Cliff Roberts administrative role. Jack, of course, would be Bobby Jones.

Did Augusta National inspire Muirfield Village, as it seems to? "Not much," Nicklaus says. "The one thing I like about Augusta National, and other Mackenzie golf courses, is that they are fairly wide open on the tee shots. But I don't think my greens are as difficult as Mackenzie's. . . . I haven't done any that severe."

Ground breaking on Jack's dream course was to be just three months after the 1972 Masters, "the end of a long, arduous process," recalls the principal partner and organizer of the project, Putnam Pierman. But at Augusta, Jack didn't think about his huge investment in money, time, and reputation. His concentration shot out like laser beams in the dark: Masters today. An elk-hunting trip with Pierman and Tom Weiskopf the day after the Masters. Muirfield Village after that.

Months later, Jack had a walkabout with Keith Duer, the head of the construction company building his course.

"That green looks a little steep," Nicklaus said.

"Trevino wouldn't have no trouble with it," Duer replied. For a few long moments Jack didn't laugh and the birds in the trees stopped chirping—at least in Duer's telling of the tale.

Although Nicklaus performed at the top of his game in 1971 (he won eight times that year), he'd also endured a butt-kicking in the two tournaments he cared about most. Both times from Trevino: a play-off loss in the U.S. Open at Merion and a down-the-list finish in the British Open at Royal Birkdale. In a six-week stretch, Trevino won the U.S. Open, the Canadian Open, and the British. So at the time most of the golf world was speculating about the chances of Nicklaus winning all four majors in 1972—"not impossible," Jack said—a rival came into full flower. The situation echoed Palmer in

1964, when Arnie seemed on the cusp of a long run of major wins, but never won another.

Jack lost the pomade and twenty-five pounds in the early 1970s and began wearing stylish, wing-collared cotton shirts from Peerless-Hathaway. His improved appearance coupled with great golf added immeasurably to his success with the fans, which led to many financial opportunities, which increased the similarity of his situation to that of Arnie at the brink of his decline. Was Nicklaus about to be replaced?

Not by Trevino, not at Augusta. Super Mex hated the place. The golf course didn't suit his low, left-to-right ball flight, he said. But what really bothered him was the precious atmosphere at Augusta National. He'd grown up in a shack by a golf course in East Dallas, a Mexican boy without a father, an eighth grade dropout. With his success at golf and a comic glibness, he'd achieved considerable fame and a small fortune. But Trevino was a sensitive man, solitary, a brooder. After his daily comedy act on the golf course and then in the press tent, the curtain came down. He'd order room service and regrip his clubs while watching TV, and wonder, perhaps, where his money had gone; through marital discord and bad management, he'd lost everything he'd made since he got out of Dallas. A star-struck teenager who ate lunch with him at halftime of a taped golf match in 1970 remembers that his hero stared at his plate while he ate and didn't utter a sound. Outside, with the cameras rolling a few minutes later, Trevino zipped out one-liners like a Vegas comedian.

His moody half delivered a locker-room tirade about the oppressive stodginess of Augusta National while Associated Press golf writer Bob Greene took notes. The resultant story offended the club, of course; his agent, Bucky Woy, urged him to own up to the remarks and apologize. But Trevino decided to say he'd been misquoted, which only kept the controversy alive. He declined his subsequent invitations to the Masters in 1970 and 1971, a shocking decision from the first or second best player in the world. Nicklaus, among others, convinced him to play again in 1972. But Lee was still ambivalent at best about Augusta. To illustrate his disdain, he refused to use the clubhouse. The defending United States Open champion changed his shoes, ostentatiously, in the parking lot. To Trevino it seemed like retaliation when a uniform informed him that the range was closed and stuck a RANGE CLOSED sign in the ground next to his practice balls. Then he had an argument with another security man and Ellis "Slats" Slater, Eisenhower's old friend, about badges. "I can drive out the same way I drove in," Trevino said.

"The Pinkerton people have more to say about running this golf tournament than the players do," said Trevino's pal Tommy Bolt after the third round. "It's not hard to feel unwanted here. But everybody's afraid to say anything at all critical for fear they won't be asked back. . . . Now I've said it. Uh-oh."

By then Trevino had shot three let-me-out-of-here rounds of 75, 76, and 77. After his postround stand-up routine for the writers, a shocking thing: between the press building and the parking lot, Clifford Roberts introduced himself and led Lee into his office in the suites building. Reporters timed the meeting: thirty-one minutes. Then they walked up to the main entrance to the clubhouse for a brief tour, ending with a ten-minute talk in the Trophy Room, in front of the glass display case that holds Bobby Jones's clubs. Perhaps the meeting wasn't so shocking after all: hadn't Cliff cultivated relationships with Jones, Eisenhower, General Vargas of Brazil, and hundreds of CEO egos at the National? Trevino was child's play compared to a future president and a South American dictator.

"I was decidedly charmed by that fellow," Roberts declared. "We've got our relationship straightened out."

"I enjoyed it," said Trevino. "He's a nice man. I'll be back next year." And he did return, but all of Lee Trevino never really showed up for the Masters. He tied for tenth a couple of times over the years, but usually he finished thirtieth or fortieth or missed the cut.

Except for the Roberts-Trevino rapprochement, the 1972 Masters was memorable for not being remembered. A 1994 article in *Golf Magazine* under Nicklaus's byline called "My Masters Memories" had not a one from 1972. Arnold Palmer recalls that the widow Eisenhower gave him a kiss on the cheek before play began. "Do your darnedest," Mamie said from the porch of the cabin. Arnie's darnedest was a 70, only two off the lead. But on the second day he got an unfavorable ruling on an embedded ball on the ninth hole, got mad, tripled the twelfth, and finished with rounds of 75, 74, and 81.

The only consistent fun for a viewer of that year's tournament lay in lip-reading. On hole after hole, someone's putt would bounce left when it should have rolled right, and the putter would say "these funky greens" or something like that. As could be expected when conditions were most difficult, Nicklaus won. Bruce Crampton and Tom Weiskopf finished second to Jack for the umpteenth times in their careers (Bobby Mitchell also tied for second, three shots back). "Giveaway golf is the only way to describe my performance in the final round," Nicklaus wrote in *My Story*, his autobiography. "I did just about everything in my power to hand the Masters on a platter to anyone who would take it." Jack shot 68-71-73-74, plain numbers, but good enough for his fourth Masters.

Nicklaus would win at Augusta twice more. In 1975, Jack prevailed in a mind-boggling shoot-out with Tom Weiskopf, the frustrated perfectionist, and the blond sylphlike Johnny Miller, who swung a golf club like a jai alai cesta. Nineteen seventy-five provided the most exciting finish in Masters history—except perhaps for 1986, a magnificent but somewhat flukish victory, since it required the intricate and unlikely eleventh-hour cooperation of Severiano Ballesteros, Greg Norman, and Tom Kite.

At some point—possibly in 1972, surely by 1975—Nicklaus joined Jones, Sarazen, Nelson, Hogan, and Palmer in the sainthood. In a sense, however, Arnie and Jack stand above the others as the only men who galvanized us, who sent a world audience completely over the moon for them as men and for the Masters as a stage.

* * * * * * * * * *

The gloomy and unsatisfying Masters of 1972 was the first held since the death of Bob Jones. Jones went out the way he lived, with dignity and a sense of humor. He converted to Catholicism from his bed at home and invited the priest to have a drink with him after the ceremony. "If I'd known how happy this would make Mary, I would have done it years ago," he said. Eight days later, on December 18, he died. Only family attended the funeral.

A more tangible reason for the Masters' off year was bad grass. A cool wet winter had caused an unwelcome emergence of annual bluegrass (*Poa annua*) on the greens. "Po" stood out in stiff, pale blotches, as if white steel wool had been imbedded in the pool table's felt. It created a visual hazard as well as an actual one; even short putts over its seed heads were unpredictable. This made scores go up, which induced certain pros to bitch. And that reflected badly on Augusta National, which made Cliff Roberts furious. The search for fast, flawless greens was an important part of his larger obsession to make Augusta National perfect. "Our greens were not only too slow for the tournament," Cliff wrote to superintendent John Graves in June 1963, "they were definitely too slow for member play." The chairman then went on at length on the arcane subject of the proper grass mixture for fall overseeding. Eight years later superintendent Al Baston was directed to use this recipe (per thousand square feet of green) for the fall 1971 planting:

25 pounds Oregon rye grass
20 pounds Penlawn fescue
7 pounds *Poa trivialis* (rough stalk blue grass)
3 pounds seaside bent

But apparently some annual bluegrass, Po, slipped through the seed supplier's quality control and blemished the usually flawless greens.

Through his involvement in such things and his willingness to seek out more highly trained minds than his own, Roberts developed a sophistication in matters horticultural and architectural. Club members Julian Roberts and Jerome Franklin knew a thing or two, and so did the USGA, and certain of the Masters players, and George Cobb, Augusta National's consulting architect. Also Jones, of course, until he became too ill to contribute. Their constant tweaking revealed both a huge budget and a rare understanding that golf courses evolve over the years. For example, sand from bunkers, deposited a tablespoon at a time from a golfer's explosion shot, changes both the bunker and the surface it lands on. Top dressing flattens a green's contours. The guy who walks behind the mower shrinks or swells putting surfaces in ways the architect never pictured. Expanding water hazards increases wind strength. Trees multiply, grow, and die.

Cobb might suggest spectator mounds here but not there and explain drainage and aesthetics, how the little hills should be blended in, like muscles on an animal. A dam at the pond on the eleventh and two bunkers behind the green? Yes. Shall we move the bridge on fifteen to the left and enlarge the pond? Yes. Widen Rae's Creek in front of the twelfth hole? Yes again. We don't need that service road between the fifteenth and seventeenth fairways, do we? No, Cliff said, take it out and grass it in. How about some fairway bunkers on the second and the eighteenth? They were duly installed in November 1966, at a total cost of $1,287 (number two) and $1,568 (eighteen).

New grass? Yes; an improved strain of Bermuda grass called T-328 developed by Dr. Glen Burton in Tifton, Georgia, was planted on the greens in 1961 and 1962, and later on the fairways. Hundreds of other courses followed suit, because, as everyone knew, the National used only the best.

A new tree to the right of the seventh green? By all means, as long as it is a pine. "Mr. Roberts always said that this is a winter course, and he wanted winter color," a member recalls. "He didn't believe in trees whose leaves fall off."

What about a new sprinkler system? someone asked in 1970. We've never replaced the original irrigation, and it's high time. Roberts put Phil Wahl on it, and the club manager produced a Masters thesis on the Seventy-five Steps in Designing and Planning Automatic Irrigation Systems and the Twenty-one Steps in Initiating and Installing Them. A wonderfully efficient Toro system was selected, after the company agreed to never advertise that it had gotten the job. But if you were a Toro salesman, you might let it slip to a potential customer that your valves and heads watered the sacred ground in Augusta.

The grass, the trees, and the water . . . what sounds like the start of a haiku was also the starting point of a slow-growing and ever more troubling problem. The National now had hungrier, thirstier grass than before. It also had the most modern and thorough means of quenching that thirst, and pine trees that fed from the same table and were already getting too much to eat and drink. Roberts was adamant that no one see a single blade of brown grass in their Masters closeup. No one thought about the bigger picture, because nothing seemed amiss. But trees and grass are not natural companion plants. Eventually, something would have to give.

****

A Southern writer like William Faulkner or Pat Conroy might have been inspired by the dense psychology of the scene: the reunion of five brothers and sisters on the occasion of the twenty-fifth wedding anniversary of the youngest sibling. At least twenty-six years have passed since they've all been together. Not since daddy's suicide. Perhaps not even since mother's suicide. It's 1947, in Seattle.

"Uncle Cliff took a real shine to me," recalls his nephew Kenneth. "I was three and a half. I sat on his lap the whole evening. . . . He wanted a photograph of all of us together, which Aunt Dot [Dorothy] did not at all want. You can see her glaring in the picture.

"Later, Uncle Cliff sent me a letter about the importance of getting a proper education. For Christmas, he sent me a little green sports coat, which I grew out of immediately. I didn't understand its significance until years later."

Kenneth gradually became aware that his famous and successful uncle was helping his (Cliff's) younger sister Dot and younger brother Bob financially and was putting at least five of his nieces and nephews through college. "He took an interest in me, too, and I was incredibly flattered," Kenneth says. "I thought of him as my second dad, and I might have been the son he never had." In Augusta, Kenneth met Mamie Eisenhower and accompanied her and two Secret Service agents to the drive-in in a limo one night and saw Robert Redford in *The Great Gatsby*. He met Gary Player when he and Uncle Cliff and the little South African simultaneously assumed the position at the row of urinals in the Trophy Room men's room:

"Uhhh, hello, Gary."

"Why, hello, Mr. Roberts."

"Uhhh, Gary, I'd like you to meet my nephew."

At Thanksgiving in 1966, Kenneth, then on leave from the army, received an invitation to dine at the National. "I decided to wear my uniform, dress greens with all my medals, and I couldn't have done anything better. We ate with the president of Texaco in the Trophy Room. Uncle Cliff couldn't have been more proud." Kenneth usually drank champagne at the club, while Cliff enjoyed a glass or two of 1952 Chateau Lafite.

When Kenneth got out of the service, Cliff paid for his final two years at the University of Washington.

A final set of memories of his uncle include Cliff's third wife, Betty, at their penthouse apartment on the beach at Freeport, Bahamas. "The top middle condo of an eight-story building," Kenneth says. "I thought it was neat. I was supposed to get it [in the will], but I didn't." When the Cadillac he'd ordered fell to the dock as it was being unloaded, Cliff had GM ship him a Corvair to replace it. He drove the golf-cart-size car like a golf cart, with one foot on the brake, the other gunning the accelerator. He was the worst driver on an island full of bad drivers. "There'd be eighty people honking at him, and I'd be slunk down in my seat, covering my face," says Kenneth. "But he'd be oblivious." After they'd navigated the trip from the airport to the condo, the old man and the son he never had took long walks together on the sugary sand, sometimes as long as ten miles a day. Cliff, then in his mid-seventies, wore a hat but not a shirt, and he told his brother's son a little about his life.

****

Only a few people saw the chairman as a gently mellowing old gentleman.

Most Cliff Roberts anecdotes depict instead a rigid, self-important man, Augusta National's designated bastard. He acquired a habit of pointedly ignoring or turning his back on people: the president of a big steel company, a Masters contestant, the mayor of Augusta. He ordered the dismissal of TV announcers when a gentle reprimand would have done the trick; maybe he'd just give the damn TV contract to another network. "Roberts had Bill MacPhail [the president of CBS Sports] scared shitless" at that possibility, says former CBS golf announcer Pat Summerall. Amateur champion Bill Hyndman approached Himself one year to express appreciation for another invitation to the tournament. "Don't thank me, thank them," Cliff said, with a vague gesture toward those who had voted Hyndman in. Then he turned and walked away.

Everybody has a Cliff Roberts story.

Golf pro Skip Alexander, April 1951: Alexander almost died in a light plane crash in 1950; his ears were burned off, and somewhat crudely grafted skin covered his face and hands. But he survived, and most people who saw him at the 1951 Masters were moved almost to tears. Cliff was not. He watched the injured man hobble out the front door of the Jones cabin, looked him up and down, and said, "Where's your badge?"

Warren Orlick, as told by Harold Martin: "Orlick, who was later the president of the PGA, was in Cliff Roberts's office in the late fifties," says Martin, a retired golf writer. "His secretary calls in and says, 'Mr. Roberts, the president on line one.' Orlick gets up to leave, but Roberts gestures for him to stay. Cliff listens on the phone for a minute, then he says 'Fuck it, let Dick handle it.' "

Bruce Fleisher, April 1969: Fleisher was invited to the 1969 Masters in honor of his victory in the 1968 U.S. Amateur, in which he wore unhemmed trousers, longish hair, and a puka-shell necklace. He must have looked like the counterculture incarnate to the chairman. "Do I remember Cliff Roberts? Does anyone forget his drill instructor?" Fleisher committed three offenses that almost got him expelled. First, he wore bell-bottom trousers during his first practice round; Roberts ordered him not to set foot on his course again in such outlandish attire. But outlandish attire was all Fleisher owned, so he had to buy a new wardrobe at a department store that night. Second, he hit a second ball to a green in practice, which earned him another visit to Cliff's office. And during the amateur contestants' dinner, Fleisher jokingly referred to the little upstairs dormitory, the Crow's Nest, as the Cat House. No one laughed, "and Steve Melnyk almost choked."

Jack Berry, April 1976: Cliff announces at a press conference that he is stepping down as tournament chairman (but not as chairman of the club) in favor of the gentleman seated on his right, Mr. William H. Lane. "Mr. Lane, I'd like to know . . ." a reporter begins, but Cliff interrupts. Mr. Lane's assignment does not begin until after *this* tournament, Roberts says; until then, I will answer any questions. Berry, impressed by this naked display of power, suggests a headline for his story in the *Detroit Free Press:* ROBERTS PASSES MAS-TERS TORCH—BUT HE KEEPS THE MATCHES.

Tom Schanher, the summer of 1976: Schanher, newly graduated from Ohio State's agronomy school, is happy to get a résumé-enhancing job at the National, even though it pays only three bucks an hour. "We had an irrigation leak one day, so we dug down and found the problem, but we didn't have the parts to fix it. So we left it exposed, just a little hole, with the dirt on a sheet of plywood. Well, Mr. Roberts was an insomniac, and he liked to drive a cart around the course at night. When he saw that hole, he went to Pipe's house [the superintendent, pipe-smoking Lloyd McKenzie, lived on the grounds]. He woke him up and took him out onto the course. And Mr. Roberts said, 'You haul this plywood off here and fill this hole *now.*' "

McKenzie says it didn't happen exactly like that. "He waited until the morning and asked me 'what that damn hole is doing out there.' I explained, and he said, 'Well god*damn*, you'd think a club of this caliber would have adequate parts to fix an irrigation leak.' We never ran out of parts after that."

No, McKenzie says, he didn't find the eighty-year-old Cliff Roberts to be obsessed with the course, just very thorough. For instance, there was the time he discovered that pinecones on occasion jammed a fairway mower's wheels or reels, which caused them to skid and damage a couple of feet of turf. Well, god*damn*, Cliff told the superintendent, why don't we hire someone to pick those pinecones up, and we'll use them as kindling in the fireplaces in the cabins? "If I saw him on the golf course, I'd approach him and ask him how his round was going and see if he noticed anything that needed to be done," McKenzie says. "You didn't want to wait for him to make a list, then call you into his office and read you the riot act."

Cliff turned eighty-three in March 1977. Alone. Unlucky in love his whole life, he and Betty were estranged; she'd moved to Denver. As he told his nephew on one of those long walks on the beach, his second wife, Letitia, had been ill with cancer when he married her and she hadn't told him. Now he, too, was ill, also from cancer, plus he'd had a stroke. Most of his friends were dead. Augusta National was all he had left, so he went there to die.

As was his custom, Roberts returned to the club a few weeks before its opening in October. "He'd only been back a day or so," recalls McKenzie. "I hadn't even talked to him." Someone saw him on the course in his golf cart in the middle of the night of September 29, not an unusual sight. He inspected the demolition work on the old Jerome Franklin house behind the first green, where a new maintenance building was to be built. Then he was gone.

When Mr. Roberts did not show up for breakfast the next morning or answer a knock on his door, a search party was ordered. One of McKenzie's men found the body on the bank of Ike's pond, to the left of the eighth hole on the Par 3 course. Walkie-talkies around the course crackled with a warning to "stay away from the Par 3," which only served to draw everyone there. Police cars, an ambulance, and a little mist surrounded the pond. Roberts lay where he died, wearing only shoes, pajama bottoms, and a raincoat. He'd shot himself through the head with a .38.

* * * * * * * * * * *

I, Clifford Roberts, of Freeport, Bahamas, declare this to be my last will, revoking all my prior wills and codicils:

FIRST: I direct there be no funeral service or other ceremony upon my death and that my body be cremated and the ashes buried at an unmarked spot on or scattered to the winds over the grounds of the Augusta National Golf Club . . .

"Tax reasons, I guess," says Kenneth Roberts about the citizenship switch. Like Bowman, club manager Phil Wahl, former office manager Helen Harris, and five others, his favorite nephew's inheritance from the multimillionaire's estate was just $5,000. Among that handful was Suzanne Verdet, Cliff's World War I paramour. She was eighty-two at the time of her old friend's death, and living in Saint Jean de Luz, a little town near the Spanish border on the Bay of Biscay. She did not die in France.

The bulk of the Roberts estate went to Planned Parenthood and to various Eisenhower-endorsed charities.

The board of governors met three days after his death and "voted unanimously to respect Mr. Roberts' wishes" to install Bill Lane as chief executive officer of the club, according to a letter from Wahl to the staff. Hord W. Hardin was elected vice chairman of the board of governors at the same meeting. "He left a legacy to be attended to and to be continued in the future by a new regime," Wahl concluded. "I pray that out of respect to Mr. Roberts . . . you will lend a hand to maintain the principles of Augusta National Golf Club and aid in continuing its greatness."

And so it came to pass.

* * * * * * * * * * *

Where are his ashes?

The leading contenders in the popular guessing game about the location of Roberts's remains are Ike's Pond, the Par 3, in an urn in the fairway bunker on ten, and "scattered to the winds" from a helicopter hovering above the National. The location of his resting place was the secretive man's final secret.

But John Derr thinks he knows. Derr, a TV/radio/film announcer at the Masters for more than five decades, was a Roberts favorite; he consumed tea and crumpets with Cliff in his suite at ten o'clock most mornings during Masters week. "We were playing the big course one day, and as we finished fifteen, I asked Roberts if my ashes might be sprinkled in the pond there." Derr had been stationed at fifteen for the first seventeen telecasts of the Masters. " 'I've spent many wonderful hours broadcasting here,' I told Cliff, and that I thought it may be the prettiest spot on the course. And Cliff said, 'Well, ahem, um, John, that's a somewhat morbid thought. And, ahem, I don't believe the club would look favorably on such a request. This is a golf club, after all, it is not a graveyard. It is not a graveyard.'

"So when I heard that Cliff had died by his own hand—which didn't entirely surprise me—I called his secretary. 'Where is Cliff buried, Mary? In New York?' 'Oh no, Mr. Derr, he was cremated.' 'He was? Where are his ashes?' 'In the pond in front of fifteen.' "

CHAPTER EIGHT

●

MTV

Larry Mize, a native Augustan, exults after his chip-in
to win the 1987 Masters.

**Severiano Ballesteros, 1980 . . . Tom Watson, 1981 . . .
Craig Stadler, 1982 . . . Severiano Ballesteros, 1983 . . .
Ben Crenshaw, 1984 . . . Bernhard Langer, 1985 . . .
Jack Nicklaus, 1986 . . . Larry Mize, 1987 . . .
Sandy Lyle, 1988 . . . Nick Faldo, 1989**

"Forty-five minutes," the hostess says. So you give your name and inch your way to the bar, where the drinkers are two deep and extraordinarily loud and happy. Waitresses and busboys hustle between the packed tables like little guys the coach has finally let into the basketball game, and they're gonna show him, boy. Frank Chirkinian strides through the bedlam, a short, thick man with a midwinter tan and a gold necklace. He pauses to kiss a cheek, shake a hand, and trade shouted insults. He acts like he owns the place, which, in fact, he does—at least part of it. For promotional purposes, he's buying a lot of the drinks and dinners tonight, the second night of operation for the French Market Grill West in Augusta. Which explains the jollity.

Parallels exist between restaurateur and Chirkinian's old job as a television sports producer for CBS. Both seem chaotic to an outsider, and both look like they'd be fun to try. "McCord! Your ad libs are sounding rehearsed again." "Margey, get this étouffée to table six." "Camera six! Show me the goddamn ball." While one of the partners will actually run the restaurant, Chirkinian could handle the swirl of diners and bartenders and health inspectors with half his brain. Producing a live golf telecast is a much bigger feat, and Frank did it for forty years. He controlled, cajoled, and cursed cameramen and talking heads into brilliance often enough to help make the Masters on CBS into the giant it is today. Only Roberts and Jones had as large a part in shaping the show.

"Frank Chirkinian *is* TV golf," says Bill Hartman, who spent twenty-one years with the CBS affiliate in Atlanta. "He's the expert, the inventor; he is the Masters guy when it comes to TV. He's a curmudgeon, and he enjoys it." His coworkers called him the Ayatollah. John Derr, another old hand at CBS, named the chapter about Chirkinian in his memoirs "I'm Calling the Shots."

The Ayatollah showed his iron hand and his salty way of expressing himself a few years ago, when he tried Gary Bender as the announcer on the fourteenth hole, the least important hole of the network's final-nine coverage. Bender, who was already in Chirkinian's doghouse for saying, "and now Smith prepares to drive from the fourteenth green to the tee," watched as Spanish star Seve Ballesteros crushed his tee ball to within ninety-five yards of the green, a sand wedge shot for him.

For some reason, although he has won the tournament twice, Ballesteros has never been a favorite of the Augusta galleries. Several Georgia fraternity boys jabbered disrespectfully nearby while Seve analyzed his shot.

"Fore, pliz," Seve called out, requesting silence. Seve trills his r's.

"Fuck you, you Spanish asshole," one of the scholars drawled. They continued to talk.

"Fore, *pliz!*" Seve repeated, more loudly this time.

From his tower behind the green, Bender told the waiting nation in his big, Ted Baxterish voice, "Seve is asking his caddie for a four iron."

Chirkinian exploded into the cue line on Bender's headset. "He's ninety fucking yards from the green! He's not going to use a goddamn four iron, you moron!" He continued in this vein for another few seconds and made it clear that Bender had worked his last Masters.

The owner sits down to dinner with his friends at the best table in the place, the one with a chair with a high back and a commanding view of the bar and the front door. It's a scene from the novel *You Gotta Play Hurt* by Dan Jenkins: a colorful and witty cast on the periphery of a major sports event, indulging in witty, earthy repartee rather than conversation. Then—perfect!—just as you finish your red beans and rice, the leading lady joins the group. She is the homecoming queen twenty years later, and still in good shape, to put it mildly. Jenkins would name her Priscilla Sue, but her real name is MJ. She's Frank's ex-wife.

Chirkinian mutters something about the high cost of divorce, then he and Frank Christian take turns imitating Cliff Roberts's throat-clearing speaking style. Christian, a former fighter pilot, is the official photographer of Augusta National. His wife is English; they met when he was in the service over there. Their daughter, a classically trained vocalist, took the best job in her field in Augusta, singing in James Brown's backup group. Dr. Paul Mahoney tells every second or third joke; he and his wife, Audrey, host a famous Bloody Mary party on the Saturday morning of Masters week. Slicker Sam sits quietly at the far end of the table, a small but formidable figure with his silver hair and jet-black eyebrows. Sam is a high-stakes gambler, or was, and he used to own a restaurant in Chicago. He knows Frank Sinatra. Jerry Matheis is a stockbroker and knows everybody.

Chirkinian points at your glass when it gets below half full; you nod; he holds his hand above his head, snaps his fingers, points, and a new drink arrives. "When this frog learns to cook, you're history." "Get that white trash out of here." "Laddie, I don't know where you've been, but I'm glad you won first prize." "The hamster's a ventriloquist." "Greg Louganis's bathing suit." The punch lines and the drinks and the laughter mount, but Chirkinian is miles from losing control.

****

A short highlight reel:
Masters Golf Tournament debuted on TV in 1956, with ten immobile cameras and Chris Schenkel as the host. Schenkel did most of the talking, with occasional comments from past Masters

champions Horton Smith, Claude Harmon, Cary Middlecoff, and Byron Nelson. The first minutes of Masters TV aired on the *Good Morning Show* in New York from seven-thirty to eight on Friday, April 6. The rest of the country got the show a half hour later, plus a half hour Friday night, and an hour each on Saturday and Sunday.

Jim McKay had the helm in 1960; the show was still called *Masters Golf Tournament.* "Look at this mob!" McKay exclaimed as a throng milled around the eighteenth green. The host chattered like a magpie, as if he was on radio, as if he'd forgotten that pictures accompanied his words. As Arnold Palmer stood over a four-foot putt to win, he backed off and looked up at the tower. McKay got the hint and remained silent while Palmer holed the putt. "If you had one comment to make on Arnold Palmer's victory," McKay asked his congenitally reticent colorman, Art Wall, "what would it be?" Not much to work with there.

Commercials were done live and were amusingly unsophisticated by modern standards. The spokesman for the Travelers Insurance Companies opened a magazine to a Travelers ad and held it up for the camera while he spoke. The other sponsor, American Express, put its pitchman on a golf cart in the shade of a big oak by the clubhouse; at the end of his spiel, he turned the cart to drive away, revealing a sign stuck to the back that read AMERICAN EXPRESS.

Roberts did everything possible to take the air out of the first televised champion's presentation, also in 1960. "Now, here are Bob Jones and Cliff Roberts," announcer Jim McArthur said, "of Augusta National Country Club." "*Golf* club," Cliff barked. "Not *country* club. Good afternoon. I am here merely to introduce Bob Jones, the president of the Augusta National. I might explain, however, this is merely a little informal ceremony that we're doing for the benefit of the CBS viewers. The tournament hasn't officially ended as yet because we still have some players out on the golf course. Bob will introduce the top tournament winners. The *apparent* tournament winners. Someone might still beat them out . . ." What a buildup; possibly neither this ceremony nor this winner was the real thing.

Jones seemed to sense the ham-handedness of his partner's

preamble, however, and saved the day. "Ladies and gentlemen," he began, "as you know, Arnold Palmer just won the Masters Tournament." Bob conducted the rest of the five-minute session in Cliff's suite with his usual grace. Defending champion Art Wall did not come down from the TV tower, incidentally, to help the new champion slip into a green jacket, a gesture that later became the linchpin of the presentation.

Cliff's fussy and overcorrect remarks hinted at his lack of comfort with TV. As Frank Hannigan astutely observed in *Golf Digest*, "Roberts deeply distrusted television, because it had the inherent power to determine the reputation of his passion. . . . He, not the network, decided who the sponsors would be, what they would pay, [and] how much commercial time they would get" (only two one-minute spots per hour for each, a fraction of the normal selling time for any TV show). Cliff nitpicked every Masters telecast, had the eloquent Jack Whitaker dismissed (allegedly for referring to a multitude of fans as "a mob"), and generally kept CBS off balance with the choke chain of a one-year contract around its neck. Above all, Roberts and Jones insisted on a dignified portrayal of their tournament, and they got it.

"Yes, we all felt constrained by the rules at Augusta," recalls Pat Summerall, who first worked the Masters in 1968. For example, "This putt's worth $10,000 to Al Besselink" or "Welcome to the $50,000 Buick Open" were stock phrases for the golf announcer, but money was never to be mentioned at the Masters. "Every new broadcaster had to go in to meet the Pope, so I went to Cliff's apartment at the end of the clubhouse," says Summerall. "He poured me a glass of scotch, which I hate, and one for himself."

ROBERTS: You know you're better known as a football player.
SUMMERALL: Yessir, I know that. [long pause]
ROBERTS: What's your handicap?
SUMMERALL: It's twelve or thirteen, Mr. Roberts. [longer pause]
ROBERTS: Well, the best golfer we've had has been Chris Schenkel, who was an eighteen. So you should be all right.

"And that was the end," Summerall says. "I was completely mystified at what it all meant."

No one at CBS ever had a tougher first Masters than Summerall. He'd been known for his grace under pressure ever since he'd kicked a fifty-something-yard field goal for the New York Giants back in the fifties. But it still seemed like a lot to handle when Chirkinian gave him the responsibility of commenting on the eighteenth hole over more experienced hands like Frank Glieber, Whitaker, and Derr.

The hot, dry 1968 Masters came down to two players at the end: Bob Goalby, who was always fighting his temper, and Roberto De Vicenzo, sweet to Goalby's occasional sour. Both played spectacularly well, but both got nervous on the final hole: De Vicenzo missed the green and bogeyed, then Goalby sliced his tee shot into the woods and barely scraped out a par. Summerall described the action in his even tones and understated style as Rob and Bob stumbled home to a thrilling tie. But De Vicenzo and his scorekeeper, Tommy Aaron, two heads-in-the-clouds guys, screwed up the scorekeeping. Aaron wrote down a four on seventeen, a hole the whole world had just seen De Vicenzo make a three on. Roberto signed the card, so the score stood.

Or did it? The Masters is neither a USGA nor a PGA event (although the USGA ties were very strong among the membership, including the first member, who'd won the U.S. Open four times) so, in theory, it could do what it wanted. The camera caught De Vicenzo sitting at the tiny scorer's table by the eighteenth green with his fist over his mouth. Summerall remembers that "Cliff called up and said, 'Don't say anyone won. There's a problem with Roberto's card.'" So while a delegation went to Bob Jones's cabin to see if he thought equity should in this case outweigh Rule 38, Paragraph 3, Summerall filibustered. He read every contestant's score, admitted that the Masters had neither a winner nor any play-off announcement, and recited the scores again. For twenty interminable minutes.

Jones decided at this, his last Masters, that the Rules of Golf should not be suspended. The higher score would count, thus giving a one-shot victory to Goalby. Few people in golf disagreed with the decision, except Charlie Sifford, who saw it as discrimination against an Argentinian. But hundreds of columnists and thousands of fans denounced the club, the tournament, even, nonsensically, Goalby. The De Vincenzo incident marked the lowest-ever point in Masters public relations. (The club tacitly admitted its culpability in the fiasco by replacing the open-air patio table the next year with a spacious scorer's tent.)

"Sixty-eight was the most shocking thing that ever happened to us, and it was the last year that Jones did the interview," Chirkinian says. But no, he says, it was not the toughest broadcast. That would have been 1967, when the American Federation of Radio and Television Artists struck. CBS management manned the mikes, and Chet O'Connell from sales said, on the air, "Here comes Tommy Walker, a member of the Aaron Cup team."

Viewers may have been successfully distracted from the audio by the video, however; for the first time, the tournament was shown in color. "When I walked into the truck and saw those color monitors, I was absolutely bowled over," Chirkinian says. "Black-and-white always gnawed at you. We were always doing *Casablanca*, always relying more on personalities." Meaning Arnie, which wasn't all bad. "Arnold found the camera and the camera found Arnold. They fell in love."

Palmer had stopped winning the Masters and Jack still had his big hips and bad haircut. Thus, the introduction of the new, permanent star of the Masters, the golf course itself—in color—couldn't have come at a better time. From that April to this, golf course superintendents all over the U.S. came to dread the Monday after the Masters. "Gosh, that course is pretty and so perfectly maintained," the callers always say. "And green. Much greener than ours." But to Cliff Roberts, it was never green enough.

"My favorite Masters? I've never been pleased with any telecast I've ever done," says Chirkinian. "I never wouldn't give my arm to go back and do it again. . . . But the all-time best is still 1975."

Nicklaus, Weiskopf, and Miller made that Masters a great tournament; Chirkinian, Henry Longhurst, and Ben Wright made it great television. Both Longhurst (London *Sunday Times*) and Wright (*Manchester Guardian*) were newspaper writers, primarily, and Englishmen. Longhurst first climbed the tower at the sixteenth hole in 1966, after Chirkinian had auditioned him at a lesser tournament the previous year. Longhurst's cultured Cambridge accent gave his commentary just the lofty quality that was perfect for Augusta and reminded the viewer that this was an international event. Although he may have sounded like an Anglican bishop, Longhurst was a rumpled, high-cholesterol bon vivant, amused both at his success in TV and at the pretentiousness of this little corner of the world of golf. "Who christened this tournament 'the Masters' no one seems quite to know, nor is it certain that the pious founders would ever have started it all if they had known what eventually they would be letting themselves in for," he wrote in 1971. "[No] mention of filthy lucre is permitted. . . . All the television directors and commentators have to submit to a solemn lecture forbidding mention of any tournaments other than the U.S. and British Open and Amateur championships and the American PGA (other tournaments on the professional tour simply do not exist)."

His colleagues remember that "Longthirst" breakfasted on bacon, eggs, and gin; that he was not dressed until he had a spot on his tie; that he could not bear to look at his image on a TV screen ("Look at the fucking monitor, Henry," Chirkinian would tease him); and that the vase with a plastic rose that was always near his chair was filled with gin, not water. He'd remove the rose, sip, and replace the fake flower throughout his long, thirsty hours up the tower.

Wright joined the crew in 1973, as the announcer at the fifteenth hole. "I asked Henry if he would critique my performance after my first day," says Wright. " 'Only if you collect me from the sixteenth tower, drive me to the clubhouse, and wet me whistle.' " By then, of course, the vase was empty.

At the clubhouse, the critique was long in coming:

"Henry, we've had five drinks . . ."

"One more."

"Well?"

"Perfectly dreadful. You prattled on like a dripping tap. Remember, my boy: We are only caption writers in a visual medium."

Tom Watson set up the most dramatic moment in Masters TV history back in 1975 by dunking two balls into the blue-dyed water in front of sixteen. The resultant delay made Watson's playing partner, Nicklaus, one of us for a few moments, a spectator watching and listening while both Weiskopf and Miller birdied fifteen. The delay, in turn, made mere viewers of Tom and Johnny as Jack putted at last from forty feet below the hole on sixteen. Weiskopf -11, Nicklaus -10, Miller -9, three holes remaining.

Nicklaus hit his putt, and the cameras captured an unforgettable tableau. Ten feet from the hole, Jack raised his putter above his head, and Willie Peterson bent his knees as if preparing to rebound a missed free throw. Chirkinian stayed with the same long shot as the ball tumbled in, and caught the simultaneous, exultant leaps of golfer and caddie. Then a close-up of Jack in extremis, teeth bared, blond hair aglow in the spring sunlight, his white pants and green-and-white shirt outlined against the shimmering pond behind him. Longhurst did not attempt to speak over the pandemonium except to say, "Have you ever seen such a thing?"

Quick cut to Weiskopf, an emotional man, trying unsuccessfully to look stoic. "Evil music to the ears of Mr. Weiskopf," said Wright, as the crowd's roar continued.

Moments later, poor Tom three-putted from the same area where Nicklaus holed out. Jack won, a shot ahead of Miller and Weiskopf.

* * * * * * * * * * *

Like the people who ran the Indianapolis 500, the Kentucky Derby, and Major League Baseball, Roberts and Jones were afraid of TV. Would anyone come and buy a ticket if they could see the big events on the little tube? Finally, reluctantly, Cliff and Bob decided in 1955 that television was inevitable. Who would lead them into this unknown electronic world?

The National Broadcasting Company (NBC) had the on-course radio broadcast rights, so it had the inside track for TV. But NBC had a formidable competitor in John Derr of Columbia (CBS). The well-met and well-connected Derr took tea with Cliff and visited Bob Jones in his cabin many times over the years, and often mentioned his company's interest in televising the Masters. Derr also befriended Augusta National office manager Helen Harris, and she was apparently charmed by him as well: when Cliff dictated a letter informing NBC that it would have sixty days to consummate a TV deal with the Masters, the letter was sent not to NBC, but to John Derr, Assistant Director of Sports, CBS.

Derr thought about delivering the "misaddressed" message to his friends down the street in Manhattan. But would they do the same for him? He decided they wouldn't. He waited a decent interval and called Roberts, who, of course, had not heard back from NBC.

"We met at Cliff's office at the Reynolds Company in New York in the fall of 1955, with the head men from Travelers and Cadillac," Derr, now eighty, recalls. "Cliff was very precise in what he wanted. He at first wanted no commercials at all. And he did not want to name our announcers but did want the privilege of approving them, which is an important difference.

"Rights fees? We paid very little, I don't remember what. But money was never a big factor; the presentation was much more important. . . . No, it's a little severe to say Roberts surrendered money for control. He just thought of the Masters as his property, and he jealously guarded its image." The Travelers, American Express (briefly), and Cadillac would be allowed to deliver brief messages, but the main product for sale at the Masters would always be the Masters itself, Bob and Cliff's version of golf heaven.

Presumably, there are no ads for hemorrhoid cream in heaven. And if paradise is sponsored at all, the commercials must be few and far between—and dignified. "Hello, I'm Gregory Peck for the Travelers," said Mr. Dignity himself during several one-minute breaks in the Masters broadcast in 1974. Peck was an inspired choice for this particular spot on this particular broadcast. He'd won an Oscar for and permanent identification with *To Kill a Mocking-*

bird, a film in which he portrayed Atticus Finch, a courageous
Southern lawyer defending a black man accused of rape; the Masters was still a year away from its first black contestant. The voice-
over in the equally low-key Caddy ads in 1974 said, "Now people
are seeing another side of Cadillac leadership." As Arnie and Win-
nie smiled and took their seats in a shiny new land yacht, the announcer reminded us that some models got twelve miles per gallon
in the city and fifteen at a steady fifty-five miles per hour on the
highway. These were Arab oil embargo days, and this was "the
Cadillac that makes sense for today."

Did the ads sell more term life and dental plans, more Fleet-
woods and Sedan de Villes? Probably. Rich men and women who
don't watch a lot of TV watch the Masters. Buying decisions are
complex things, particularly for expensive items like cars and insurance, but the scarcity of commercials and their association with
this blessed golf tournament undoubtedly increased their impact.
"People are so cynical about advertising, but the Masters ads take
some of the cynicism edge off," says Pat Madden, an executive with
a San Francisco agency. "They say, 'I don't hate this advertiser as
much.' That's like a precious island in the sea of beer ads."

This continuing triumph of clarity over clutter costs the advertisers surprisingly little. Cadillac and Travelers pay the networks
approximately what the networks pay the Masters. According to
writer John Steinbreder in the May 1997 *Golf Digest,* USA Network,
which shows the play on Thursday and Friday, pays about $1 mil-
lion for TV rights; CBS has the weekend, and pays $2.5 million; for-
eign broadcasters like Tokyo Broadcast System chip in $3.5 million.

Free-market capitalism is stood on its ear at the Masters. The
$7 million in TV rights fees? They could triple it tomorrow; the U.S.
Open isn't nearly as good a show, and it gets $21 million. Logoed vi-
sors for ten dollars? They'd still fly off the shelves at twenty. Parking, food and drink, and most of all, tournament badges for one
hundred dollars, all are spectacularly underpriced. The tournament
turns a profit of about $7 million after taxes, a lot of money but
peanuts compared to its potential.

TV earns far less. "CBS may even lose money on the Masters," says Mike Hiestand, who writes about advertising and media for *USA Today*. "But you know NBC, ABC, and Fox would love to have it. The whole theory is 'We're a network, and events like the Masters are what make us special.'

"A lot of it comes down to client entertainment. You can get a lot more big shots to come schmooze with you at the Masters than if you've got, say, the Houston Open."

Hospitality and money are joined in two identical dark green buildings tucked away in the woods to the right of the first fairway. Their floor plans are simple, just four bedrooms arrayed around a large common area. The club built the houses in 1996 for the exclusive use of Cadillac, Travelers, and CBS during Masters week. Augusta National owns the buildings, of course.

You picture the ecstasy of the leading salesman for the Western Region for fiscal 1998 when his boss tells him his extra effort has paid off. "You're going to the Masters, Harry! Two tickets for the Monday and Tuesday practice rounds for you and Amber, and you stay at the company's house by the first fairway. Whaddaya think!" Harry will love it, of course. The ironic result of the uncommercialized Masters was that it became filled with Harrys and Harrys' bosses. Especially the bosses. Cadillac entertains its suppliers of alternators or shock absorbers. CBS cements a relationship with an advertiser or a big affiliate station with some clubhouse badges and on-site lodging. Travelers makes inroads with any big employer with big insurance needs.

"This has become the corporate Woodstock," wrote John Helyar in *The Wall Street Journal*. "The corporate jet volume forced Augusta's general aviation airport, Daniel Field, to build a control tower that's used one week a year. The membership of Augusta National itself is a Who's Who of corporate America: CEOs like Citicorp's John Reed and General Electric's Jack Welch, [and] billionaire investors like Warren Buffett and Jackson Stephens."

A happy crowd gavottes under the sheltering limbs of the Tree—the big water oak between the putting green and the clubhouse. There's Doug Sanders, once the tour's number-one reprobate, telling a writer he's found the Lord. Golf instructor Wally

Armstrong would like you to know he has a new video. Agents of famous golfers are willing to listen to a new shirt or equipment deal. Magazine editors and advertisers joust. Earl Woods, Tiger's father, sits in the shade on the clubhouse side in a blue canvas director's chair, answering questions into a fuzz-covered microphone. The Tree for the businessman–golf fan is as the Mall for a teenager, but with cheaper food and fewer nose rings.

* * * * * * * * * * *

Augusta settled itself into its present layer cake in the 1980s. At the top of the heap is the Hill, encompassing the Country Club and the National and the best shopping and all those lovely old homes. West Augusta–Columbia County grew like mad and spawned housing developments with prefixes. The various "Gardens at," "Courtyards of," and "The Village at"s contain wide, tree-bordered streets and lovely homes ranging from the $160,000s to the $500,000s. "Nouveau riche," says a cynical Hill dweller. South Augusta has grown, too, but remained "what it's always been–redneck." Downtown is what it is. "They're trying to revitalize, with the River Walk and some restaurants, and I think they're succeeding. But the shopping is not there yet."

Neighborhood is as important in Augusta as it is anywhere, but church is vital. Hard data doesn't exist, but in both attendance and number of churches, the Garden City seems world class. The different Christian sects and denominations are comfortable enough to poke fun at each other: the new, grand-looking First Baptist Church is sometimes referred to by those who worship elsewhere as Six Flags Over Jesus; some locals call St. Mary's on the Hill–a Catholic Church–St. Gucci's; and "The only problem with Baptists is they weren't held under water long enough" is a line almost as old and familiar as "Jesus Saves."

"Intellectually, we can say that all people matter, but in a practical way there are those we don't care about," says Pastor Daniel McCall from the pulpit at Reid Memorial Presbyterian. "But you have never looked into the eyes of a person that God does not care about." The Chancel Choir sings: "Life is light that fadeth never / Life is here, today, forever." You are still attempting to digest this food for thought when you shake the pastor's hand by the front door. Then you go home or to a restaurant for another feast of roast beef, green beans, mashed potatoes, and pecan pie.

The Mize family lived this ritual and loved God and golf and the Masters as so many in Augusta do. Charles and Elizabeth Mize and their three kids worshipped on Wednesdays and Sundays at First Baptist and played when they could at the Country Club. Charlie Mize worked for the phone company, and his employer kept him and Elizabeth and the three kids moving around—Atlanta, Macon, Savannah—but they always moved back home. And they always returned for the Masters, even when it meant having to rent a house for the week.

Charlie's friends at the telephone company handled communications for the Masters, so fourteen-year-old Larry got a job putting up red and green numbers on the scoreboard at the third hole. Picture him jumping up and down on the scoreboard scaffolding when his hero, Nicklaus, made another birdie and Larry got to hang a lower red number next to his name. Picture him endlessly practicing jump shots in the driveway and chip shots in the yard. And picture young Larry Mize picturing things: he met a girl named Bonnie in high school and could see her as his wife; they were married after she completed her studies at the University of Georgia, and he at Georgia Tech. A hundred times he looked at Augusta National from the ninth fairway at the Country Club. He'd walk to the fence and look through the wire at the verdant, empty thirteenth fairway and the plateau of the twelfth green and the eleventh green and its little pond. No one was ever around; he could have scaled the fence and hit a few shots without being detected. But he was picturing things then, too. He never snuck on and he declined invitations to play the National, because he'd fantasized that someday he'd play there during tournament week.

Charlie and Elizabeth's single-minded son could see other things, too. "He's very, very religious," says Charlie. "Much more than I am." Adds Mrs. Mize, very quietly and seriously: "I'm a Christian—a Baptist. Larry's a born-again." They don't fully understand him.

Larry would like to explain. "The birth of my son in 1986 inspired me," he says. "It removed my separation from God. . . . God can't allow anything that's not perfect to be with him. Like if someone gave you a glass of water, but with one drop of cyanide in it." After a wrenching, six-hole play-off loss to Greg Norman in the 1986 Kemper Open, Mize began attending the Tour's Wednesday night Bible study classes. Trying to become the pure, clear glass of water he'd pictured.

Within a year, he won a big tournament. The ten-year anniversary of that win has brought him here at seven A.M., to the Warren Baptist Church on Washington Road, two days before the 1997 Masters. He's the featured speaker in the Fourth Annual Augusta Golf Breakfast.

"On Friday, I was in the last group, and they were watering the greens behind us as soon as we finished the hole," Mize says, recalling the 1987 Masters. "And I remember when they put the water on the third green, it just rolled off, like the green had been waxed. Like off the hood of a car." A thousand people in the church, recent consumers of pancakes and sausage, nod and smile. Those greens were *fast* in 1987.

Mize shot 70, 72, and 72, two behind Roger Maltbie and Ben Crenshaw, one behind Greg Norman and Bernhard Langer. "When I got to the tenth hole on Sunday and saw that I was one shot off the lead, the butterflies in my stomach started to fly in formation." The people in the pews chuckle.

Jodie Mudd started fast and took the lead; then Maltbie led; then Mize, after birdies at twelve and thirteen; then Crenshaw, after Larry hit his four-iron second shot into the water over the green on fifteen. Seve Ballesteros putted from above the hole on sixteen for a share of the lead, but the ball hit the lip and spun away. And Seve held his arms out and threw his head back in his crucifixion pose, and spectators laughed at his extravagance.

Mize crunched his drive on eighteen and ripped a nine iron to six feet above and to the right of the hole. He knew he needed the putt to have a chance at a play-off. He made it. "When he birdied eighteen, I told Elizabeth I wasn't feeling too good," says Charlie Mize. She gave him a two-milligram Valium. Larry went into the Butler Cabin to wait. Seve saved a par from the right side bunker on the last hole to tie Mize, and Norman's perfect putt to win refused to go in. A sudden death play-off began forthwith.

"Oh my God, that's my baby playing with two giants!" Elizabeth Mize whispered to herself.

Her baby hit his drive 320 yards, thirty yards past the giants.

The blond Australian two-putted from the back fringe. The dark-haired Spaniard three-putted from the same area and trudged back up the hill to the clubhouse in tears, his caddie and a Pinkerton trailing two respectful steps behind. The Augusta boy had hit a seven iron to about eight feet, and straight uphill. "If you're ever gonna win your first Masters, you're in the best opportunity right now you'll ever be," said Ken Venturi on TV. But Mize babied the best opportunity he'd ever be, and he and Norman went on to the next hole.

On eleven, Larry again drove far past Greg, even though Norman was normally the longer hitter. Norman had birdied twelve, thirteen, fifteen, and seventeen just to get in this play-off, and he continued to fire at the play-off pins. But too long; his iron to eleven stopped on the green but well past the stick. Larry's turn.

"Often I watch him, not the ball," says Charlie Mize. "He swung and did this [spins his head away in disgust], and I just closed my eyes." The mishit seven iron finished in the bail-out area, thirty-odd yards to the right of the target.

You know from a thousand replays what happened next: Mize bumped the ball with a short follow-through sand wedge on a line a foot to the right of the hole. The first bounce was short of the green, the second bounce on the fringe, then the slow, smooth roll to the center of the flagstick. And in. Larry jumped and whooped and looked to the sky, and in the center of a crying, hugging multitude, his parents swear they felt the earth move.

Jack Nicklaus, the outgoing champion, helped Mize into his jacket in the ceremony on the putting green. And Larry picked up David, his one-year-old son, his inspiration, and held him above his head like a trophy.

The cheers died slowly, and so did his golf game. Mize played poorly for a few years after winning the Masters, but came out of his slump when he came to appreciate the transient nature of beauty and of beautiful moments. " 'All the glory of man is as the flower of grass. And the grass withers and the flowers fall away,' " he says from the pulpit near the end of his talk. "Peter, Chapter One. That's one of my favorite verses."

CHAPTER NINE

•

Communion

Eldrick "Tiger" Woods with Nick Faldo in 1997.

Nick Faldo, 1990 . . . Ian Woosnam, 1991 . . .
Fred Couples, 1992 . . . Bernhard Langer, 1993 . . .
Jose Maria Olazabal, 1994 . . . Ben Crenshaw, 1995 . . .
Nick Faldo, 1996 . . . Tiger Woods, 1997

Perhaps it's no more than an ironic sidebar in the story of this perfect garden: Augusta National is having a little trouble with its trees.

Like Arabs and Jews or lions and hyenas, grass and trees compete for the same food, air, water, and sunlight, the same *space*, and success of the one may mean death to the other. Trees throw out shade, dead branches, and acid from fallen leaves, bark, and needles. Grass counters with greater numbers, the ability to creep, and its own soil-modifying chemicals. Trees predominate in the forest, and grass rules the meadow.

But in the artificial environment of a modern American golf course, the two antagonists are expected to live in peace. Since the playing surface matters more than the wooden obstacles or decorations on it, trees almost always get short shrift. No superintendent has yet been fired for allowing a weeping willow to wilt, but brown-tinged greens or fairways are a frequent prelude to an exit interview. Dr. Jim Watson, a horticulturalist who works for Toro, speaks for an entire industry when you ask him about the problems grass causes for trees on a golf course. "I usually think of it the other way around," he says. Toro makes mowers and irrigation systems; no such industry grew up around trees.

If a tree survives the root cutting of golf course construction, the shock of transplantation, the invitation to disease or harmful insects caused by mowers scalping roots and string trimmers cutting bark, a slower death can await. Drought-tolerant pines, for example, don't know when to say when when several hundred inches of sprinkler water is being served. Minerals in irrigation water that may have a positive effect on the grass may sicken the tree. Herbicides can cause trees to develop thin cell walls. And a banquet of high-nitrogen fertilizer, gravy to the grass, can be poison to a nearby tree, whose feeder roots can extend a surprising distance from its trunk. The root spread of an evergreen, for example, is only slightly less than its height.

But the biggest problem faced by the golf course tree is the widespread assumption that it is immortal. True, trees live a long time; a loblolly pine, for instance, reaches maturity at about 150 years, and can live three centuries. And a tree-human analogy holds in terms of diet: if either eats or drinks too much or ingests too much of the wrong thing, it shortens its life. And maybe it doesn't look so good in middle age.

"This is a widely reported and easily understood situation," says George Blakeslee of the University of Florida School of Forest Resource and Conservation. "No mystery to it: pines are born and bred in a nutrient-poor, pH-poor [acidic] environment. When they get a lot of high pH water, it predisposes them to disease. We need to train golf course people to treat trees more gently, with more respect—and, on the other hand, to leave them alone."

Since the summer of 1931, Augusta National has had the most thoroughly watered, fed, and chemically doctored golf turf on earth. Scores of newer, less efficiently maintained courses in the Southeast have had serious problems with prematurely aging trees; therefore, it would only be surprising if Augusta National *didn't* have a tree problem.

How big a problem? One man with a unique perspective is Desmond Muirhead, the architect of over one hundred golf courses and the author of two books on trees. "Since I first visited the course with my then-partner Jack Nicklaus [in 1972] Augusta National's once-powerful trees have matured," Muirhead says. "Many of them look like frail old men. They are already taking some of them down.

"There's a parallel to obese people, who, as you know, don't live as long, and are more susceptible to disease. We dig our graves with our teeth, you know."

That significantly overstates the problem, according to Augusta National's horticulture department: "The trees at Augusta National are of varying ages and species. Some trees are now reaching maturity, while others are in their later stages. The club has been replanting trees for many years, and the mature trees are continually monitored. There is no isolated problem. Our horticulture program is on-going and integrates the entire golf course and surrounding area."

Deciphering this rare communiqué from the club is a little like reading tea leaves, but *Some trees are now reaching maturity, while others are in their later stages* must refer at least in part to Augusta National's most numerous type, the loblolly pine (*Pinus taeda*). Loblollies, their lower limbs self-pruned up to a hundred feet, create an awe-inspiring effect of cathedral pillars at the National. They form the primary barriers between the fairways and around the perimeter of the course, providing the background and shadow for all the beauty and drama 150 feet below their swirled peaks.

The club has been replanting for many years. You can't replace a 150-foot tree with another 150-footer. Especially not a pine; because of the difficulty in keeping their long taproots intact, large, transplanted pines are often very slow to establish. Another limiting factor is the impossibility of moving very big trucks and digging equipment on and off the tightly confined course. Then there are the unusual underground intrusions of electrical, telephone, and television cables.

Ten or so thirty-foot trees a year are transplanted at Augusta National. "That's a big tree, but you can do it if the root ball is big enough," says arborist Jeff Trojacek. "But wind would be a problem, especially with a pine. You'd have to stake it."

There is no isolated problem. This, apparently, responds to this question: "Have you isolated the problem?" In another sense of isolation, however, you can look out from the high ground by the clubhouse and see the difference in greenness and vigor between the trees on the perimeter of the course and those deeper in the woods, out of reach of sprinklers and fertilizer. Many of the on-course pines have faded like old denim.

Our horticulture program is on-going. "On-going" is corporate speak for unceasing, and of this there can be no doubt. No one should underestimate the quality of the grounds staff at Augusta National or its budget (approximately $2 million a year, but with no practical limit). The most modern methods of diagnosis and cure—aerial infrared photography, vertical mulching, deep-root fertilization, tree injection—are all within the club's reach. Maintenance practices have changed, with an eye to the pines and other trees as well as turf and April bloomers. For example, the maintenance crew has stopped raking up every dead leaf from beneath the trees on Magnolia Lane. By removing its natural food and mulch, the ground under golf's favorite driveway trees had turned to hardpan a few years ago, which was causing nutrients and water to run off. Which could have eventually led to . . . better not to think about that.

Augusta National's tree trouble is not a cautionary tale of rich men failing to control nature by throwing money at it; golf course tree decline strikes the great and the small. Perhaps the lesson is that maintaining a golf course is an unnatural act that can have un-intended results. But Augusta National's budget allows it to play God, and money abhors a vacuum. Within certain natural limits, the club can have the course it wants. Fewer, smaller trees once grew on Augusta National, and the course was more easily maintained be-cause pine needles weren't cluttering every bunker and fairway as much and screwing up the soil. Sam Snead could cut the corner on thirteen. It was windier in the old days, to be sure: "Yes, I noticed that," says Byron Nelson. "They used to have tents blow down and everything." Maybe that was a better, tougher golf course than the wind-blocking giant pine version.

"People at golf clubs tend to become such tree huggers," says Ed Connors, an engineer and golf course builder. "Look at pictures of Pinehurst in the 1930s, when it had a wide open, links look. It's anything but that now. You've got to keep trees at bay. Their nutri-ent and water needs, and their shade, all are bad for grass.

"Winged Foot East had the world's biggest elm tree by its ninth green, and it caught the world's biggest case of Dutch Elm disease. They cut it down, and the turf around that green went from awful to perfect. . . . What happens when an old course loses a bunch of trees? You get a better golf course."

****

The golf course evolved, and the club's leadership changed, and the ghost of Cliff Roberts hovered over both.

If Roberts was the George Washington of Augusta National chairmen, his successor was the William Henry Harrison. Like the U.S. president who caught a cold during his inaugural address and died thirty-one days later, Bill Lane never got a chance to leave his mark. "Bill got the job mostly because he was very competent and well liked, and because he was very close with Slats Slater," recalls an old member. "Slats was quite influential at the club." Eisenhower's fourth for bridge (or golf) had a major financial interest in Lane's food brokerage business in Houston.

Lane presided over the tournaments just before and just after Cliff's suicide, but became ill on Monday of Masters week in 1979. Hord Hardin filled in when Lane could not answer the bell; he was elected chairman following the 1980 Masters. Two months later, Lane died.

Hord W. Hardin was a lot like Harry S Truman. Both were from Missouri, both were stiff as a board in front of a camera or microphone, neither enjoyed anything close to unanimous approval, and both faced comparison to powerful leaders (meaning, of course, FDR and Roberts; Lane's brief tenure had no impact). "Hardin was a trust officer in a bank—not a very prestigious position," says that same member. "He was the least popular of our four chairmen. The basis on which he was chosen caused a lot of strain among us." Meaning? Several sources mention a piece of paper on which Cliff may or may not have scrawled the names of suitable chairmen, and the lines he may or may not have drawn through all but Lane and Hardin. In the atmosphere Hord created at the club—

"conversations would stop when he walked into the dining room"—it was not considered a good idea to inquire too deeply into how he got the job.

On the other hand, Hardin loved private country club golf, he looked good in a blazer, and he had the urge to administer (he'd spent twelve years as a USGA committeeman and two years as the association's president), precisely the qualities the job demanded. The TV contracts were in place, after all, and the tournament and club operations institutionalized.

"This tournament was so well organized by Mr. Roberts, my function is more or less that of continuing what he set in motion," he told the *Chronicle* in 1987.

"I'm convinced if we didn't have the kind of members we have, somehow that would trickle down into the Masters and affect it. We try to be very careful only to elect to membership people who are basically golfers. Not just good players, but people who think the game is important and should be preserved, not used."

Hardin is usually credited with or blamed for two bold changes during his otherwise conservative administration. He acquiesced to those who wanted the National caddies out of the Masters, and he converted the greens to bent grass. Bent is a northern grass that would ordinarily die in the heat of a Georgia summer, but it is a faster, smoother putting surface than rye grass seeded over Bermuda, and it looks greener on TV. Roberts, not Hardin, was really responsible, however; it was his last big project. After years of planning and discussion, he ordered the experimental planting of fine-bladed, smooth-putting bent in the fall of 1977, on the chipping green on the east practice area. The Par 3 got bent in 1978, and the big course greens were sterilized, aerated, sanded, and seeded with Penncross Creeping Bent in 1980. But Augusta cooked in a particularly hot summer and a lot of that northern grass just said no. That fall the members were forced to live with the horror of five temporary greens—on six and on the always problematic tenth, eleventh, twelfth, and thirteenth. From too hot, the weather quickly got too cold, and the second planting wouldn't germinate. Superintendent McKenzie saved the day when he covered the greens in plastic and inflated the covers with warm air. With the installation of double rows of misting heads around the greens, the grounds staff was able to keep the grass cool enough to thrive during ensuing summers.

"Now the greens are unreasonably fast, much too fast for their steepness," said Dave Marr shortly before his death in October 1997, expressing a sentiment widely shared among the players. Administrators argue that very fast greens are the only way to maintain the old course's integrity, now that modern equipment has shortened it so much. (How much? "Three to four clubs," says Ken Venturi.)

Hardin reigned until 1991. "Hardin was resisting retirement, but then acted decisively to install his own candidate," it was reported in *Golf Digest* in August 1991. But he didn't resign, as it said in the papers, and he didn't choose his successor. "I want to talk about how to make this club fun again," Calvin Coolidge told a meeting of thirty members around the time of Hord's ouster. Comparing long-faced Jackson Stephens of Little Rock to the pinch-faced Vermonter who was the thirtieth president may be a stretch, but both Silent Cal and the new Augusta National chairman served with some reluctance, and both were businessmen who possessed an economical way with words. What's causing all this unemployment, Mr. President? someone asked. "Too many people not working," he replied. . . . "Hord would talk to you for an hour," a newspaper editor recalls. "But it's hard to get a word out of Stephens. You measure his speech in geologic time, and he gives you this slow, country-boy look, but he's smart as hell."

And rich as hell: when a new member bragged during a clubhouse card game about his net worth, Stephens shut him up by asking, "Want to cut for it?" and meaning it. He made most of his first billion in oil and gas and in Stephens, Inc., a treasury bond trading company his brother Witt founded in 1933. His large early investments in Wal-Mart and Alltel, a telephone company, also did exceedingly well. He was a major political supporter of his naval academy classmate Jimmy Carter. Another testament to his power is that he got University of Arkansas football coach Frank Broyles into the club. Broyles is the club's only "celebrity" member. Stephens's power at Augusta National is such that the chairman-in-waiting, Joe T. Ford, is also from Arkansas and also from Alltel. Joe, not Jack, represents the club during the post-Masters green jacket ceremony on TV.

Stephens, a generous man, has reportedly given thousands of shares of Alltel stock to former National employees with inadequate fixed incomes. When an impoverished football player recruited from Florida showed up in Little Rock many years ago without a winter coat, Stephens escorted the youth to a men's store and bought him something in gray wool. The football player was Pat Summerall. Some suspect the chairman also is giving away some of the estimated after-tax tournament profit of $7 million—but privately and anonymously, so the club is not hounded by those seeking help.

As much as any of his predecessors, Stephens believes in allowing Cliff Roberts to run the tournament from the netherworld: "Cliff's our Bible," he said in his annual meeting with the press in 1997. "The way he ran it is the way we assume it should be done. . . . Our primary objective is to maintain the philosophy that was handed down by Cliff and Bob Jones."

But Stephens and Hardin faced a politically correct world Roberts and Bob never dreamed of. When a reporter asked the chairman of the golf club in Alabama that was hosting the 1990 PGA Championship if Shoal Creek Country Club had any black members, Hall Thompson said no, and you can't make me (Thompson, coincidentally, was and remains an Augusta National member). The resultant public relations firestorm led to the PGA's announcement that it would not sanction tournaments at clubs that weren't racially mixed. Then the USGA followed suit, then the PGA Tour. A crisis loomed for Augusta National. What would Mr. Roberts do? Cliff would rather have eaten sand than allow some outside group to monitor the membership for ethnic diversity, but he'd also dedicated a lot of his life to making the Masters a success. The club decided the continued existence of the Masters transcended other considerations. Just weeks after "Shoal Creek"—the new shorthand for the birth of American professional golf's affirmative action plan—a black man named Ron Townsend received an invitation to join Augusta National Golf Club. Townsend, who owned the CBS affiliate in Washington, D.C., accepted. Charlotte insurance executive Bill Simms became the club's second black member in 1994, but resigned in 1997 over work problems unrelated to his membership.

Other gusts rippled the National's flag in modern times. A time-carding, drug-testing subcontractor took over its caddie program; two members were dismissed for selling guest privileges; the club and the 1996 Atlanta Olympics flirted briefly with golf as an exhibition sport with the National as its host, but nothing came of it; and President Clinton gave a speech at Augusta State University, but his hoped-for invitation to play golf at you-know-where did not materialize. Trifles, all of them, compared to the Masters of 1997, when the Golfer Formerly Known as Eldrick blew through Augusta like a hurricane.

* * * * * * * * * * * *

Sadly, sweetly, the flowers of Augusta come out two weeks before the tournament. Premature bloomication disappoints most Augustans, who prefer Masters visitors see the city at its prettiest. Something in the fragrant air tells you to visit all the old familiar places, and all the people you've been meaning to see. Because who knows if you'll ever be back?

The dusty, arthritic Bon Air has become, inevitably, a retirement home. Sure, you can look around, says the lady at the desk. The ballroom? You'll need a key. Here. You're welcome. Up the stairs and to the left. The gaping lock looks like it could be opened with an unsharpened pencil. You whistle "In the Mood" to test the acoustics, and then the big narrow room is silent. Cloudy light through dirty windows illuminates the delicate crust of ancient paint on the ornate, eighteen-inch-wide ceiling trim, big chunks of which are missing. On the dark brown hardwood floor are faint tracings of something—the chalk outline of a body? No, a shuffleboard court.

Across the street is the Partridge Inn, the last of the old hotels. A huge wooden building, the Partridge creaks and pops at night like old bones, as if after a hundred years the nails are still getting used to the lumber. From your bed you hear sighs and coughs in adjacent rooms or the sharp scratch of a key in a lock from the hall. When you turn on the window-unit air conditioner, it sounds like an idling diesel truck.

You eat again at Luigi's, lasagna, and an ouzo on the rocks for dessert, and examine the signed photographs of happy Masters champs on the wall.

The following morning at ten, Mayor Larry Sconyers is happy to meet you in his office. Yes, *the* Larry Sconyers, Boss Hog, purveyor of the best pork-pig sammich in Georgia. His restaurant received national acclaim as the occasional caterer to the White House during the Carter administration. "Consistency and big portions" have been the keys to success, Sconyers says. "My daddy said, 'I don't want to get up from the table and feel as hungry as when I got here.'"

The mayor discusses the problems of consolidation (Richmond County and the City of Augusta have merged), the difficulty of applying business principles to government, and the fractiousness of the commissioners. What, you ask, does the Masters mean to the city? "For us not having anything to do with it, it's one of our greatest assets," His Honor says. He puts Barry White of the Augusta Convention and Visitors Bureau on the speakerphone to give you the 1996 numbers: about 217,000 attended, and spent, conservatively, $215 each per day outside the gates. Hotels tripled or quadrupled their rates. (Shantu Patel, general manager of the Days Inn on Wheeler Road, multiplied his basic rate by five and still filled up.) Total economic impact: about $108 million.

Often you hear about the tension between Augusta and the Masters. Local retailers get bullying letters from the National's lawyers over highly doubtful cases of trademark infringement; Augustans whose daddies and granddaddies supported the tournament when it was nothing to complain about losing inherited rights to a ticket; Bryant Gumbel asks in a TV special what the tournament donates to local charities. But $108 million spreads a lot of love.

After the Masters but ahead of Sconyers in Augusta's hierarchy of stars is James Brown. "James Brown Enterprises—The People Man" reads a brass plaque embedded in the sidewalk out in front of the Godfather's office on Medical Center Drive. The sign by the door of the single-story brick building informs you that "Television-Recordings-Movies-New Talent" is the business within. The reception room has sleek black furnishings and imitation leopard-skin wallpaper, but it never seems to contain the People Man. He's touring or recording or rehearsing . . .

"James Brown was my manager, in 1983," says Lynne Houston. She sits at your table for the last minute or two of her break between sets at Henry's Piano Bar on Washington. She leans back to blow cigarette smoke up into the smoky air. Spangled white dress, blond hair. "He bought the rights to six of our songs but never recorded them. I love him dearly, but—"

"But you better catch him either right before or right after he's lost all his money," says Jeff, Ms. Houston's husband. "He's made and lost several fortunes." Brown is no icon in his hometown, where they know his failures better than mere fans from elsewhere around the world. For example: Georgia and South Carolina courts sentenced Brown to six years in prison in 1988 for fleeing the police after a complaint that he was carrying a shotgun in the building next to his office in Augusta, looking unsteady on his feet. The police punctured his pickup truck with twenty-three bullets, and James drove six miles on his wheel rims. He served a year and a half, then endured a period of work-release at the Lower Savannah Work Center, an incomprehensibly severe punishment for the only crime he was charged with, a traffic offense. Obviously, he doesn't want to talk about it.

Having failed to even say hello to James Brown, you bid a tentative good-bye to Augusta's golf courses. Again you play Forest Hills and the Patch, the muni course that hugs the runway at Daniel Field. A friend invites you to play the Country Club. Like a tourist, you pause for long moments on the ninth hole to peer through the fence that borders the National. The twelfth green reminds you of the best shot Gary Player ever hit, a hole out from a buried, downhill lie in the back bunker. The thirteenth reminds you of the perfect drive Bernhard Langer hit there in the final round in 1993, and of the perfectly awful second shot Billy Joe Patton hit in 1954. The eleventh is Larry Hogan Mize and Ben Hogan.

The azaleas and every ornamental tree on the place are in bloom. You whimper a little bit at the beauty of the place, and at its inaccessibility, then hurry on to finish before dark.

> The low grass loaded with dew
> the twilight stood as strangers do
> with hat in hand, polite and new
> to stay as if, or go
>
> A vastness as a neighbor came
> A wisdom without face or name
> A peace, as hemispheres at home
> And so the night became
> —"Evening" by Emily Dickinson

* * * * * * * * * * *

I tell you what.

Lee Trevino popularized the indispensable golf pro expression of the 1970s. As in "I tell you what, it rained so hard last night, my alligator shoes started to walk out the door" and "I hit the ball good today, I tell you what." After that country-boy stock phrase faded came the odious "bottom line" of the eighties. "Bottom line, I just didn't putt well today." That accountant's verbal tic died with trickle-down economics, only to be replaced by the transcendent, touchy-feely use of the word "about," especially in a "not about—not about—about" construction. "It's not about money. It's not about endorsements. It's about winning." "Putting is what it's all about." "About" users see the big picture, and feel—bottom line—the essence of things. I tell you what.

Earl Woods is an "about" man. Whether from his military training, his tours of duty in the Mysterious East, the discrimination he experienced as a black man in white America, or all three, Woods wastes no time on trivia. Missions defined and missions accomplished, goals and a global perspective, that's what he's all about. How can I help my child become a golf champion? Earl Woods has a plan. Buy his book. The Masters? "The average golfer that goes there is blown away with Magnolia Lane and the history and tradition," he said when his son debuted at Augusta in 1995. "That doesn't impress the black golfer. Black golfers have nothing in common with Bobby Jones, no historical ties with Bobby Jones. They prevented blacks from being here for many, many years."

Deacon Palmer, Charlie Nicklaus, and Colonel Bob Jones fathered sons like Earl's, but there the similarity ends. First of all, they were white men: a golf pro, a pharmacist, and a lawyer, none of them Green Berets or anything like it, none of them married to Kultida Punsawad of Bangkok, Thailand, or anyone like her. Earl Woods's perspective and the height of his profile in his son's life set him apart. Golf history had seen Tiger several times before, but it had no precedent for Earl Woods.

He played baseball for Kansas State. "I was the first black player in the history of the school and the history of the conference," he told *Executive Golfer* publisher Ed Pazdur in 1996. "We would go on baseball trips, like to Memphis. And I would have to eat and sleep on my own. . . . We played the University of Oklahoma in Norman. The team would stay in the dorms and I would have to drive to Oklahoma City and get into a black hotel."

After college, Woods served twenty years in the Army: one tour of Germany, two of Vietnam, one of Thailand. "I was assigned as an advisor to Lieutenant Colonel Nguyen Phong," Woods said. "Phong and I were in combat all the time. Because Phong fought like a tiger, I named my son Tiger in his honor."

In Thailand, he met Kultida, an army secretary. "The reason we didn't marry in Thailand was because the command chaplain had to approve it and you had to be interviewed. No one, other than me, can determine who I marry and when! I went back to the U.S. and made arrangements for her to come over and we got married in New York [he, for the second time]. That was in about 1965."

Eldrick was born December 30, 1975, the same year Lee Elder became the first black man to compete in the Masters. Earl placed a sawed-off golf club in his baby's crib. Little Eldrick hit balls from his walker at six months, took up the game at age two, and won more juniors events than he and Big Earl could count. At age fifty-six, Earl quit his job as a contracts negotiator for McDonnell Douglas to take his twelve-year-old son around the country to play in golf tournaments. "Put yourself in his place," Earl said. "Say you're in Africa and you're the only white guy playing. How would you feel? He had me for support, for help, for guidance, and for strength."

And put yourself in the father's place, pulled by the instinct to protect his son and pushed by financial realities. His two pensions did not make him rich, and travel was expensive.

From a distance Mr. Woods looked like just another athletic stage father trying to live or relive his life through his kid. He seemed unusual only for the chip on his shoulder and for the lengths he'd go, like hiring a sports psychologist for Tiger at age thirteen. "I view myself as a person who was chosen by God to help my son to his appointed destiny," Woods told Pazdur. "I was selected and prepared to be Tiger's father. Tiger's mother was selected and prepared to be his mother." Tida taught the child Buddhism, and Earl exposed him to his Protestant faith.

After Tiger spoke to the press on the day he turned pro, Earl took his turn. "There is no comprehension by anyone on the impact this kid is going to have, not only on the game of golf, but on the world itself," he said. His increasingly grandiose evaluations reached an embarrassing crescendo when, in the pages of *Sports Illustrated*, he compared his son to Indian religious leader Mahatma Gandhi. He's tried to tone it down since.

At least he didn't screw the kid up. On the contrary, Tiger's biggest fans are the people who know him best. And Tiger's best friend, he says, is his dad. So forgive the father of the prodigy for his pride. Tiger Woods won six consecutive USGA championships, three Juniors, and three Amateurs, his fifth tournament as a professional, and the full-court press of late-twentieth-century adulation.

He also won a fortune from Nike and Titleist the day he turned pro, something like $60 million. "It wasn't about the money," Tiger said. "It was about happiness."

* * * * * * * * * * *

Compared to Masters past, the 1997 traffic seems more snarled, the walking scalpers more numerous and purposeful, the ticket have-nots more desperate. "It's Nike," everybody says. "They're buying up every badge." Demand is driving prices to unheard-of heights.

Practice-round attendees suffocate each other. The problem isn't so much that too many tickets have been sold, explains Chairman Stephens at his press conference, but that attendance is nearly 100 perfect. In other years, you could count on some no-shows.

Two Augusta boys break away from the mob and head for the exit, not even bothering with the highlight and finale of the three-day warm-up, the Wednesday afternoon Par 3 contest. "It used to be fun, when you could move around and drink a beer," Danny says. "Now, we play golf during the Par Three." He and Mike walk to the lawn of the Stephens cabin, where Mike's dark blue Cadillac is parked. "What the hell, let's go down Magnolia Lane," Mike says, waving jauntily at spectators and uncertain security guards while he glides down the sun-dappled tunnel. The Caddy rolls southeast for forty-five minutes, over the pine-covered hills of Gracewood and Hephzibah to Waynesboro, where Sherman's outriders jab-stepped toward Augusta during the Civil War. At noon the big car's tires crunch the gravel parking lot of the Waynesboro Country Club, and Danny and Mike disembark for the Lauderdale. A Lauderdale is not a fort in Florida but Georgia-speak for a scramble-format competition. And Waynesboro CC is not Augusta National, nor are the golfers thereon Masters in any obvious sense.

The front nine is a search for what Walt the Pharmacist calls "the beer zone." Tom from Atlanta reveals that he has a book coming out, *The 364 Letters of Marilyn Monroe and JFK*; Mully the Lumber Broker observes that he's never read a book without the word "throbbing" in it. John the Cigar Man wails that his ball has rolled slap out of bounds ("slap": *Ga., adv.*–"completely"). With the bets even, the Lauderdale devolves into a cozy tensome on the back nine, five against five, like a basketball game. "Miss it, miss it," Tat the Banker whispers sincerely and quite audibly at a crucial juncture, and Danny and Mike's team falls one down with one to play.

The eighteenth at WCC is a 420-yard par four with woods and single-family dwellings on the right, and a pond and bunker crowding a too-small, sloping-away green. Team Tat scatters the ball all over creation, and lies two, forty yards left of the green behind some trees. Danny, an insurance man who's had difficulty finding his beer zone, answers with the best shot of the day, a high, faded five iron to eight feet. He putts first and makes it for a hard-fought tie, and all ten participants seem happy to keep their twenty-dollar bills. We'll get you sumbitches next year, they all say, and slap backs and shake hands. "Things like this are the best part of the Masters," Tat the Banker says. "The reunions." Danny and Mike head back to Augusta in a celebratory mood.

Mike pushes in a tape. The Allman Brothers, Georgia's greatest rock band, begins the musical interlude with "Statesboro Blues" while Statesboro, Georgia, forty miles to the south, recedes in the distance. Then a little Led Zeppelin, followed by an extended set of Beach Music, the make-out sound track for Georgialina boys and girls of a certain age. We're talking about the Tams and the Drifters here, not the Beach Boys or Jan and Dean. Mike, who's in personnel at the bomb plant (otherwise known as the Savannah River Site), completes his seated pantomimes of Richard Betts and Jimmy Page with his impression of Jerry Butler performing "Mr. Dream Merchant."

Danny hurries home to shower and change. He's got two pool parties to attend tonight, maybe three.

* * * * * * * * * * *

Everyone's talking about Tiger at the first pool on the Hill, and about the insane prices being paid for a badge. Tiger is the first player sold in the pool (no one says Calcutta anymore), for $460. But you know something, and don't want Eldrick anyway. For just

$70, you buy a guy who drives the ball and attacks pins like a young Nicklaus. Three months before he'd shot 28-34—62 at Pebble Beach, a course record, and almost won that and a handful of other tour events.

Yet despite his Vandyke, his Oakleys, the dip under his lip, and his disrespectfully low scores, David Duval, twenty-five, is a throwback. His father, Bob, was a golf pro, and so is his Uncle Jimmy, and so was his grandfather, Henry, or "Hap," as they called him at his club in Schenectady. As a boy, he worked for his dad for minimum wage, pickin' up the range, cleanin' out the golf carts, connecting himself to the club professional tradition which died out in big-time golf twenty-five years ago. Duval, twenty-five, also has ties to the gentleman golfer era of Bobby Jones. Like Jones, Duval graduated from Georgia Tech, and he *reads* in his spare time, and not just *Golf World* or Michael Crichton. Recently he's been wading through Ayn Rand, the author of deep, phone-book-thick tomes like *Atlas Shrugged* and *The Fountainhead.*

"No, I never pushed him at all," his father says. "Sure, he played other sports. Baseball, mostly, third base and pitcher. Pretty good hitter. Don't throw him a low fastball."

"I have some goals, but not a whole lot of them," Duval says on Tuesday. "If you get too specific, you lose sight of your progress."

On Thursday he shakes Byron Nelson's hand on the first tee, then blasts off, seemingly as cool within as the chilly sixty-degree day. He hits the green on ten of the first eleven holes, but he's scrambling for pars, because all his birdie putts but two are from the wrong side of the hole. On twelve, Augusta National's mystery hole, Duval hits a seven iron over the green. Chip, chip, putt, putt, and he has a double bogey, and a jaw that won't unclench for two holes.

When his drive drifts a little left on fifteen, Duval punches an iron short of the pond, sixty-four yards from the hole. He lines up the shot from behind the ball, exhales like a woman in a Lamaze class, rolls both shoulders, then steps to the plate. His sand wedge to the back left pin lands ten yards onto the green, bounces forward a foot, then spins violently backward. The grandstand crowd's voice starts low, then rises excitedly as the ball reaches the edge of the green, then falls back down to the key of D minor when it slips into the water like a little turtle. Duval, refusing to give in to emotion, walks back sixteen paces and drops another ball. He can take a swing at an eighty-yard shot, maybe hit it close and save a six.

Line up, cleansing breath, shoulder rolls, hit. Skid, spin, slide, and back in the water, the same goddamn thing. Duval's nine on fifteen plus sixty-nine on the other holes equals 78, and awkward moments for the supporters who encircle him between the eighteenth green and the clubhouse. Only with his blond wisp of a girlfriend, Julie McArthur, can Duval manage any animation. To the others, he can only manage a shell-shocked "Man, I hit it damn good."

"He hit fifteen greens. You're supposed to shoot three-under, not eight over when you do that," states Buck Levy, a friend from Colorado. "On sixteen holes, he's one ahead of Tiger. But on twelve and fifteen, he's nine behind." Tiger, omnipresent Tiger, has shot 70, two shots off the lead. He made two and three on the twelfth and fifteenth, where Duval scored five and nine.

"I've got an extra badge for Sunday." "Can you believe Tiger's back nine?" "I'll sell you Nick Faldo for ten bucks . . . five." "And she's down to here, and out to there, and up to here . . ." A woman at the Thursday party is describing the outlandish architecture and clothing of some young hussy at the tournament. Which reminds you of the walk up the hill to the eighteenth green today: a sweet young thing, Jell-O on springs, walked arm-in-arm with her swain. Behind them trudged two game but osteoporotic women wearing hats decorated with badges from Masters past. "Showin' it all, ain't she," remarked one dowager dryly, almost loud enough for the girl to hear.

* * * * * * * * * * *

Danny answers the phone on Friday morning. "Oh, no," he says. "Oh, no." He hangs up the phone and sits down heavily, his face vacant. What? "Allen Caldwell shot himself last night. I can't believe it. He was a good boy, too. I just can't believe it." Caldwell, a local man, brokered Masters badges. He'd buy low from longtime customers he knew and sell high to a "hospitality company," which packaged the tickets with lodging, food, and maid service. But as a veteran of the badge wars told the *Chronicle*, buyers for several corporations had come into town and turned the market upside down.

"The prices basically doubled overnight, and whoever he was supposed to be getting them from sold them to somebody else for more money," the broker said. A gray-market badge that had sold for $3,000 in recent years was this week fetching $8,000 and up.

Dead men and Masters badges. . . . A few years ago Augusta National security discovered that about twenty deceased and imaginary CBS employees were being issued badges. One of them, a Mr. Dark, was a lighting specialist. The club took the credentials back, and stern letters were undoubtedly written, and the incident became a cocktail party story. A man kills himself over Masters tickets and that's what you think of.

Duval shoots 72 on Friday and misses the cut. Woods shoots 66 and grabs the tournament by the throat. The Augusta National Communications Department issues a bloodless statement reminding us that selling badges violates club policy and its agreement with badge recipients.

On Saturday morning, you find yourself at a funeral home downtown. You stand there in your tennis shoes and red windbreaker with people in dark suits and dresses; Danny knows these people and must pay his respects before going out to watch the third round. Allen F. Caldwell III lies in an open coffin, a handsome man, mustache, age forty. His wife sits close to someone on a little bench near the front door, her right hand over her eyes, her shoulders heaving. Their kids stand near their mother and look bewildered.

The stakes are high at the Masters.

* * * * * * * * * * *

Many of the old members had gathered on Wednesday at a local church, another ritual in the ritual-laden week. They bowed their gray heads and summoned the memories of old friends that time has taken away.

Perhaps on one of those Wednesdays, when the cool of evening meets the warm, fragrant day, the prayed-for will come back to meet the praying.

If Ron Green, Sr., could be in the room during the visitation, he'd address Bobby Jones with humility and respect. He's covered the Masters forty-three times for *The Charlotte Observer*, "but I still like to be awed by it." Green would ask Jones if he thinks the golf course should be changed, and if he ever thought the Masters would become as big as it is, and he'd like to hear about the flavor of the first tournament, if it was at all serious. "And so many people say they wouldn't 'let' Negroes in the tournament, which wasn't true. I'd like to have Jones and Roberts discuss that."

Byron Nelson would talk with Roberts about the stock market. "I think Cliff would say, 'They've lost their cotton-pickin' minds' in the market today. But he'd adjust to it. He was the most brilliant business executive I've ever known.

"I'd like to talk with Jones about the difference in the players today, and about the golf course. I hear people say they ought to have rough. But it wouldn't be the Masters anymore. Jones's philosophy was you still need to hit the ball in the proper spot."

Tom Weiskopf echoes Byron, but with more fervor. Weiskopf's history at Augusta National is unique: as a player, he finished second four times; he worked as an interviewer and analyst for CBS-TV for twelve years; and in his second career as a golf course architect, he's studied Augusta National like a monk poring over the epistles of St. Peter. "I think Jones, Roberts, and Mackenzie would be amazed and complimentary as to the presentation—the TV and the tournament management," Weiskopf says. "And I think they'd be surprised—but not pleasantly—at the changes in the course.

"What's happened is what I call the Augusta Syndrome: because of the tremendous financial returns to the club as a result of the tournament, they can afford to experiment on the course every year. As a result, Augusta has become like a cadaver in an anatomy class. No basis for comparison from one era to the next. If they don't stop hacking away at the body, there won't be anything left. What separates the Masters from the other majors is that everyone knows what happened to Curtis Strange at thirteen or what Arnold did at seventeen, and that adds tremendous interest." Eleven architects—not counting Roberts—have touched up the work of the maestro, Mackenzie.

"Neither Jones nor Mackenzie would like the changes," Weiskopf says. "If they were alive today, you'd see a much different golf course. I don't know what, but much different."

John LaFoy, who apprenticed as a golf architect at Augusta National, would ask a reanimated Roberts why so many people thought he was a jerk. *Sports Illustrated* writer Jaime Diaz would get Jones off to the side and ask him what he ever saw in that jerk Roberts.

Billy Fuller, the superintendent at Augusta National from 1981 to 1986, would ask Mr. Jones to please leave the church with him. He'd show Jones the modern club and ball, and the changes to the course, and Tiger's record-setting score—eighteen under par—in the 1997 tournament. "And I'd ask him, 'What would you do to fix our game?' "

Desmond Muirhead would ask Mackenzie if it was the scotch that killed him and if he'd had a previous life. And was he coming back?

"I'd ask Roberts to leave," says *Golf Magazine* editor Jim Frank. "I'd pour Jones a big glass of bourbon. And then I'd just listen."

In my version, a soft green glow like radioactivity would emanate from Cliff, Bob, Mac, and the other visitors. The living and the dead would sit quietly in the pews at Reid Memorial and listen to the choir in the loft sing, in Jones's honor, "La donna è mobile" from *Rigoletto*. Ike is on his old bench, fifth from the front, left side. The round metal collection plate is passed, and you strain to see what Cliff and big-bucks Pete Jones put in. There is no sermon. This group has heard enough and delivered enough sermons. Instead, we shake hands with our neighbors. "Peace be with you," we say.

In the final part of the ceremony, Frank Stranahan hands the bread and the wine to Roberts, who passes it to Tiger Woods. And on and on it goes, from golfer to member to total stranger, because what we want here is not inquisition, but communion.

AFTERWORD:
A COLD, GREEN
SHOULDER

Mark O'Meara, 1998

"Y ou can't *do* that!" said the member, desperation coloring his Georgia accent. "I didn't know we were on the record!" But we were, and one of the man's comments made it into the first edition of this book, to his great regret. Yet in this and at least a dozen subsequent phone calls he remained remarkably polite. Reconciling the Southern gentleman's code and the *omerta* of the Augusta National Golf Club was obviously not easy, but he did it with impressive grace.

The little crisis required two weeks of faxes, phone calls, and sleepless nights. The attribution of one particular quote was painstakingly reworded, excising the man's name in future printings. When it was over, I thought Mr. X. and I had become friends, as adversaries often do. I was wrong.

In the press building on the day before the Masters, I saw him, wearing his member's green jacket, smiling and greeting old pals from Masters past. Our eyes met. The smile disappeared. His withering look said, "You bastard," and he abruptly turned away.

"Tell your friend he ought to get his facts straight," another member growled to a mutual friend. What facts? our friend asked. "I can't say," the member replied.

Others in the green brotherhood had their problems. One reviewer bemoaned what he perceived to be attacks on "defenseless" Augusta National. Well, the rich and fiercely litigious club is many

things, but defenseless it ain't. Just ask CBS, Cadillac, Travelers, disinvited TV commentators Jack Whitaker and Gary McCord, or anyone who ever used the Masters logo without the express written
consent of the club.

Most people who read the book were generous, however, including two I didn't expect. The Godfather of Soul loved it. We visited at his radio station at Eighth and Broad on the afternoon of the
day I got such a cold green shoulder in the press building. "Come
in, come in, God bless you," James Brown said in his unmistakable
growl. After a fifteen-minute discussion of his life and his place in
The Masters, I found myself behind a microphone in the control
room. And for a further fifteen minutes, the listeners of WAAW, Soul
94.7 FM, endured my responses to Mr. Brown's off-mike questions.
The tuxedoed DJ played Brother James's hit "Sex Machine" as
background music over the last few minutes of the interview.

Early one morning the following week, the phone rang, and
a low, uninflected voice said, "This is Frank Stranahan." Just a
minute, I said, fumbling for my lawyer's number. But Stranahan was
not contemplating a lawsuit. On the contrary: "Best goddamned
book I ever read," he said. "I only wish someone had had the guts
to tell the truth before now.... See, everybody hated and feared
Cliff Roberts. But I could afford to do what I wanted."

After such praise and a brief stay in the close-in suburbs of
the *New York Times* bestseller list, only one thing bothered me:
What about the trees? The April 1998 issue of *Golf Magazine* and
Chapter 9 of this book simultaneously revealed a real scoop, the
premature death and aging of the predominant species of trees at
Augusta National. So where were the wire service stories about the
structural problems in golf's cathedral in the pines? Where were the
features, the columns, the helicopter-mounted minicams? Nowhere.

"Yes, that's surprising to me, too," said *Golf* editor Jim Frank.
"I would have thought there'd be some follow-up."

Neither apathy nor conspiracy caused the silence, in the
opinion of *Forth Worth Star-Telegram* sportswriter Jimmy Burch.
"The newspaper business is very here and now," Burch explained.

"If you tell me a tree is going to fall down in ten years, that's not a story; if it falls down today, then we're interested.

"And I've seen a lot of people crying wolf on nature stories like this over the years. I just think if there's really a problem, Augusta National will take care of it."

****

Problem? What problem?

"After fourteen months of denying that Augusta National needs to be toughened up, or Tiger-proofed, club officials announced that Tom Fazio will modify the course in time for the 1999 Masters," reported *Sports Illustrated* in June 1998. "Fazio will lengthen the par-5 2nd hole by 25 yards, bringing a bunker on the right side of the fairway into play; raise the green at the par-4 11th [by two feet] to create a new, difficult pin placement behind the pond in the back left corner; cut down the mounds on the right side of the landing area on the par-5 15th [and replace them with five or six clusters of pine trees] to keep drives from hitting them and bounding down the fairway; and add 15 yards to the par-4 17th." With further modifications to the fairway bunker on the second and to the dam by the eleventh green, and the excavation of the mounds by the fifteenth green, you have the most thorough remodeling in the club's history.

In the summer of '98, Augusta National looked as though bombs had exploded in its verdant turf, and men and machines scrambled in the heat to repair the damage.

But a bigger bombshell than the remodeling was the elevation of Hootie.

As the bulldozers dug and scraped the sacred ground, William Woodward "Hootie" Johnson, sixty-eight, was elected the fifth chairman of the Augusta National Golf Club. Johnson, a member since 1968 and the club's vice president since 1975, replaced his close friend, slow-talkin' Arkansas bond daddy Jackson Stephens.

Johnson is the father of four daughters. He's married to Pierrine, a former cheerleader, and is known as a behind-the-scenes player in business, civic projects, and philanthropy. He was an outstanding football halfback for the Greenwood High School Emeralds, and a mediocre one for the University of South Carolina. "He couldn't see without his glasses," says Johnny Gramling, the Gamecocks' quarterback in 1950–51. "That hurt his chances of playing."

The family business is banking. With his father, Dewey, and his brother Wellsman ("Bubba"), Hootie helped build and merge a little bank in Greenwood, South Carolina, into Bankers Trust of South Carolina. Which merged with NCNB. Which became part of NationsBank Corporation. Which merged with California-based BankAmerica in April 1998, a staggering $60 billion deal.

In *Time* magazine's ten-page cover story on the creation of the fifth largest bank in the world, Hootie Johnson's name is not mentioned. His colleague (and fellow member of Augusta National) Hugh McColl gets all the credit for engineering the deal, but those in the know say that Hootie had a lot to do with the huge merger of money and power.

Will Hootie be another Cliff?

On the one hand, Johnson says, "I hope that they'll say about me that I was a good steward of Bobby Jones and Clifford Roberts. That's the only mark I'd like to leave." On the other, in the early seventies he appointed M. Maceo Nance to serve on the board of Bankers Trust. Nance is a black man, and the first of his race to serve on a bank board in South Carolina. Johnson also joined the National Urban League and took an active role in its promotion of black-owned businesses. "It would have been far more convenient to pay lip service and concentrate on building his bank," says Elliot Franks, the former director of the Columbia (S.C.) Urban League. "It took a certain amount of courage to be on the front lines."

In November 1998, Hootie Johnson did something else Cliff Roberts would never have done. The *Chronicle* put the news on page one: "Augusta National Golf Club, the exclusive playground with a reputation for secrecy, dropped its guard for the first time Friday [November 13] by publicly announcing $3 million in charitable contributions." Three nonprofit organizations received

$1 million each. Two were local, the CSRA Community Foundation, a clearinghouse and grant-giver for Augusta Charities, and Fore! Augusta, the fund-raising entity for the Georgia Golf Hall of Fame, which plans to build a museum "attraction" in downtown Augusta. The third recipient was First Tee, a national group with plans to build free, three-hole courses for disadvantaged urban kids.

"Augusta National Golf Club believes that our service to the game of golf is the Masters Tournament, and we will never allow that event to be compromised by practices or policies designed solely to raise money," said Johnson in the press release announcing the gifts. "To do so would be contrary to the spirit and ideals established by our founders. At the same time, we are pleased that we are able, at times, to share with the golf world and the Augusta community to whom we owe so much."

It wasn't the giving that was unusual, of course; the club had cleaned up its balance sheet and indulged its philanthropic urge for years. But never before had it told the world about it.

And that last phrase—"to share with the golf world and the Augusta community to whom we owe so much"—those words would never have passed Cliff Roberts's lips. He saw things the other way around: that golf and Augusta owed him and Bobby and the Masters.

Chairman Johnson's surprising overhaul of the club and the tournament continued through the fall. By dismantling the creaky and arbitrary set of rules that denied invitations to scores of deserving players over the years, Johnson hoped to kill the widely held perception that the Masters has the weakest field of the four major golf championships.

He began his announcement with a little lie, a tip of the hat to the founding fathers. "Our existing qualification system has served us well," Johnson said. "However, our new methodology better reflects the changes in golf, and will ensure that the best players worldwide are invited to the Masters each year."

Henceforth the Masters will rely rigidly on the Official World Golf Ranking and other published lists to determine its entrants. Thus the tournament becomes less the invitational it's always been and more the straightforward "you're in or you're out" event the world seems to demand. For all its historic abuses and oversights, however, something will be lost. The new Masters will be somehow less romantic and at a still greater remove from the event conceived by Jones and Roberts in 1934.

But Johnson does not see himself as the new broom cleaning up the messes left by his predecessors. On the contrary, he embraces the legend of Cliff, who always called him Hootie, never William, Johnson recalled. "He liked me, and I liked him.... I think he counted me among his closest friends, and that was important to me."

"Mr. Roberts was told once what a great tournament the Masters was. He said, 'Thank you, but we really never get it right.' We still feel that way."

BIBLIOGRAPHY

Apel, William. *Harvard Dictionary of Music.* Cambridge, MA: Harvard University Press, 1944.

Brown, James, and Bruce Tucker. *James Brown: The Godfather of Soul.* New York: Macmillan, 1986.

Cashin, Edward J. *The Story of Augusta.* Richmond County (Georgia) Board of Education, 1980.

Derr, John. *Uphill Is Easier.* Pinehurst, N.C.: Cricket Productions, 1995.

Ellison, Ralph. *Invisible Man.* New York: Random House, 1952.

Ely, Mervin Patrick. *The Adventures of Amos 'n' Andy: A Social History of an American Phenomenon.* New York: Free Press, 1991.

Harris, J. William. *Plain Folk and Gentry in a Slave Society: White Liberty and Black Slavery in Augusta's Hinterlands.* Middleton, CT: Wesleyan University Press, 1985

Heller, Peter. *In This Corner . . . !* New York: Da Capo Press, 1973.

Jones, Robert T., Jr., and O. B. Keeler. *Down the Fairway.* Minton Balch & Company, 1954.

Lewis, J. C., and Harvey Z. Yazijian. *The Cola Wars.* New York: Everest House, 1980.

McClure, Rupert Hughes. *Music Lovers' Encyclopedia.* Phillips and Co., 1903.

McCormack, Mark H. *Arnie.* New York: Simon and Schuster, 1967.

Mitchell, Margaret. *Gone With the Wind.* New York: Macmillan, 1936.

Oliver, Thomas. *The Real Coke, the Real Story.* New York: Random House, 1986.

Pendergrast, Mark. *For God, Country and Coca-Cola*. New York: Charles Scribner's Sons, 1993.

Price, Charles. *A Golf Story*. New York: Atheneum, 1986.

Rice, Grantland. *The Tumult and the Shouting*. New York: A. S. Barnes and Company, 1954.

Roberts, Clifford. *The Story of the Augusta National Golf Club*. New York: Doubleday, 1976.

Rosaforte, Tim. *Tiger Woods: The Makings of a Champion*. New York: St. Martin's Press, 1997.

Rowland, A. Ray, and Helen Callahan. *Yesterday's Augusta*. Miami: E. A. Seeman Publishing, 1976.

Sampson, Curt. *The Eternal Summer*. Dallas: Taylor Publishing, 1992.

Sifford, Charlie, and James Gullo. *Just Let Me Play*. New York: British American Publishing, 1992.

Slater, Ellis D. *The Ike I Knew*. Ellis D. Slater Trust, 1980.

Stowe, Harriet Beecher. *Uncle Tom's Cabin, or Life Among the Lowly* (originally published 1852). New York: Bantam, 1981.

Taylor, William R. *Cavalier and Yankee: The Old South and American National Character*. New York: George Braziller, 1957.

Wilson, Ken, and Ken Bowden, editors. *The Best of Henry Longhurst on Golf and Life*. London: William Collins and Sons, 1979.

INDEX

ABOUT THE AUTHOR

CURT SAMPSON is the author of four other books, including the bestselling biography *Hogan*. He lives in Bristol, Texas, with his wife and two children.